REBUILDING WALL STREET

"After the Crash of '87, Fifty Insiders Talk about Putting Wall Street Together Again"

Mark Fadiman

PRENTICE HALL
Englewood Cliffs, New Jersey 07632

Prentice-Hall International (UK) Limited, *London*
Prentice-Hall of Australia Pty. Limited, *Sydney*
Prentice-Hall Canada, Inc., *Toronto*
Prentice-Hall Hispanoamericana, S.A., *Mexico*
Prentice-Hall of India Private Limited, *New Delhi*
Prentice-Hall of Japan, Inc., *Tokyo*
Simon & Schuster Asia Pte. Ltd., *Singapore*
Editora Prentice-Hall do Brasil, Ltda., *Rio de Janeiro*

© 1992 *by*

Mark Fadiman

10 9 8 7 6 5 4 3 2 1

Library of Congress Cataloging-in-Publication Data

Fadiman, Mark.
  Rebuilding Wall Street: after the Crash of '87, fifty insiders tell about
putting Wall Street together again / Mark Fadiman.
    p. cm.
  Includes index.
  ISBN 0–13–753013–7
  1. New York Stock Exchange. 2. Stock-exchange—New York (N.Y.)
3. Stockbrokers—New York (N.Y.)—Interviews. 4. Stock Market Crash, 1987.
I. Title.
HG4572.F33 1992
332.64'273—dc20   92–23931
                                                                                      CIP

ISBN 0-13-753013-7

PRENTICE HALL
Professional Publishing
Englewood Cliffs, NJ 07632
Simon & Schuster. A Paramount Communications Company

Printed in the United States of America

To my mother and father

ACKNOWLEDGMENTS

I would like to acknowledge, first of all, the help and support of my wife, Cindy. Professionally, many people have been kind to me: certainly everyone interviewed in this book, and others who I'm leaving out either for reasons of space, forgetfulness or because of the sensitivity of their professional positions. I'd like to mention the following: James Michaels, who gave me my start; Donald Moffitt who showed me how to compose business articles; Phil Hawkins, who tried to teach me the difference between price and yield; Jack Fitzgibbon and Phil and Cathie Petrosky who provided valuable insights about this book in manuscript; Jay Peake, who drove me down to Wharton one day; Ronald Cohen, who took a chance on an unproven author; Drew Dreeland, who provided many pertinent editorial suggestions; Phil Ruppel, who believed in this effort and picked it up; my delightful agent Anita Diamant; and, finally, Martin Mayer who, in the late stages, provided lunch along with an insightful interview.

I'm not academically grounded in financial writing; any mistakes in this book are certainly my own and have occurred despite the best efforts of others to eradicate them. If I've unintentionally forgotten to credit the works of anyone whose insights or statements I've had the good fortune to use, I apologize in advance.

CONTENTS

PART TWO
The Evolution of Current Market
Difficulties   69

PART THREE
Free Market Solutions   161

FOREWORD
Five Years from Black Monday and Counting—Trading Toward the Millennium . . .

Nothing during the last decade has more deeply influenced the way we Americans live, our prospects for the future, or the options available to us to alter those prospects than the operation of our financial markets.

During the 1980s, the stock, bond, futures, and options markets yielded wealth at rates not previously imagined. Notwithstanding those terrifying days in October 1987, the stock market tripled during the decade. And thanks to Paul Volker's (and his successor, Alan Greenspan's) use of interest rates to control inflation, the 1980s became a golden age for government bondholders. These investors, who for the first 80 years of this century had given their savings to Uncle Sam for a return that averaged just a couple of percentage points above inflation, in the 1980s found themselves getting four, five, and even six points above inflation.

Yet, ironically, the unprecented 1980s markets bonanza was rarely perceived as such. Indeed, the emotion driving most market participants most of the time during the 1980s was *anxiety.* For one thing, few felt they understood what was happening in the markets, which—thanks to a growing arsenal of high tech communications, trading systems, and investment products—began behaving in ever more mysterious ways. Anxiety was further fueled by the irony of market high after high occurring even as the nation's structural economic problems steadily worsened through the decade.

Ascendant in the markets of the 1980s, confusion now rules the markets of the 1990s, where investors are left to ponder how a near depression suports the case for investors paying more than 20 times annual earnings for the average share of stock, or a government bond yield that is quadruple the rate of inflation.

Never was the time more ripe for a work such as this one by Mark Fadiman. Thanks to a brilliant plan, crisply executed, Mr. Fadiman has captured the entire sweep of major innovation in the nation's financial markets over the past 15 years—often in the words of the very people responsible for the innovations. What results is a unique, fully comprehensive structural view of our markets, sure to be valuable to a wide range of readers from the merely curious to committed students of the markets to market professionals and regulators alike.

Mr. Fadiman's great unifying theme is the march of technology. This book makes clear that the computer revolution has remade the trading and investment landscape over the past 15 years in much the same way that television reshaped mass communications a generation before. Just as Marshal McLuhan found that, with television, "the medium is the message," one could cite today's array of computer-based trading systems, strategies, and products to justify an observation that "the product is the market."

Such is the case, for example, with many of the so-called "program trading" strategies, which tend to nudge stock prices steadily higher over time. Accordingly, as I observed in my book about Black Monday 1987, program trading not only was the principal cause of the day's 508-point market plunge, but also had a great deal to do with the market's explosive rise in the 1984 to mid-1987 period. I also submit that if you subtract program trading from today's market environment, prices would drift down toward those levels justified solely by fundamental valuation principles—about half of current market levels.

Nobody is going to turn off program trading, of course—or the other powerful new equities, fixed income, options, and futures markets trading strategies. Instead, as Mr. Fadiman so skillfully relates, still greater innovation lies ahead, especially in capabilities for trading partners to interact.

In the world Mr. Fadiman and many of the visionaries he talks with see gleaming out at the millennium, ever greater improvements in electronic market communications and trading capabilities may make it possible to one day turn over the financial markets entirely to investor principals.

In such a world of perfect information made available to all market participants on a real-time basis, there will be no need for intermediaries, be they stock exchange "specialist" market makers, brokers, or even today's high-powered institutional money mangers. All of us, it seems, will one day be able to trade directly with one another, using our home PCs.

Premised on a consensus among market participants that fair and efficient markets are the best haven for investment capital, such would be a rationally consistent and, indeed, much-to-be-desired outcome.

But, after a couple of decades of watching investors and traders from a perch at *The Wall Street Journal,* I have little trouble with that premise. I haven't met any traders who were interested in fairer or more efficient markets, only in more profitable ones.

Also, if the most powerful market participants try to influence the market environment to the greatest extent they legally can, then it would seem that these very same participants can be expected to offer the stiffest resistance to any change that would narrow their advantage.

Finally, I'm not sure there ever will be a way for technology to replace the stock exchange specialist—to make markets under all circumstances. And is a 10 percent, 15 percent or even 50 percent improvement in market efficiency and trading productivity under normal conditions worth it if it involves the risk of illiquidity at times of market stress? I wonder.

Maybe it's a phobia related to my age, but I keep remembering that back in October 1987 it was the NYSE specialists who had the white hats, and the computers (or at least the guys loading them) who wore the black ones. While the computers spewed out wave after wave of sell program orders on the floor of the NYSE, the specialists somehow managed to keep most Big Board stocks trading most of the time.

Having constructed a system in which a specialist's entire advantage over other market participants stems solely from his or her position at the head of the order flow, the stock exchange could (perhaps cynically) be confident that he or she would move heaven and earth to perpetuate that privilege—and, so, the trading from which it flows.

Meanwhile, on Black Monday in the theoretically more efficient NASDAQ market, hundreds of callers to OTC trading desks at brokerage firms around the country—even at some of the industry's prestigious firms—got only busy signals, caused by telephones intentionally left off the hook. Nonetheless, it is NASDAQ these days that advertises itself as "the stock exchange of the 21st century."

Among the many authoritative sources Mr. Fadiman talks to about the coming shape of the financial markets, I guess I most closely identify with the view of the American Stock Exchange chairman, James Jones, who expects that tomorrow's markets will need to rely on new roles for *both* people and technology.

Whatever financial markets systems may evolve in the future, you most likely will be able to find at least their roots right here in Mr. Fadiman's wonderfully comprehensive and comprehensible book.

Tim Metz
April 1, 1992

INTRODUCTION

I remember we walked down to the New York Stock Exchange (NYSE) on the day of the crash, October 20, 1987, and stood in front of the huge, stony facade where the line of sightseers patiently waited to see what a 500-point drop looked like from inside on the trading floor. The line snaked around the block. The media was staking out the exchange. It seemed like a war zone, there were so many cameras and minicams. Baggy-jacketed specialists and floor brokers emerged every now and then to take a break. They looked dazed, as if they didn't know what had hit them. But everyone knew, I suppose, deep inside. Whatever it was that was wrong with the market had finally caught up with it.

At the time tumbling Dow was as incomprehensible to me as it was to the line of amazed visitors. The crash seemed dreamlike, divorced from anything real. The numbers ticking down were just that, digits separated from tangible items of investment or trade.

The week and then the month of the crash passed. The financial industry did not crumble; there did not seem to be an impending Depression. I continued reporting on Wall Street, but now I wanted to understand what had happened. Unfortunately, the more I tried, the more elemental gaps I found in my comprehension; I couldn't seem to get below the surface. I read articles in major business journals; most did not seem to tell me what I wanted to know.

I moved to *Investor's Daily* (now *Investor's Business Daily*) and used my position as the paper's Wall Street reporter to interview a number of industry executives about the stock market and financial issues. I questioned others on assorted securities industry events—the limited partnership and penny stocks deals that were blowing apart at the time.

What I learned was fascinating: The market's difficulties were not necessarily economic or the result of a sudden onslaught of greed combined with devious program trading. Perhaps they weren't even simply the result of economic cycles—the inevitable boom-bust prized by hardheaded financial economists. No, I was discovering from articles and interviews there were certain problems peculiar to the American securities industry—difficulties recognized even back in the early 1960s, after the big stock market drop of May 1962.

I began to firm up my reporting. I would explore two issues: How the stock market crash of 1987, which seemingly threatened the underpinnings of the nation's credit system, could have occurred; and why so many individual investors were ill-treated through penny stock fraud, and junk bond and limited partnership mis-pricing in the 1980s.

Over the next year, I formally interviewed about 150 individuals inside and outside of the securities industry. I talked to many others during the course of my day-to-day reporting. I read a number of books, some of them popular, some more complex, about financial services. I also requested articles—hundreds of stories, or parts of stories—from electronic news services: the *New York Times, The Wall Street Journal, Barron's,* the *Chicago Tribune* and the *Washington Post,* much to my wife's dismay when the credit card bills arrived.

At first I attempted a narrative form, but I wasn't satisfied. Then I tried another way, condensing first-person interviews from the tape-recordings and notes I'd taken. I was happier with this result, though it entailed much fact-checking and, ultimately, reworking of interviews with my subjects. Since many of the issues were of considerable complexity, at least on the surface, I gave my subjects the right to review their contributions for the sake of accuracy; and this, of course, resulted in further complications.

Eventually, the book resolved itself into what it is today: A combination of what I'd originally set out to write—a narrative of the ongoing growing pains of our financial industry, with special emphasis on Wall Street—and individual interviews representing a variety of viewpoints on important issues. The interview technique is, I hope, one that will help attract a wider audience for this kind of book than is ordinarily the case.

Meanwhile, in the narrative sections that remain, I've recorded events—recent and historical—as I believe they occurred, based on my research and interviews. I tried not to shy away from conclusions, just as I've chosen subjects with the most interesting and, in some cases, controversial things to say. The *status quo* has its defenders, but many of these interviews are about changing or improving how the current system operates. I do hope the narrative reinforces the interviews and vice-versa. But I'm sure the reader will notice loose ends and may well come away with very different opinions than mine.

Why This Book Happened

It was the best of times for Wall Street in the early 1990s. Pre-tax earnings for soared to record-breaking levels of about $5.5 billion. Small investors, facing the prospect of declining interest rates, flocked back to equities, investing billions through mutual funds or discount brokers. The Big Board broke 3000 and just kept going higher.

Yet it was the worst of times. The NYSE still reeled from market surges and drops, though collars and other regulations had been cobbled together to provide some protection. The small investor was back in the stock market—but was it out of choice or merely because there was for the moment, nowhere else to go?

It seems evident the difficulties the securities industry and, indeed, the country face—problems that were apparent in the late 1980s—have not been solved. In many cases they're still just beginning to be addressed by regulators, politicians and industry executives.

In the 1980s, the securities industry helped create and then profit from three powerful, evolving trends. The first was the rise to prominence of the options and financial futures markets. The second was the explosion of new non-Exchange traded instruments, such as limited partnerships, penny stocks, and junk bonds. All these trends interacted, in some cases, damagingly, with the financial industry. The former evolution resulted in the stock crash of October 1987. The latter resulted in billions in paper losses for individual investors.

The third, and perhaps most dramatic development, was the growth of computerized, electronic information delivery systems. These systems allow industry professionals to make rapid, powerful investment decisions. Unfortunately, exchange-based derivatives trading and automated systems—when combined with a regulatory system that encouraged order flow through a handful of Wall Street firms—gave rise to market "games" in the 1980s that continue today.

Suspicions about Wall Street have arisen because the firms stand in the middle of enormous order flows by historical accident and regulatory design. Traders for a firm's own account often occupy the same trading room as those filling orders for institutions. Perhaps the trader, legally or not, buys and sells both for the customer and the firm. Wall Street's name for the delicate partitioning that separates the broker's interest in its own profit from its client is "Chinese Walls." In the 1980s, too many of Wall Street's Chinese Walls were paper-thin and easily punctured. "Frontrunning is simply a cost of business," one big institutional money manager told me crisply.

The crash of 1987 came with startling suddenness (though it is hard to avoid the conclusion that some professional investors and regulators knew it was building). It cost hundreds of billions of dollars of paper wealth and chased numerous investors out of the market while the Dow commenced a strong upward surge in 1988 and 1989 on relatively thin volume.

The crash was only one of the factors that damaged the nation's pocketbook and confidence in the later 1980s. The other factor can be broken down into at least three main areas: penny stock fraud, limited partnership devaluations with its attendant real-estate/banking problems, and the collapse of the junk bond market.

By the late 1980s, a sad scenario for individual investors became apparent: $50-$100 billion locked in under-performing limited partnerships, according to New Jersey-based Stanger & Co.; $10-$20 billion lost to penny-stock fraud, according to state regulators; and $100 billion or more invested in junk bonds that had moved down precipitously, according to *The Wall Street Journal* and New York-based *IDD Information Services, Inc.,* which tracks issuance.

Up to $200 billion, altogether, were invested in products that soured in the late 1980s. Add in $200-$300 billion from the Savings and Loan (S&L) crisis, plus billions more lost to small consumers who sold out stocks at their lows in late 1987 and never reinvested, and the damage soared for small investors as the 1990s opened.

Wall Street was certainly not solely at fault in selling products that faltered in the late 1980s. But just as surely those products would not have been so popular without Wall Street's bankers and marketers. Writing in the *New York Times* in late 1989, Henry Kaufman, a longtime critic of the junk bond market, pointed out: "For many firms in the

securities industry, the franchise they once had will not be recaptured
. . . That trust has been shattered . . . In the more concentrated U.S.
financial structure of tomorrow, conflicts of interest will flourish. This
will invite governmental intrusion, less innovation and, ultimately, a
more inefficient allocation of capital."

The North American Securities Administrators Association (Nasaa)
found in a late 1980s survey that "widespread manipulation and other
schemes," mostly involved in penny stock fraud, were costing consumers
$2 billion annually, a total for the 1980s that may have reached $20
billion. Nasaa also found, in another survey, that certain so-called financial
planners were involved in investment schemes that cost consumers up
to $400 million or more annually.

Nasaa executives have suggested that the industry establish a strict
code of ethics similar to that functioning for the medical, banking,
and legal professions; additionally, the possibility of energetic litigation
aimed at securities fraud would have a deterring effect. This would
be one way of decreasing domestic malfeasance.

Ultimately, what may be necessary to diminish fraud and increase
trust in the financial marketplace is a three-pronged attack: more competition through aggressive deregulation, increasingly rigorous standards
of professional behavior (alongside the emergence of agency—i.e., fee-
based—brokers); and finally, the application of computerized technology
to all facets of the market, including the execution of the trade.

Sunshine Through Automation,
Deregulation

The automation of the financial marketplace—using computers to
facilitate full price exposure of retailed instruments—might have ameliorated at least some of what happened in the 1980s.

And what the industry refers to as "sunshine," produced by automation, would be of benefit not only to the financial industry. According
to an article on the S&L disaster in an early 1992 winter issue of
the *Washington Monthly*, "regulations requiring confidentiality of thrift
examinations help keep the industry's deep trouble under wraps." The
Washington Monthly concluded that the secrecy laws should be repealed
as part of a larger effort to clean up the S&L mess.

The same lack of information haunted three of the most problematic financial vehicles of the 1980s—limited partnerships, junk
bonds, and penny stocks. These all-too-often disastrous investments

had one common link; prices were not easily obtained by the average consumer and historical data was, pretty much, unavailable.

Junk bond prices were—and still are—mostly available to a select group of Wall Street traders. In the 1980s Drexel Burnham Lambert Inc. dominated the primary market: It priced and issued bonds. Merrill Lynch & Co. dominated the secondary market: It bought and sold a large percentage of junk bonds. There were also mutual fund junk prices available in the newspaper, but these did not, of necessity, reflect much of the market. Limited partnership prices were not easily available, and the information disseminated quarterly was not always reliable; penny stock prices were often listed in the "pink sheets" and not easily acquired by ordinary consumers, especially those who chose to invest in them.

Wider dissemination of securities prices is practical. It's probably no coincidence that Bloomberg L.P. terminals, placed at buy-side firms and disseminating fixed-income prices, are said to have considerably narrowed spreads in the last few years. IBM-compatible, DOS-based PCs—well within the reach of the average investor as well as the institutional investor—now offer most of the power of Wall Street's heavier Unix platforms.

In addition to a wide dissemination of securities prices, a thorough, measured, regulatory overhaul of the nation's financial industry is probably needed. In fact, when you scratch the surface of a variety of financial problems (a good, big scratch to be sure) the difficulties usually seem to be the same: Excessive government regulation setting up, codifying and even guaranteeing a rigid business construct that gets everybody into trouble when it's badly and abruptly deregulated. (Of course the industry, whatever it is, is often not deregulated at all; it remains exactly what it has been minus a few, important safeguards.)

This seems to be what happened in the S&L fiasco in which thousands of small banks crashed, costing taxpayers hundreds of billions in deposit insurance payments. The outpouring of books and documents on the subject are beginning to document what really went on. To begin with, the S&L industry was set up to give people credit to purchase homes. But as our financial industry evolved, especially in the 1970s and early 1980s, S&Ls failed to compete. They had to lower the amount of interest they charged on loans while paying more to borrow money from other sources.

Instead of shutting down what it helped create, the federal government mounted a bail-out effort ; the government decided to loosen reporting restrictions. That meant S&Ls could carry hidden bad loans on their books while growing their way out of their problems during the 1980s. Only it never happened. Once S&Ls didn't have to report losses, they were free to make risky investments that were—as has been pointed out numerous times—guaranteed by government deposit insurance. Profits flowed directly into the pockets of S&L operators while red ink—some $200–300 billion—flowed in the opposite direction, eventually to be staunched by taxpayers.

The S&L debacle shows the degree to which government and industry can become intertwined; and so it is, on occasion, with our large and profitable financial services industry.

In the 1980s, the stock market crash was a kind of S&L disaster for Wall Street: The same problems that battered our S&Ls at least in part gave our stock market difficulty. That's because Wall Street and its exchanges evolved in some ways into nearly as artificial a construct as the S&L industry. And just like the S&Ls, our government and its regulators—beholden to various interests—kept trying to patch up the system to gratify powerful constituencies.

Ironically, the place where regulations would do the most good in the consumer sphere were the places where regulations, even those on the books, were least applied during the 1980s. And "let the buyer beware" still seems most often invoked when it concerns the little guy about to invest his life savings in a sure thing—that's not. Even taking into account certain spasms of virtue in the early 1990s, tough rules still don't seem to be applied where they would do the most good. Meanwhile, they are manufactured and debated endlessly as they pertain to markets in general—as if government itself can build and maintain a satisfactory financial environment through political jaw-boning.

In an editorial, April 23, 1992, *Wall Street Journal* editor Robert Bartley spells out the causes of the Tokyo stock market crash. "The guiding philosophy here," he writes, "is to be suspicious of either 'bubbles' or 'panics' as explanation for market phenomena. Mass psychosis may sometimes happen, but more usually there is a cause. Japanese prices would not have soared so spectacularly if Japanese investors had more outlets abroad. Or Japanese policy could have promoted more consumption and less savings."

But what Bartley and others find obvious in foreign markets is not often mentioned in regard to the U.S.: Government control (read regulation)—aided and abetted by the industry itself—leading to crashes, panics and abuse of individual investors.

Regulations and the Market

The computer revolution has remade the trading and investment landscape over the past 15 years, and the results are often unexpected and sometimes painful. A less obvious challenge our marketplace faces is not automation but the interaction between industry and government. To illustrate the problem, here's small sampling of rules that have had a fundamental impact on the structure and performance of our financial industry over the last half century:

Glass-Steagall, which set up the split between commercial banks and Wall Street firms; the McFadden Rule that still makes it hard for banks to expand beyond state lines; Rule 390 that mandates that Wall Street firms cross trades for their own account on the floor of a recognized physical stock exchange; the Short-Short Rule that says mutual funds can't get more than 30 percent of their income from transactions that are less than 90 days in length without losing tax advantages; the 1940 Act which mandates, in part, that all sellers of mutual funds must charge the same prices for the same products; diversification rules from the 40 Act that put institutional funds at a disadvantage versus Wall Street's proprietary traders; the Employee Retirement Income Security Act, (Erisa) which codifies through Prudent Man how pension plans have to provide for employees, and what they can and can't invest, especially as regards non-U.S. investing.

In their well-documented book, *The Troubled Money Business*, Richard Crawford and William Sihler write—as Peter Drucker in *The Unseen Revolution* pointed out in 1976—that "pension fund investment is bringing socialism to the U.S.." While pension plans were originally a private sector response to worker need, the 1974 passage of Erisa overhauled laws covering pension plans and established minimum requirements that created a massive funding need among corporations with plans. By the year 2000, pension plans may be the largest form of financial institution, alongside some equally big mutual funds.

In March 1991, the Pension Benefit Guaranty Corporation (PBGC) reported that businesses across the country might be underfunding their plans by $14 billion more than the PBGC's potential assets. A tax-payer bailout of the pension industry would probably not go down any better with the public than the current S&L bailout. In an interview in this book, the well-known bond-writer Jim Grant says banks "should be allowed to fail." What about other financial entities?

Pension plans have already had a tremendous effect on the financial industry. For one thing, management is often short-term: Pension plans tend to buy stocks that do well and sell the ones that don't. Also, as Sihler and Crawford point out, the concentration of capital in the hands of a relatively few money managers and plan sponsors eased the way for takeovers in the 1980s.

Economist Charles Trzcinka, also interviewed in this book, has made an impact with an article in *The Wall Street Journal* calling for the deregulation of mutual funds. Now Wall Street's regulatory body, the Securities and Exchange Commission, has said it would like to do away with 1940s rules that set mutual fund price controls.

Like pension plans, mutual funds were a creation of the private sector that eventually became subject to stringent regulation. As it stands of this writing, a financial planner cannot offer a client a specific mutual fund for less than the customer can purchase elsewhere—at, say, a big broker. This lack of price competition has squeezed the financial planner at the expense of the Wall Street salesman.

Fee-based agency business—the idea that an independent representative can deal with an individual client untrammeled by sales considerations—has suffered as a result. Some of Wall Street's biggest firms throughout the 1980s profited tremendously from "asset capture" as their salesmen energetically flogged in-house products. Whether firms will be able to maintain their growth and size in a deregulated mutual fund market remains to be seen.

Industry executives like Michael Lipper of Lipper Analytical Services Inc. think the biggest Wall Street players will be more competitive than independent financial planners because of economies of scale. Yet the most unbiased financial advice may come from planners who do not sell products for a living but charge fees for their services. Such professionals might well benefit from mutual fund deregulation: Another example of how deregulation—rather than more regulation—can encourage trustworthy investment information.

Whether the SEC will be able to follow through with its stated intention is also uncertain. One of current chairman Richard Breeden's more unfortunate accomplishments at the SEC has been the evisceration of its group of economists built up in the 1980s. Trzcinka worked on a mutual fund study at the SEC.

It's true the SEC under Breeden, a self-proclaimed "tough cop," the agency has been a more vital and gutsier body than in the 1980s. Still, the question remains: How truly objective can a regulatory organization be? Bureaucracies are not often sympathetic to fundamental reform. More likely they are apt to listen to the industry's largest players—the very participants they're supposed to regulate. When the administration switches, or when the current deregulatory push lags or confronts a determined industry lobby, the SEC and other financial regulators, may well return the kind of business that did not serve the nation especially well in the 1980s or 1960s.

It is also noteworthy that two of the financial industry's less-regulated secondary marketplaces, in bonds and foreign exchange, weren't so troubled in the 1980s—at least not so publicly troubled—as the more highly-regulated futures and equity markets.

An accretion of regulations throughout the decades since the Depression helped codify a kind of three-part securities industry layer cake with pension plans and mutual funds on the bottom, money managers in the middle and Wall Street on top where the icing is. Even now, a handful of firms, historically in concert with the NYSE, are exposed to much of the market's order flow and can reap benefits from their position within the nation's capital-raising mechanism.

The situation has been complicated by computer trading, electronic execution mechanisms, and a dizzying variety of new markets and instruments. Expert systems and neural networks, two components of so-called artificial intelligence, further erode traditional investment techniques. Such new technologies make use of computer-generated overviews of investment patterns involving customized universes of securities rather than individual stocks and bonds.

The somewhat incestuous structure of the financial industry—once encouraged by regulators as a way to keep tabs on the market—is increasingly detrimental to the nation's, and even the world's, financial stability as technology places more and more financial power in the hands of a relatively few bankers and brokers. The result: Pension plans funds are sliced up for program trading, and retail investments are diced by huge commissions that are extracted regardless of the efficacy of the investment, as in the case of limited partnerships. The plan or retail customer, the "ultimate consumer"—a favorite term of Howard Schwartz, president of the agency dealer Lynch, Jones & Ryan—ends up enriching Wall Street and, on occasion, its physical exchanges.

The influence of regulatory design is subtle as well as obvious when it comes to financial markets. As an editor of *Investment Management Technology,* I've been made aware of institutional resistance to technology or different ways of doing business. Asset management evolved out of bank trust departments, and Glass-Steagall only reinforced the supine behavior of the money management industry relative to its more active and agressive sell-side, Wall Street.

A good example of how Wall Street and its satellite hedge funds can dominate may be seen in the autumn 1991 Treasury scandal where Salomon Brothers Inc. was accused of buying up bonds to squeeze the market. A New Jersey money manager, Three Crowns Limited Partnership, filed a lawsuit alleging several firms colluded with Salomon. The firms, Steinhardt Partners Ltd., Soros Fund Management, Caxton Corp. and Luttrell Capital Management met with Salomon executives at Caxton's New York offices in March 1991 to discuss the attractiveness of the notes, the suit alleges. The firms then bought the securities, restricting the supply of notes in circulation and creating a "squeeze" in which Three Crowns was caught.

It is easy to blame such behavior, if proven, on greed or dishonesty. Yet executives on Wall Street are not any better or worse than people anywhere else. The ongoing concentration of securities information and order flow in few hands is what needs to be changed.

After the difficulties of the 1980s, that at least some of the above securities-related regulations are under attack is, I believe, no coincidence. The Short-Short Rule may be done away with during the next round of tax legislation; Glass-Steagall is gradually crumbling as banks market mutual funds and securities and assume underwriting powers. Defined contribution (DC) plans—that allow investors to make some of their own pension choices—as opposed to defined benefit (DB) plans (in which companies choose for participants) also may hold out hope of altering the financial industry's comfortable business practices. New regulations affecting DC plans are being codified as I write.

The domestic securities industry's regulatory structure is gradually evolving; the challenge for the future will be to insure that the established securities industry and its main regulators do not throw up so many roadblocks, or so distort the process of deregulation, that Wall Street—or some other specific industry group—gains in a new age what has been excised from the old.

In another April editorial, the *Journal's* Bartley, points out how the 1980s represented *Seven Fat Years*, the title of a book of his on what really happened last decade. In excerpts, Bartley says that rather than being a time of greed when an exploding budget deficit nearly sank the economy, the 1980s, from beginning of 1983 to the end of

1989, the economy grew at a 3.5 percent clip—compared to a 1.6 percent rise during the previous ten years.

Bartley isolates the sparkplugs of economic prosperity: Treasury Secretary Paul Volker's tight monetary policy that kept inflation down and President Ronald Reagan's tax cuts providing economic incentives. Additionally, he cites America's entrepreneurial tradition which flowered in the 80s. He also says a second industrial revolution is changing an industrial economy into an information economy, in which the predominant activity is collecting, processing and communicating information.

The financial services community is in large part involved in this change. Unfortunately Bartley, despite his persuasively optimistic vision, and others who share his point of view, often don't have much to say about the regulations that shape and control the dissemination of financial information.

The intersection between government regulations and private enterprise in this country contributed to some of the more problematic developments of the 1980s. But this intersection is not an abstract issue going forward: Financial markets, here and abroad, are growing not diminishing in importance as lines between banking and dealing blur. An *Economist* magazine survey in May 1992 documented how different forms of mediation that separate banking from securities trading and underwriting are being torn down around the world.

Mediation is the term used by the financial industry to describe what happens when someone makes a profit by putting together buyers and sellers. Much profit in a free market stems from mediation. Department stores are physical intermediaries for the buyer (the shopper) and the seller (the company producing the goods being purchased). The financial industry makes a profit no differently than any other kind of business. Wall Street firms put together buyers and sellers through brokerage or securitization. Banks take in loans and lend out money—another way of putting together the buyer (the entity receiving the loan) with the seller (the depositor providing the cash).

The Economist survey points out that the securitization of assets is replacing banks old-fashioned method of taking in deposits and then lending them out at a profit. If securitization is the wave of the future, than market structure, more than ever, becomes a determining factor in the health of our international marketplace. And market structure has always been subject to political struggles.

The Best of All Worlds

The gradual coming together of different kinds of financial services under one roof is not by itself cause for dismay. But bigness combined with what Washington Beltway insiders call "regulatory capture"—in which regulatory decisions are made to promote narrow industry interests—is worrisome despite changes regulators are making or contemplating.

There are alternatives. As *The Economist* pointed out, the U.S. has become the second country to legislate weak banks out of existence through the Federal Deposit Insurance Corporation Improvement Act. The core of the FDICIA act is a series of measures mandating regulatory intervention when a bank's capital falls below certain levels.

A guiding principal behind the FDICIA rule is that it mandates what regulators can and can't do. The idea of writing a law so tightly it restricts regulatory latitude may be a way to deal an inconsistent interpretation of rules and enforcement from one administration to the next. Of course, in this country the rules are written by congress—but that's a separate problem.

We probably don't need more regulation restricting economic and financial activity; we do need to concentrate in a disciplined way on injecting more players and more capital into the system. The result would not only provide a more vibrant economic structure but also could allow—in addition to new electronic trading nets—the continued emergence of agency brokers and traders to take the customer's part.

It's always easy to believe, like Candide, that the present system must be the best of all possible worlds since it has just come down to us this way. But a recent book by the financial writer Martin Mayer *Stealing the Market* documents many of the same abuses in the financial industry that my subjects did.

While Mayer's conclusions are not, in many cases, those I agree with, I do believe in his analysis of the workings of our financial industry. His perception, in fact, is not so different than those of the authors of *The Troubled Money Business*; as with the S&L debacle, a consensus among some informed financial observers would seem to be evolving. It is not, necessarily, that financial innovation is bad or that our capital market structure has been hijacked or "stolen" by speculative instruments. There are fundamental problems with our current financial system, observers seem to be saying. The argument is over what's to be done: Causes are not so much in doubt as solutions.

In the 1980s a rigid financial industry structure was haphazardly deregulated and the results were seen in the S&L losses and the 1987 stock market crash. The same half-baked deregulatory impetus aided penny stock criminals and other kinds of white-collar scam artists.

In the 1990s I hope we'll seriously crack down on retail financial fraud and give some thought to truer, more far-ranging financial deregulation affecting the markets. Unlike financial industry observers, executives and regulators who call for more studies and more rules specifying what can and can't be done in securities markets, I believe we should be removing regulations to further increase competition.

It's unfortunate our federal politicians and agency officials find market structure issues so much more fascinating than the work of policing consumer fraud. It's also unfortunate that the media often decline to challenge this attitude. A review in a major business magazine declared last spring: "Sure there's room for reform on Wall Street, but by and large the system still works." For now it does. But not so well. Times are a-changing.

PART ONE

■ ■ ■

RETAIL DIFFICULTIES

■ ■ ■

*In the 1980s, there were two different kinds of market abuses
perpetrated by Wall Street. The second and third sections of this book
deal with market structure difficulties within the current regulatory
framework—how they occurred and how they might be alleviated. This
section deals with the first kind of market abuse: consumer fraud
perpetrated on individual clients by various groups within the financial
industry as it is currently constructed. I have chosen to put this section
first in the hope of gradually easing the reader into some of the more
complex issues that occupy the later sections of this book. But abuses,
whether aimed at individual consumers or institutions, stem from the
same systemic difficulties: too much power, too much information, too
much regulatory leverage in the hands of too few people.*

No one knows how much money has actually been lost through
investment in Wall Street's largest consumer fiasco, limited partnerships,
but estimates of troubled partnerships have ranged from one third to
90 percent. To some extent, partnership damage will be determined
by price rebounds in real estate and oil and gas, the areas where most
of the estimated $100–$200 billion or more in partnership investments
are located. The more time that passes while these markets remain
soft, however, the more punishment is inflicted on the millions of
individual investors partnership portfolios. With the federal government
dumping $200–$300 billion worth of real estate from failed thrifts
onto the market, the chances of $50 billion worth or more of real-estate
limited partnerships recovering their projected value any time soon is
somewhat doubtful.

1

The lack of information available to investors in limited partnerships aggravated the problem. Partnership sponsors or general partners are required to mail investors regular reports on the status of their investments. But often these reports are late, and many times the reports may give little indication of the underlying problems of the partnership until suddenly a distribution is diminished or cut off entirely.

According to executives at the limited-partnership research firm, Stanger, public partnerships—aimed at the smaller investor and fully registered with the SEC—from 1981–1990, totaled about $75 billion at the decade's end. About $10–$12 billion of these partnerships, specifically in oil and gas, plus up to $2 billion in Sun Belt real estate were not performing up to expectation, according to Stanger figures. These partnerships failed to meet projections of paying investors a quarterly or annual dividend in addition to a hefty cash-out value at the end of a five- to seven-year period when the partnerships supposedly matured.

Meanwhile, about $40 billion in private partnerships, sold mostly to wealthy investors, had a poorer track record. Perhaps half of all private partnerships were in some kind of trouble by 1990. Up to $35 billion, or between a quarter and a third of all limited partnerships offered since 1981, have underperformed—as *Investor's Daily* pointed out in a series of articles.

Perhaps the most insidious, costly, and least known of Wall Street's limited partnership excesses lies in its contribution to the hundred billion dollar S&L bust.

One of the chief prophets of doom and gloom in the 1980s was the well-known investment banker Felix Rohatyn of the prestigious Lazard Freres & Co. investment bank. Rohatyn summed up the 1980s in especially glum terms in a spring 1990s article for the *New York Review of Books:* "The use by unscrupulous bankers of federally guaranteed deposits to rescue a savings and loan industry that should have been liquidated a decade ago will ultimately cost the taxpayers between $300 and $500 billion; ten years ago the costs would have been limited to perhaps $10 billion. The colossal amounts of money wasted by the savings and loan industry in investments in worthless real estate, in junk bonds, in speculation and corruption of all kinds could have been invested in new, productive investments. . . ."

The grim legacy is easy to trace. To begin with, in the 1960s congress passed legislation that did away with an S&L tax-advantaged reserve fund that was supposed to cushion S&Ls against Depression-style insolvency. Then in the late 1970s era of high inflation S&Ls offered customers lofty rates of return to lure their deposits. In the low interest 1980s, S&Ls found they could not continue to pay the high coupon rates they had promised these customers. Enter one of the decade's first meaningful deregulatory efforts: congress allowed thrifts to lend money to investors for purposes other than financing their homes—the reason why thrifts had been created in the first place. The consequences of this loosening of the thrift investment limits were disastrous. Thrifts immediately began to offer cash to riskier businesses. The shakier the venture, the more interest the S&L could charge on the money it lent. The other big deregulatory change came in 1982 when a law went into effect doubling the federal insurance on thrift deposits to $100,000. The law attracted many new savers to S&Ls, which, flush with cash, poured money into ever riskier investments.

Financial executives have skillfully maintained a wall between the thrifts and Wall Street. But the two separate industries were fatefully interlocked in the 1980s. Firms began to offer investors shares of "jumbo" certificates of deposit. These S&L products offered risk-free high rates of return, and thrifts competed to guarantee Wall Street the highest possible interest rates for these big investor deposits. The weakest thrifts—the ones that needed the money the most—competed the hardest.

By using its massive marketing leverage, Wall Street helped raise cash for thousands of thrifts. But since the cash went to the highest bidder, Wall Street was actually helping contribute to the destabilization of the industry. The only way thrifts could fulfill their promises to investors of extremely high rates of return was to plunge into ever-riskier development projects. Here is where Wall Street found another niche. The shaky projects S&Ls invested in throughout the decade were partly financed by Wall Street through more than $50 billion worth of real-estate limited partnerships offered throughout the early and middle 1980s. Such partnerships are truly the flip side of the S&L crisis.

During the easy-money 1980s financial con men peddled billions of dollars of worthless real estate. Assuming the title of general partner, a crook might approach an individual account or a securities firm with a flimsy but professional-sounding venture and receive marketing and sales help. Cash in hand, the general partner could then turn around and ask a thrift to add in additional cash to the speculative development.

It was also very simple. All you needed was the "Big Idea." Say, to build a resort motel in the middle of a desert. Then you needed a title: General Partner would do. Assuming this title, you approached a variety of "sponsors," syndicators, and individual accountants and began to market your Big Idea, your Vision. The sponsor might wrap your Vision in impressive statistics, projections of potential business duly attested to by the accounting industry. A prospectus would be drawn up and meetings would be scheduled. A syndicator—a regional brokerage firm or even a national Wall Street firm—would agree to facilitate your Dream. A group of high-powered brokers would sell your project to the general public. You would return to your favorite bank with millions of dollars backing your idea.

A former executive recounts: "I once told the board at Shearson [evaluating a limited partnership] that I thought a particular product was an abomination. They intended to market it as a conservative investment, but they were also going to highlight a huge return. How the hell can a conservative investment return double digits like that?"

But the reality of the system at Shearson and elsewhere was not only that bad deals were forced through because they were so lucrative to market; today as assessments of the true damage from mob-rigged, spendthrift S&Ls climb ever higher, investors have realized an even more horrible fact—they're paying double. According to industry observers like Scott Miller, the now-failing limited partnership an investor bought in the 1980s is the same partnership that the investor's thrift also invested in.

The damage through the end of the 1980s was not limited only to limited partnership products. Many Real Estate Investment Trusts (REIT)—a slightly more liquid real estate investment—sold by big firms also stumbled in the late 1980s. Both REITs and limited partnerships solicited cash in much the same way—via promoters trying to raise money by offering potential clients shares and units in planned projects—or in the income streams from such projects. The REIT market is thought to be between $10 and $20 billion: The market is also, apparently, heating up again as I write and the real estate cycle begins to turn.

Prudential Securities Inc. (formerly Prudential-Bache), along with other firms, energetically marketed REITs in the 1980s. The tale of Prudential is instructive because it illustrates how competitive pressures can result in the marketing of questionable products, which is as good a reason as any for reducing Wall Street's monopoly over the selling of such products.

When the huge insurer Prudential Co. bought the mid-size firm of Bache & Co., one business magazine commented dryly that Prudential had purchased a piece of the "shlock." Prudential realized it needed special leadership to raise the industry opinion of the company and not-so-incidentally to insure higher quality recruits for the firm. The man they picked was George Ball, a top E.F. Hutton Inc. executive.

Like Peter Cohen, his counterpart at Shearson, Ball wanted to build his firm into a "financial supermarket," a firm that could offer an array of services to an entire universe of financial customers. In the world of the mid-1980s stock market boom, nothing looked so attractive as the ability to be all things to all people. Ball spent a lot of money pursuing his dream of building a top-notch firm. He routinely offered brokers $100,000 in "up-front" money—bonuses—for leaving their firm to come to Prudential. He paid vastly inflated sums to top analysts to lure them to Prudential. As a result, even before the 1987 crash, Prudential-Bache's resources were being strained by Ball's Project 1989.

To fund Prudential's growth, Ball demanded more production and profits out of the firm's one truly substantial business, its brokerage group. In truth, Wall Street's biggest securities sales firms like Merrill Lynch and Hutton, before it went out of business, had been contemplating expansion ever since May 1, 1975, Mayday. On this date, by law, securities commissions were deregulated and discount brokers like Charles Schwab & Co. began chipping away at Wall Street's profits. But with the 1980s boom giving rise to inflated expectations, the pressure to sell questionable products with high up-front payouts to brokers and to the firm increased.

Prudential turned to marketing so-called closed-end funds that offer commissions. The firm's first great mid-1980s success may have been First Australia Prime Income Fund that raised $850 million. After this fund, the firm promptly began churning out closed-end funds at a phenomenal rate, former retail executives recall. Ultimately, the firm would sell in excess of $10 billion in closed-end stock and bond funds, and over $50 billion in mediocre mutual funds managed by parent Prudential. It was the fund-of-the-month, brokers joked. Buy 12 and get the 13th free.

Top retail executives at the firm fought against the trend. "The projection and analysis was flawed," says one retail executive. "It got to a point where it was difficult to make a decent analysis. If it wasn't a plain-Jane municipal fund or a plain vanilla corporate, you just knew that the due diligence was a mess."

By marketing at least $10 billion in limited partnership syndications and other real-estate products, and another $10 billion in closed-end funds, the firm gradually compromised its client base. By the time the selling spree was over, *The Wall Street Journal* estimated that Prudential and its parent insurer might be facing liabilities of up to $2 billion from customers with failed or failing investments.

Another firm identified with sour closed-end funds is the mid-sized Wall Street brokerage firm of PaineWebber Inc. PaineWebber had substantial involvement in at least three closed-end funds that came under attack in the late 1980s by investors who wanted them to be converted to more traditional open-ended investments.

Closed-end funds so often underperform the marketplace that the SEC issued a report in the late 1980s recommending changes in the way such funds were marketed. According to the SEC, closed-end funds, especially equity funds, almost invariably move down 10 to 15 percent starting a mere 12 days after they are offered. Such products tend to run in cycles.

A recent peak of country fund offerings may have been reached with the New Germany fund offered early in 1990. The $375 million fund, offered by PaineWebber, charged up from its $15 per share price to close at $22 million by first day's end. In fact, the performance of the Germany fund reminded at least some Wall Street executives of the last gasps of the 1960's Go-Go years when the infamous Manhattan Fund generated so much demand that management had to raise the offering by millions of shares.

The predictable and poor performance of certain closed-end funds was aggravated in the late 1980s by so-called "penalty-bid" practices at major Wall Street firms. Firms had been increasingly assessing penalties against their own brokers to prevent them from marketing newly issued securities to short-term traders who planned to hold such investments for just a few hours or days. Such a practice is called "flipping"—buying and selling back stock in IPOs and closed-end funds soon after the offering to realize small gains.

To curb flipping, underwriting groups levied longer "syndicate penalty bids" that attempted to fix the price of new issues. Brokers who sold the new securities below that price faced the loss of their commissions even if they were trying to protect a customer. Firms—harkening back to an older Wall Street—also began to extend the time of the penalty bid and to insure the actual physical delivery of securities so that individual sellers and brokers could be traced.

Meanwhile, another practice, bid stabilization, the routine practice of selling short to cover against share redemptions, was also extended. The two practices, taken together, tend to freeze the investor in a downward spiral. Of course, the investor didn't usually know about that until it happened.

Such practices are the result of Wall Street's monopoly over certain financial products—and the archaic regulatory standards that have facilitated it.

As we head into the 1990s, Wall Street's powerful selling machines are turning more and more to marketing so-called wrap fee products. For a stiff fee of up to three percent of all assets invested, a firm will assign a client a special money manager and undertake to shift assets, free of charge, from among a series of specially chosen funds.

As Wall Street's large brokerage firms continue to emphasize asset management over the stock tip of the past, the industry's usual conflict-of-interest difficulties will resurface. Consumers in ever-larger numbers will place their cash with Wall Street's "financial consultants" who, for a flat fee, will be glad to recommend one of several funds that their own firm happens to manage. The conflict-of- interest between managing money and selling products designed to capture client cash flow will blossom again.

Wall Street big retail drummers are in many cases public entities and must make money for their shareholders. They are in the sales business first and the investment-management business second. If it were not so, then Wall Street firms would not seek, as they do, to retrieve their salaries from a consumer's initial investment but would be content to retrieve a portion of the profits on the back-end.

This will never happen.

Penny Stocks and Junk Bonds

So long as a few powerful Wall Street firms sit between the buyer and the seller at the center of the world's biggest economy, "the tail will wag the dog." Wall Street's profit pressure, self-inflicted or not, leads to ephemeral financial trends.

Pressure for profits led firms like Prudential-Bache to develop and market products with little or no track record and dubious prospects for success; consumers paid the bill. Pressure for profits on Wall Street also drove the mergers and acquisitions (M&A) business. The trend may have peaked with the $20 billion privatization of RJR Nabisco, authoritatively documented in *Barbarians at the Gate*. It imploded along with the retail empire of Canadian-based entrepreneur Robert Campeau. Helped by Wall Street's bankers and generous dollops of junk, Campeau assembled more than $7 billion worth of retail outlets before going bust. His lingering series of defaults helped crush prices of the junk bond market and cost investors in other junk issues billions—to say nothing of Campeau's own bondholders and bank lenders.

Things change rapidly on Wall Street, but perhaps nothing is truly new. The M&A trend mimicked the conglomerate build-up of the 1960s when companies like ITT and Gulf & Western acquired dozens of companies in an effort to cushion recessionary cycles. In the 1980s privatization was supposed to concentrate the corporate mind via a huge debt hangover, but as the deals escalated—leading too often to corporate bankruptcy—small bondholders often ended up paying the bill. Meanwhile, as in the 1960s, the securities industry raked in fees.

In many cases, Wall Street is the victim of its own success. It cannot resist "driving a stake" through the heart of its most successful financial schemes, in the words of one caustic Wall Street observer. When it does, the media may turn brutal. Not equipped, apparently, to ask big questions about systemic difficulties, the media energetically pursues the most banal of current events: the loss of capital and the fall of recently lionized financeers, for instance. Perhaps the most outstanding example of this is epitomized by the rise and fall of Drexel and the relentless press scrutiny of its leading banker, Michael Milken.

Drexel's business was driven by Milken, the king of junk, whose career was first chronicled by Connie Bruck in her *Predator's Ball*. Bruck traces Milken's great vision that the high-yield market—the market for bonds that fueled the activities of small companies deemed to be high credit risks—was not truly more subject to default than investment-grade bonds of companies deemed better risks.

Armed with studies that apparently showed this was true, Milken joined the third-rate banking firm of Drexel in the mid-1970s and gradually began to build up a list of companies whose high-risk credits he marketed to an increasingly expansive roster of institutional buyers—banks, insurance companies, and money managers of mutual funds and pension funds. As the market expanded, Milken moved from selling bonds to creating issues, using a vast network of buyers and traders to ease the insurance of even the riskiest credit into the marketplace.

Labeled "junk" by Wall Street's half-fearful, half-envious rival bankers, Milken's high-yield shop churned out billions of dollars' worth of bonds, eventually helping to create a market of some $200 billion or more. By then other outfits like Merrill Lynch and First Boston Co. had clawed their way into the action. But Drexel was still doing more than half the business, according to *IDD Information Services.* By 1986 little Drexel was one of Wall Street's biggest money machines, spinning revenues of $5.3 million and earnings of more than $500 million. *BusinessWeek* magazine published a front cover with Milken standing astride a tiny globe, his head in the stars.

It turned out later that Milken had been shockingly well compensated for his efforts. He received an impossible $500 million bonus in cash and securities the year of the *BusinessWeek* cover story. But already the market had turned. There simply wasn't enough product to fuel the machine: That's what always happens sooner or later, on Wall Street. Milken must have begun underwriting weaker credits simply to keep the tail wagging. Quantity became more important than quality. Just as with Prudential, spinning out new limited partnerships and closed-end funds, Drexel churned out junk not to fill a need but to turn a profit.

On Monday, February 12, 1990, the situation became unglued for Drexel. Milken, by then, had been forced to resign and would shortly end up in jail. Institutional customers, aware that Drexel had no credit line from its banks, turned their backs on the firms that had made them rich and then, in some cases, poor again. On Tuesday, Drexel's parent defaulted on $100 million in short-term loans, and the firm declared Chapter 11. By Wednesday the phones had been removed from the firm's ninth-floor trading room. Drexel was finished as a major Wall Street player.

In Los Angeles, Benjamin Stein visited the legendary junk bond offices of Milken and wrote in *Barron's:* "The office that was the center of the empire, the trading room for junk bonds has been converted into a litigation defense file room. . . . In the center of the room, a shredder sits, humming quietly. . . . Maybe it just looks like a really successful boiler room that has just been busted. The lawyers have fled with their money, and only the desks and the phone lines remain. It certainly does not look like an investment bank."

According to Stein, Milken's whole market was a kind of Ponzi scheme kept afloat by propping up inferior issues with the public's money. If Milken's junk bonds had been of superior quality, the market would sooner or later have perceived that: Drexel would not have had to warehouse issues it could not sell; Milken would not have had to reward buyers of certain issues with partnerships in other issues; the commissions would gradually have come down because sellers would have found an ever bigger pool of buyers, as they had in Treasuries and high-grade corporates. Selling would have been easier, and salesmen would not have been able to charge so much for their services.

This is not a convincing argument. The junk bond market does exist, it continues in the 1990s, and it brings some investors and issuers profit—in some instances, depending on the level of the credit, big profit. Writing in *The Wall Street Journal,* the Hudson Institute's George Gilder pointed out that many of America's successes in the 1980s in fiber optics, cable, and the cellular phone industry were funded by junk. "Conventional venture capital could not meet these huge demands. It was Milken and Drexel that summoned the hundreds of billions of dollars in high-yield securities the new order required."

Ultimately Milken was brought down by one of the ring of buyers he used to manipulate the market he created: Ivan Boesky, the arbitrageur-turned-convicted-financier and state's witness. Milken pleaded guilty to flouting six relatively obscure securities regulations and went off to a San Francisco pen; but his fall left reverberations that found a harsh echo in a recent book, *Den of Thieves* by *The Wall Street Journal*'s front-page editor, James Stewart. "Could it happen again," Stewart asks. "If nothing else, the scandals of the 1980s underscore the importance of the securities laws and their vigorous enforcement."

One could be more sanguine about the possibility of more enforcement of the industry's dizzying array of rules and regulations if the industry—aided by the government and obliging lawyers—had not already been successful in insulating itself from some of its most egregious missteps. Sometimes it seems our regulators and legislators are too involved in the political process to be entirely objective.

In the 1980s, for instance, the industry finally got what it had hoped for, an SEC chairman, John Shad, who had spent his career on Wall Street. A senior executive of Hutton, and later on, of Drexel, Shad seemingly eviscerated the oversight efforts of the SEC—the nation's top securities regulator—in the 1980s, while talking tough about insider trading.

While the SEC railed about market manipulation, real-live fraud spread throughout the country. Investors were tricked into buying junk funds with retirement money; penny stock operators made billions;

limited partnership fraud and S&L fraud spread across the land. Additionally, while it would be nice to think that even though oversight had been lacking, the nation's legal system would provide remedies after the fact, this has not proved the case either.

The lack of alternatives for investors faced with mounting investment losses is one of the more startling aspects of our economic and legal system. While investing by its nature deals with risk, most fair-minded individuals would probably agree that where the investor has been bilked, legal recourse is a reasonable alternative. Unfortunately, in this country, such alternatives are not always available. That is because the Supreme Court has ruled that customers who sign arbitration agreements with securities firms are bound by them and must submit to arbitration if they have grievances. Because of the Supreme Court ruling, many of Wall Street's biggest retail brokerage firms have made signing arbitration agreements virtually mandatory. The situation is exacerbated by the arbitration process, which for the most part is supervised by the industry itself—the NYSE, the American Stock Exchange, or the National Association of Securities Dealers (NASD)—all "self-regulatory organizations" involved in the securities industry.

In addition to Supreme Court-mandated arbitration, unwary investors face other difficulties. They may be in for a shock if they do not choose litigators carefully. Some lawyers demand money before they will put a client's name on a class-action lawsuit. And then, when it comes time for the action to occur, these lawyers will settle on behalf of clients for relatively small sums. An investor, therefore, who has lost $5,000 or $10,000 may pay a lawyer $500 for the privilege of having his name attached to a class-action lawsuit and realize only, say, $700 in compensatory damages—for a total net of $200. But this investor, along with others who have forgone the class-action lawsuit, may not reopen the case once it has been settled. This is another reason, legal sources say, that firms are not entirely averse to class-action lawsuits and even in some cases may encourage them.

Conclusion

In the 1990s U.S. firms will be jockeying for position in an increasingly competitive international market while contending with the fallout of the 1980s. It is noteworthy, however, that some responses to 1980s difficulties involve increased price dissemination. The NASD is working on no less than three projects that seek to electronically present information on markets that were previously not easily accessed:

penny stocks, junk bonds, and American Depository Receipts (the instrument whereby American investors can buy and sell foreign stock on domestic exchanges). These products are all to be presented on electronic "bulletin boards," accessible first by the industry and later on through securities information vendors.

In fact, legislators and regulators have been steadily addressing oversight issues in the 1990s. Congress and securities regulators have tried to protect investors with legislation that makes it harder for the industry to market risky investments to unsuspecting buyers. The SEC has obtained additional civil powers of enforcement to stop insider trading and market manipulation. Even blind pools and other kinds of publicly issued shell companies that are floating invitations to penny-stock fraud have come in for some attention, though not enough.

In the coming two-tier securities system, individual investors and the big international banks are simply not going to be on the same footing (not that they ever really have been). The nation's top enforcers and policymakers should probably stop pretending that the system can ever make it so. That means the deemphasizing of market manipulations such as insider trading or "stock-parking." These kinds of crimes do cost the public money. But worse still, for the individual, are the kinds of petty fraud and high-powered sales hype that deprive old people of the money they need to live on and struggling parents of income to support their families. Insider trading may affect one security or another; a single crooked salesmen can ruin a household and blight the lives of innocent investors.

There are kinds of market manipulations that move markets, but these systemic opportunities are the result of the way the securities industry has developed. To make a significant dent on market manipulation, regulators and politicians will probably have to confront the way the securities industry is structured. The fundamental problem is that too few individuals have too much access to too much information.

Automation can make it more difficult for the industry to conceal the failure of certain products. Additional players in the retail market selling products in different ways to the consumer might mitigate some of the damage from powerful Wall Street sales arms. Mayday, and the introduction of competitive commissions began to give the consumer a lower pressure alternative to the purchase of stocks through a full-commission broker. The collapse of Glass-Steagall might inject more competition into the market and do even more to erode Wall Street's consumer franchise.

There are other measures that could prove effective. Merit regulation, the idea popular at a state level that certain phony issues have telltale signs that can be detected in advance and stopped, should be re-examined at a federal level. At least one former top Nasaa regulator thinks the securities industry needs to invent for itself a professional code of ethics similar to those that are in operation for doctors and lawyers. Such a professional code would be legally enforceable and would dramatically simplify notions of what constitutes wrongdoing within the industry. Mutual fund deregulation also holds promise. If fee-based or portfolio percentage-based financial planning ever overcomes Wall Street's opposition, investors will begin to benefit from the only kind of truly disinterested investment advice available.

The well-known securities lawyer Norman Poser has written that the industry itself ought to reconfigure the way it does business. Rather than brokers receiving a commission for selling a product, they should be put on a salary; this would remove the incentive on the part of salesmen to pursue products with the biggest "ticket" or payout, at the expense of the investors. This might be useful now that so many brokers are dressing up their salesmen as mutual fund marketers and even as financial consultants, despite clear-cut conflicts between advising a client and marketing a product.

For the speculator or the sucker—too often one and the same among the public—there will always be the shadowy sure thing, the hot tip not to be resisted. At least, in an optimistic future, our most reputable institutions won't be peddling them.

1

■■■

Brokerage

"There is zero possibility that Wall Street can clean up its act."

■ Tom Saler

Tom Saler was a broker in the early 1980s for Dean Witter Reynolds Inc. and the regional brokerage Robert W. Baird & Co. Unlike other securities-industry professionals who hung in through the boom time of the mid-1980s and the unraveling of the late decade, Saler bailed out early to write a book about his experiences: Lies Your Broker Tells You: What to Watch For and Still Achieve Financial Security.

I was a high school music teacher and left to become a stock broker. I had some experience in playing the stock market so when I left teaching, the stock market seemed a good alternative. I wanted to be an investment professional. I thought I could act in the best interests of my customers and my own best interests. It didn't work out that way—you were just being paid to be a sales professional. Look, by the time you add on transactions costs the average investor is better off in a no-load index fund, one that tracks a market.

The longer the period you look at, the more managed money underperforms the market. Now add on the fees—and broker fees are greater than what professional money managers take. The idea that a professional salesperson can generate ideas that consistently can beat the market after transaction costs is ludicrous.

It took me a couple of years to figure out the research on Wall Street wasn't much good. It sounded impressive, but the results weren't impressive.

The brokerage business motivated salesmen by telling them their best interest was also the customer's best interest. But that's just not true. Just because you make money doesn't mean the customer will out-perform the market. From the standpoint of the individual investor and his dealings with the customer, the biggest empty promise the broker sells is that he can predict the future. The entire financial services industry is built on this myth.

Limited partnerships were probably the most abused investment. The motivation for selling them was the huge up-front commission—an eight percent payout to the firm, and the broker might keep most of it. Limited partnerships were so lucrative because they were a tougher sell.

Junk bonds are more positively correlated to the business cycle—in a recession junk prices were more likely to move down. I think investors were probably not adequately informed.

They certainly aren't informed about penny stocks. A thinking investor would understand how tilted against them the risk-reward ratio is.

Selling a bad investment is always made easier if the customer does not have the facts. You can't make rational investment decisions without historical data. For instance, real estate is a commodity, it has cycles, and you have to learn from cycles. But I doubt that too many brokers educated their customers about the cycles of real estate before selling them limited partnerships invested in real estate. History is the starting point for financial markets. It's easier to sell an instrument without a track record.

There is zero possibility that Wall Street can clean up its act. What customers want is more honesty after a decade of greed. That's what Wall Street thinks it's hearing from the media. So they'll repackage their product to promote honesty. But as long as you have a commission driven system, it doesn't matter if you're honest. The system puts you at odds with the customer.

There's no substitute for being informed. All investing starts with a study of history. If investors are willing to study, they'll discover they can do better on their own.

I've started a non-profit organization to educate investors about the reality of the securities industry. I want to teach people how they can improve their investing. I'll be giving counseling free of charge. There will be classes, informational brochures, legal referrals, and lots of historical data.

2
■ ■ ■

AGENCY BROKERAGE

"I don't have any reason to think that this smear of financial planners has happened by accident."

■ RICHARD BANDFIELD

Richard Bandfield started out in the insurance field and then shifted over to the securities industry, eventually serving as director of personal planning for Shearson/American Express and Prudential-Bache. He currently runs his own personal financial counseling firm, Bandfield Associates, in New York City.

In most cases, investors don't read the prospectus of a security offering to really figure out the pros and cons of what's being offered to them. No matter how much conscientious effort may have gone into developing disclosure requirements for the protection of the public, the average investor finds prospectuses unreadable. What they really need, and want, is good professional advice—someone to sit down with them and explain what it's all about. The trouble is that the typical relationship between a broker and a client is more often purely a sales relationship. That's not what consumers want.

There was an outstanding marketing research study conducted in 1979 by SRI International—formerly Stanford Research Institute—of Menlo Park, California called "Financial Planning in the 1980s." It's the definitive study on the subject, with its findings based at the time on the most extensive in-depth personal interview survey ever conducted.

The SRI study showed that the public was very unhappy with the traditional product-oriented marketing and delivery system for financial products and services. They typically didn't believe the marketing claims made by vendors.

They said that what they really wanted was a trusted relationship with someone who understood their unique goals and circumstances and was technically competent to help them establish a strategic financial plan.

They also wanted someone who would assist them in identifying the types of financial products and services appropriate to their goals, and would help them to select the most suitable vendors and specific products or services for purchase.

The SRI study was an affirmation of a concept that was just evolving in the 1970s. The development of computers was making integrated financial planning practical for the first time, and the SRI study showed us the way to go.

When Shearson asked me to help them to develop a client-centered financial planning service I was initially skeptical about the extent of their corporate commitment. But they made me a corporate senior vice president and supported me in my efforts to create a really effective service consistent with SRI's findings. Our financial planning department, in consultation with the client, the client's tax and legal advisers and the broker was able to help clients develop a strategic plan, identify appropriate types of assets and make specific recommendations with a high degree of professional integrity.

By limiting the service to qualified clients we generated fees and commissions averaging nearly $10,000 per client, simply by showing customers appropriate financial strategies to fit their unique personal circumstances. That was our revenue goal, and we created substantial additional income for brokers, managers and the company. It was ex-hilarating to see that client-centered planning really could work.

The day came, however, in December of 1983 when my initial fears were realized. Senior management changes had occurred, support had clearly faded and finally Shearson shut down its financial planning service without advance notice or explanation. In its place they introduced a computerized, product-centered financial planning program for use by brokers through a sales support group. I learned about the decision when everybody else did, when the routine company announcement memo reached my desk, and to this day I have no idea what the thinking was that led company officials to decide to junk financial planning—and the substantial investment that had been made in its development.

In the meantime, George Ball had moved from Hutton to Prudential-Bache and under his leadership the company had been running a very effective advertising program designed to position Prudential-Bache as The Total Financial Planning Company. He had a reputation of being supportive of personal financial planning, having built and then maintained a very effective department of 120 or more employees during what had been very difficult times for the company. I was pleased when I was invited to join Prudential-Bache to be a part of his team.

As with Shearson, I had misgivings about the company's true commitment to client-centered planning. My concerns lessened when I was given a copy of the firm's financial training manual to review. It was completely consistent with the SRI study findings, and didn't reflect the traditional product-oriented approach that was characteristic of most Wall Street firms.

Unfortunately, financial planning never really got off the ground at Prudential-Bache. I realized early in the game that my skepticism had been well founded when I was told that the training manual used to recruit me had never been utilized and, in fact, its use was not permitted because it did not represent the firm's product-oriented philosophy. I'd been sold a bill of goods.

Tremendous losses in late 1983 led to an austerity program at Pru-Bache that included the termination of programs that did not contribute to the firm's bottom line. The total financial planning concept was immediately discarded, and I found myself put out with the trash.

While I had concluded from my experience that cost-effective, integrated, client-centered financial planning required a minimum staff of 10-12 staff members, I found that by 1984 most financial institutions able to support such a staff had lost interest in financial planning. About the only way left for a financial planner to practice was by establishing an independent firm, which I eventually did.

The fact is that Wall Street firms are basically marketing driven. I'm not saying that this is either good or bad—just that it is a fact that must be recognized. I have never understood why a client-centered service department couldn't co-exist in a firm with product-oriented marketing activities, but fee-based client-centered financial planning has been abandoned by every securities firm of which I'm aware, so there must be a reason. I'd love to know what it is.

The securities industry has the responsibility in our economic system of raising or securing capital for businesses, as well as governments, ours and others. They don't raise capital by providing financial services to individuals—they do it by aggressive marketing, which has nothing to do with a client-centered system. In retrospect, it was almost inevitable that most of these institutions would corrupt the client-centered concept cf financial planning by turning it into simply another product to sell, and another means of marketing whatever other products they had to sell.

I don't mean to single out the securities industry. The banks and insurance companies have done the same thing, hiding their marketing efforts under the cloak of financial planning, and calling their salespeople financial consultants or financial planners to mislead potential customers into thinking that they are being given objective advice rather than a sales pitch.

The securities industry, along with all the other financial services industries, has done a remarkable job of resisting the forces of change which are clearly threatening to their established way of doing business. Do they want the public, through financial planners, telling them what products and services they should be selling? How can they be comfortable if their representatives are truly representing their customer's best interests rather than those of the firm?

Tight control of a security firm's sales force is critical to accomplishing its corporate marketing objectives. The securities industry has been very successful in preventing its representatives from straying off the path laid out for them by their employer.

To a large extent the securities business has prevented pressures for change by co-opting the regulators. Dual licensing, for example, has largely been eliminated. That means, if you're a broker, that you cannot sell products through more than one firm. You work for one firm, and represent its interests to customers, not the other way around. You're controlled by your employer, even though your title might represent you to the public as something else.

I can't speak for the rest of the country, but in the metropolitan New York area the availability of client-centered financial planning has practically disappeared. But the public continues to be dissatisfied with the way securities are marketed by most firms, and ultimately I predict that their voices will be heard and major changes will result.

Meanwhile, the media is trying to fill the vacuum by playing the role of financial counselor. Their advice, usually developed by writers who are not educated or experienced in the topics they write about, is often arbitrarily limited by space and time, and is often seriously flawed or incomplete.

I feel very strongly that publications which give financial advice should have to be registered as financial advisers and should be held accountable for their advice, just as individual advisers are.

What the public told SRI in 1979 that they wanted was the creation of a new class of professional advisers. While many individuals and institutions responded to their cry, their efforts have largely failed because they have been blocked by established institutions, outdated regulations, and an openly hostile environment created by both.

The financial planning profession has taken a phony rap as far as purported abuses are concerned. An examination of the actual reports of studies made of claimed abuses by financial planners makes it clear that most of the abuses attributed to financial planners have been perpetrated by salespersons who merely called themselves financial planners to dupe their victims. While SRI defined financial planning as a profession in its report in 1979, the public perception, and the perception of many regulators seems to be that a financial planner is someone in the business of hustling securities by any and all means. I don't have any reason to think that this smear of financial planners has happened by accident.

For some time I've been calling myself a financial counselor rather than a financial planner to avoid being thought of as something that I'm not. If I were developing regulations for the protection of the public, the first regulation I'd recommend would be to prohibit anyone from calling themselves a financial planner unless their financial planning services are rendered only when they have been retained on a fee basis by clients. They'd also have to subscribe to a professional pledge to put their clients' interests above their own or the companies they represent. Right now that isn't the case.

3

▪▪▪

MUTUAL FUNDS

*"**W**all Street has occasionally used its marketing muscle to funnel money into areas where it doesn't belong."*

■ GERALD BEIRNE

Gerald Beirne is an outspoken stockbroker whose views on various securities issues have been quoted in national publications such as BusinessWeek. *One concern of Beirne's is the way the big mutual fund companies do business. Of course, life may change radically for these big funds, and also for Wall Street if true mutual fund deregulation occurs.*

I went to Columbia University where I majored in music and art history, a not necessarily inappropriate preparation for Wall Street. For a while I was with a clothing manufacturer and then I answered an ad for a stockbroker. I got my Series 7 and was hired as a full-time stockbroker in 1975.

Clearly mutual funds are an honest way to invest. Bond funds are an appropriate way to invest too. But there are some concerns that investors should be aware of. When the investor reads any claim that is out of line with the current market, a higher than normal yield for example, that should be a red flag.

For example, First Investors in New Jersey was cited by *The Wall Street Journal* with touting junk bonds with high yields as a come-on. Their marketing skills resulted in a market distortion. The result was a flood of investor money into a speculative arena that would never have attracted it in the first place. Add to this the billions sucked into the same market by Drexel and crew from shady insurers and the S&Ls, and it's easy to understand why junk bond prices were artificially high during this buying binge. When the collapse finally came, the customer found himself with a shrinking asset—and with poor prospects for recovery when interest rates turned down.

This is how the marketing works. In the mid-1980s, for instance, Treasury yields started to drop. That's because inflation had slowed. But the mutual funds could still claim high returns based on past performance. That made big bond funds attractive. You could get a high yield and the safety of a government investment.

For the next couple of years, money poured into these funds. That's one reason so much money moved into mutual funds in the 1980s. One fund went from $800 million to $8 billion under management in just a few years. But it was all based on past return. And in fact, the funds couldn't maintain the past return on new investor's money because interest rates were lower and new investments were paying less.

Managers started offering enhanced funds. That means the income is enhanced by an option-writing strategy. That works just fine until the market moves down instead of up. And one day, of course, it does—as investors found out in 1987.

A lot of these funds suffered from a crippling redemption rate. To stem the tide, funds are sweetening their yields. But what they're doing is disguising a portion of their returns. Some of their distribution to investors is actually coming from capital, not from the interest earned on capital. In summary, just as the S&Ls exploited a federal guarantee on deposits to attract money into overpriced real estate, Wall Street has occasionally used its marketing muscle to funnel money into areas where it doesn't belong.

It's this sort of thing—even in mutual funds which are as well-regulated as any consumer investment—that make additional demands on investors to look before they leap.

4

■ ■ ■

CLOSED-END FUNDS

"The major investment banks have been very unfair to the investor."

■ TOM HERZFELD

Tom Herzfeld is a leading authority on closed-end funds. Headquartered in Miami, Florida, his research firm tracks hundreds of funds; he has over $200 million under management invested in various closed-end investment companies.

I went to Wall Street after I completed my Army service; I was 22 or 23 at the time. I became a stockbroker and then a year or two later I bought a seat on the Big Board—the NYSE—with two colleagues and we formed a member firm.

I have always specialized in closed-end funds. As a trainee I took a course on the then-obscure industry of closed-end funds. That's when I was hooked. The pricing mechanism is, of course, that closed-end funds have market risk built into them because the issuer won't redeem an investor's share at the underlying value of the securities. The investor has to find another investor to buy his shares. And that means that closed-end funds' shares, which trade on various stock exchanges, may cost more or less than the securities of which they're made up—that is the premium or discount.

When other brokers were trading glamour stocks, I was trading sleepy closed-end funds. People knew almost nothing about them at the time. And that provided some great opportunities so long as I stuck with funds at wide discounts.

I always had what you might call a low tolerance for risk. I think my partners, on the contrary, had a much higher one and so I finally decided to go it alone. In 1981 I formed Thomas J. Herzfeld & Co., the nation's first stock brokerage firm specializing in closed-end funds. A little later I moved to Florida and formed in addition the first investment advisory firm specializing in closed-end funds.

Today, through our advisory firm and our affiliated brokerage firm, we're managing $200 million for all types of clients both here and overseas.

Closed-end funds are a great investment but buyers should, of course, avoid buying them as new issues. The SEC has pointed out that equity funds can move down very quickly, between 10 and 15 percent, once the underwriter stops supporting the issue.

Closed-end funds tend to be issued in cycles. In the 1980s, many believed that because of the high yields of junk bond funds, they wouldn't decline. But as we know, as a group junk bond funds performed awfully in the early 1990s—the underlying value of the securities that make up the funds crumbled during the Milken crisis and the recession.

Recently there was a big wave of municipal closed-end funds being issued, and one hears the same kind of optimistic talk. But bond funds as a whole tend to trade about four percent below net asset value. It's when they get down to that level that they become attractive. Not before.

People have taken a beating in new issues of closed-end funds, especially country funds. And I guess if I had to suggest changes for the industry, it would be in the mechanism in which new issues are launched. It would help if underwriters would not be so greedy. If the new issue is such a good idea, why not reduce underwriting fees to one or two percent on an initial offering. Additionally, it would be a good idea if investors would be able to put back their shares to the funds after a year or so and receive the net asset value of their investment. The SEC has been considering this idea as part of its review of the Investment Company Act of 1940. I think, on the whole, the major investment banks have been very unfair to the unsophisticated investor, though fortunately there are signs of improvement lately.

5

■ ■ ■

INVESTOR REGULATION

*"Times have changed but the individual investor can't
take advantage of it yet."*

■ ROBERT GORDON

*As chief executive and founder of Twenty-First Securities Corp., Robert
Gordon is one of the few successful entrepreneurs on Wall Street at
the turn of the decade. His interest in securities began even before
he was old enough to be a broker; today his clients include the Walt
Disney Company and Chanel Inc.*

When I was 12, 13, whatever, I started following stocks and
graphing them.

I became a broker at 21. When you're a stockbroker and the
market goes up you look like a genius and you get referrals. When
it goes down you lose referrals and your book is burnt out. So I
gravitated to investments where I didn't have to be right or wrong
all the time, to non-traditional products like tax arbitrage.

After I went out on my own I started specializing in different
hedged strategies, selling sophisticated financial products to professional
investors.

When you're a broker you're told not to go elephant hunting.
But I really felt that we had the ammunition. I knew if someone was
a professional and he looked at what we had they would appreciate
it, act on it and put money into it.

These days we run about $2 billion. The crash of 1987 was the best thing that happened to us because our clients didn't lose money—so we could prove our hedged strategies worked.

It was very powerful to see that our hedging strategies worked in 1987. In the mid-1980s, most big institutions were hedged in futures, not options because it was cheaper to hedge with futures. But when the crash of 1987 came, they found it wasn't so cheap after all. They lost billions.

The individual investor works on a lot of emotion, and emotion is usually wrong. When you're a broker you're taught what motivates people is fear and greed. I always sold the logical investment. I found stocks to be a very harried business. And I always remember the Will Rogers line—the customer is more concerned with the return of his money than the return on his money.

There are changes going on that can allow more rational investing. If the regulators would let us, we could offer our hedged products to small investors. Right now only the wealthy can afford them. But I could offer a mutual fund, only a lot of what we want to do, what I want to do, is presently illegal under the 1940 act regulating what fund managers can do with public money. We'd like to see the Short-Short Rule removed. We'd like to see the diversification rules of the 40 Act reexamined. Times have changed, but the individual investor, for the most part, can't take advantage of it yet.

6

■■■

STATE REGULATORS

"The SEC and Wall Street have tended to look down on Nasaa."

■ LEE POLSON

An enforcement attorney with the state of Texas for 11 years, Lee Polson came to Washington as executive director of Nasaa's Washington office in November of 1987. Jim Meyer, then Nasaa president, offered him the job. "It sounded interesting so I took it. I was ready for a change anyway."

State regulators and their organization, Nasaa, have often been at odds with the outfits that do the same job at a national level. In fact, because of its unique position, Nasaa has squared off with a variety of industry and small business interests as well as regulators.

Both the SEC and Wall Street have tended to look down on Nasaa as a kind of weak sister without the regulatory muscle or know-how to have consistent, industry- wide influence. But more recently, especially during the 1980s, the states were called on to do the job the federal regulators didn't seem interested in doing. I mean the nuts and bolts regulatory work at a grass-roots level that defended people from being defrauded.

That's always been Nasaa's mission, and it's always been a source of tension between Nasaa on the one hand and the NASD and the SEC on the other.

The way the SEC was set up diverges from Nasaa's philosophy. That's because the states often impose various merit tests on securities registrations to determine whether or not the offerings are possibly fraudulent. But the SEC, from its very inception, has observed a mandate to withhold such judgments.

That was a big argument when the SEC was being set up. The industry argued that if the SEC could stop issues from going public that sooner or later they'd keep an Edison or Ford from raising money on the grounds that whoever heard of a box that produced moving pictures of a horseless buggy. So the SEC adopted it's present mandate. So long as information is properly and legally presented in a prospectus, the SEC will pass on that registration and allow the issue to become public.

States have tended, individually, to take stricter approaches. The most stringent type of merit is fair, just and equitable merit. That's a series of definitions that an offering must fulfill and that opponents claim must by definition be arbitrary. *Caveat emptor* is the slogan of the SEC. Let the buyer beware.

It's true Nasaa is a more parochial organization than the SEC. Our members tend to see first-hand the damage that corrupt securities offerings can do. Our members are on the front line.

Nasaa is composed of state regulators from across the country who perform a variety of state security functions. Membership in Nasaa is voluntary, and the organization derives income from fees collected by the NASD which administers tests that brokers must take to become registered.

Nasaa's regulatory territory extends beyond the U.S. to Canada, Mexico, and Puerto Rico. State regulation began in 1891 with adoption by Kansas of the first so-called blue sky laws. The association itself has been around 15 years longer than the SEC. The phrase was coined by a judge long ago who said the schemes hatched by some stock crooks had no more substance than a "square foot of blue sky."

The markets didn't grow much in the 1970s, but they certainly grew through the famous bull market of the 1980s. Federal oversight of the securities market under the Reagan administration did not expand, and in fact the amount of federal regulation of the securities markets decreased. As complaints grew, states took up the slack.

Section 19c-3 of the Federal Securities Act of 1933 was passed in the early 1980s—that required increased cooperation between the

SEC and Nasaa with emphasis on small business issues. An early result of state-federal small business initiatives was Reg. D and its counterpart in the state realm.

The idea of Reg. D was to increase access to the capital markets by small business. There were many partnerships that took advantage of Reg. D, small public offerings too. It was the last major attempt to create a sane structure of limited offering exemptions. But it was subject to some abuse. Partnership investments and small offerings have always been the subject of abuses.

There was some debate about shelf registration, where a firm can fulfill SEC disclosure requirements in advance of an offering, and then have the offering ready to go whenever they want it. But most of the companies using shelf registration are the big ones. And those are exempt from state rules anyway.

Edgar was of more concern. Beginning in the mid-1980s, they began to talk about Edgar—an electronic filing system. Shad's idea was that this information would be so fascinating that every dentist would want an Edgar, and that would help pay for the system. His time line was shorter than 1992. It was a priority of his. I didn't think then that it was realistic. The data are popular but not that popular.

I would say the 1987 stock market crash was the seminal event of the decade, for all securities regulators including Nasaa. It caused us to believe there were major shortcomings in the way the market dealt with investors.

The 1987 crash has been one of the most studied events of the last half century. Coincidentally, it occurred shortly after Nasaa opened its Washington office. After the crash we put in a hot line. We were not equipped to handle the volume—but the bottom line was too many investors knew too little about what they had bought. I don't think the SEC was pleased. They've always had a consumer office but we had a more aggressive program.

We began to advocate that someone should establish a toll-free 800 number full-time, and that proposal was rolled into the penny stock bill.

In the 1990s my big concern is making sure the grass-roots protection stays in place and is as effective as today. I want to insure that the Edgar gets running and that the states have efficient access to the system. Nasaa is probably going to enhance its own electronic systems in any case.

Globalization is going to be an issue in the 1990s, and states will have to find a way to regulate their positions and deal with the SEC's efforts at the same time. I would say Nasaa's idea of merit regulation is closer to the way more foreign governments deal with securities disclosure than the federal government's idea.

7

■ ■ ■

PENNY STOCKS

*"**I** used to go around from state to state, to legislatures, like a poster child."*

■ ROYCE GRIFFIN

Royce Griffin's parents were schoolteachers, and such pedagogical role models may have spoiled him for numerous careers. Griffin graduated from Harvard and later received a law degree but chose to work in the public sector. In Arkansas he prosecuted corrupt Bond Daddies who sold fraudulent municipal bonds to western and southern investors.

In 1981 he moved to Denver, where he took over the grandly titled Colorado Division of Securities with all of nine staffers and with office space opposite the state capital.

I got to Colorado right at the hottest part of the market. It was unlike anything you can imagine. I used to go around from state to state, to legislatures, like a poster child. I'd tell them, Don't repeal merit legislation the way you're planning. You have to give your regulators the power to keep crooked deals off the market. Look at what's happened in Colorado. I was invited to testify in Texas, in Illinois, in New Jersey, all over.

Our legislative efforts were successful. For several years, in the early and mid-1980s, lobbying efforts were made to weaken state securities laws and to do away with merit regulation. It happened in Colorado, which never had any strong laws to begin with, but most other states held firm.

The new law in Colorado, passed in early 1981, made it legal to sell any security which was offered in more than one state, without any form of state registration or review.

You'd sit in your office and read prospectuses they were sending in and you'd know how outrageous the offerings were. The NASD wasn't going to stop it because they had people on the regional board from these penny stock firms. The SEC was 2,000 miles away.

All you had to do was read to get the picture. One offering disclosed that one of the principals had exchanged 50 bins of earth worms for his insider stock. That's kind of funny because earth worm farming is a classic fraud. The promoters approach the victims and say, We'll give you worms and equipment, you raise them and we'll buy them back. They never buy the worms back. Another variation does the same thing with silk worms and moths. Grow the silk and we'll buy it back. They just need something, anything to sell—anything with a time lag so they can collect money on the front end with no intention of performing as promised at the end of the growing season.

A gold stock offering was even simpler. They raised $500,000 and they were going to give that money to the president of the company to go down to Liberia and buy gold for half price and bring it back to this company. Subsequent reports revealed that the scheme didn't work and that most of the money had disappeared.

Then there was a real high-tech deal. This outfit was going to manufacture and sell sawhorses. They even illustrated the prospectus with black and white photos of sawhorses. They raised three million dollars.

I've seen more elaborate offerings illustrated with color photos. There was this restaurant with a brothel decor. The idea was that the waitresses would dress like 1890s prostitutes and diners would come in for the experience.

You couldn't read prospectuses of Denver offerings without laughing out loud. Many of the deals provided that most of the proceeds could go to retire debts owed to insiders. No real capital was being raised at all. I concluded that the penny stock market was a fancy con game. I had little respect for those people who were making fortunes selling worthless securities.

My first secretary was an elderly lady, and she got very irritated with me once. I remember she told me that not everyone could afford stocks trading on Wall Street. She thought the penny stocks were giving ordinary people a chance to invest. That was the attitude in

Colorado. It ran very deep during the boom, but they didn't realize these cons go all the way back to the 1800s and the mining frauds, and in the 1950s there were uranium stock frauds, very similar except in magnitude to the penny stock boom of the early '80s.

I already knew how these offerings would turn out. Almost all penny stock offerings have the same story. First it goes straight up and then it goes straight down, and when it starts to fall you don't get anything back. It's very much like the children's game of musical chairs—when the music stops the trouble starts.

The penny stock houses were energetic. Some would cut up phone books and give out columns to salesmen and have the salesmen call everyone in that column. Or they'd hire former service managers from auto dealerships. A guy used to run the shop, and they'd have him call service managers all across the country. That's what's called recruiting new blood. When you'd bring someone in from the outside who had contacts and credibility and could bring in as yet untapped and not yet burned investors to replace the losers from the last deal.

I spent every year that I was in Colorado lobbying and trying to change and strengthen the law. The local securities industry hired the best and most expensive lobbyists to see we were never successful. There was so much fraud we couldn't begin to dent even the openly illegal deals. The state had stripped away our regulatory powers. If a security was offered in more than one state, we could sue only if we had evidence of outright fraud. We were swamped with fraud, but we still had no power over the brokers.

Unregulated deals where there was no SEC involvement—that was an area we could attack. Mortgage brokering was a fertile area for us. What promoters would do was advertise a kind of CD—a cash deposit on which they promise to pay you interest. You weren't supposed to be worried about giving them your money because they would pledge a mortgage of theirs on a specific piece of property against your loan. The only trouble was they would secure about fourteen other loans with the same property. And needless to say most of these so-called mortgage brokers never had any intention of paying the money back.

The mortgage brokers were able to attract investors because they would offer such high interest rates—fourteen to twenty percent and sometimes higher. That's how I got involved. I'd scan the ads and I'd target outfits offering impossible rates of return.

I remember we went to the office of one mortgage broker who has since fled to New Zealand. We made copies of the paperwork of this fellow and figured out what he was doing. I recall a meeting in my offices with his lawyers where they offered me a deal. The lawyer said she'd let me off the hook if I'd simply apologize to the guy, and she started ticking off other things they wanted. It was truly bold. After the fifth or sixth thing, I asked her to leave. She was shocked. This was not the way regulation was supposed to work in Colorado. We went to court and the promoter immediately filed for bankruptcy. Charges were filed and he fled the country with a million dollars of other people's money.

The list of victims who bought these kinds of deals, it was always the same. Elderly people, people who can't take care of themselves. People who buy platinum over the phone.

Eventually I decided the best way to attack the penny stock problem was to get other states with real laws involved. The other states had a reason to get involved since investors all over the country were being victimized.

I knew who I wanted to get on board from Nasaa, and we used Nasaa funds to partially fund the multi-state project. Our first discussions were at a Nasaa Enforcement Committee meeting at Big Sky, a Montana ski resort. There was a good deal of enthusiasm for the project from the start.

Philip Feigen, the enforcement director in Wisconsin, was at the meeting. We became good friends: I thought Phil was just about the best lawyer in the country doing state securities work. Later on he came to work for me and took my place as state commissioner when I left.

What we decided to do in Montana was to simultaneously raid a dozen operations and see if we couldn't find sales practice violations, like selling stocks in states where the brokers weren't registered. When we struck, we did so with auditors from 15 states, and found violations in every firm we visited. Some firms were registered in two states but doing business in fifty. Years later, the states were still using what was found in prosecutions.

In 1985, I became president of Nasaa for the typical one-year term. I got a chance to meet John Shad. We hit it off to some degree. He seemed to like me, but trusted me like a nephew from the frontier, a person unfamiliar with the real securities industry.

Shad's priorities were things like developing an electronic registration system called Edgar and implementing a book entry system for the purchase of securities that would replace the settlement process involved in the actual delivery of these issues.

It seemed to me that these priorities didn't have much impact on individual investors, but they were the love of his life. I was little shocked by his lack of familiarity with the street crime security issues I'd seen in the penny stock market. Investor protection was not a term to be found in his usual vocabulary.

He'd explain to me about how Wall Street worked and what the real levers of power were. He invited me to several securities roundtables that the SEC sponsored. One dealt with insider trading and included both Ivan Boesky and Lloyd Jefferies—both later convicted of securities crimes. Another roundtable was about doing more with less, which was something Shad was also focused on. The industry kept on soaring and he kept asking for budget cuts for his agency.

A lot of what he was doing, I disagreed with, but I couldn't say he was insincere. Ours was a disproportionate relationship of power. I did the best I could to get the investor protection message out. I testified at budget hearings in opposition to more cuts.

At every opportunity, Shad asked for less money while the number of broker-dealers in the country doubled and the actual number of complaints about securities offerings went up 150 percent.

By the end of my term I was somewhat cynical about securities regulation in general. Despite Shad's protestations, there had been a substantial diminution in the protection to investors across the country.

After my term as Nasaa president I went to work for Representative Edward Markey (D-Mass.) as senior counsel for financial issues. He'd just become chairman of the House subcommittee dealing with securities oversight. I ended up working more on insider trading and market reform issues than on penny stock issues because of the 1987 stock market crash.

I left Washington in 1989 and ended up in New Mexico involved in a special regulatory project rewriting that state's securities rules. I must admit I watched with a certain amount of amazement when the new SEC chairman David Ruder came to Colorado and declared war on penny stocks. He surprised a lot of people.

I think you have to do a lot more than is being done to really combat securities fraud now that it is a nationwide problem.

I believe that the relationship between a broker-dealer and a registered rep. and between a stockbroker and a client is not generally treated in the brokerage industry as a fiduciary one. My relationship with my banker if he's managing my trust and with my accountant is a fiduciary relationship—that means they have a duty to put your interest above theirs. In such situations the law implies a higher standard of care. You don't see that higher standard when you go to see a car dealer—or oftentimes a broker.

Instead of this higher standard, you have exchanges and self-regulatory organizations each purporting to police its own rules of fair practice. These rules are incredibly complex and often difficult to understand. They do not generally serve as an adequate replacement for fiduciary behavior. I think that fiduciary responsibility should be clearly articulated in the 1934 Act.

I would also clarify the principal and agent relationship in the industry. If one of your employees is cheating a client, I would hold the firm responsible as well, with no exceptions.

Vicarious liability for securities firms is one way to describe what I would like to see put in place. The SEC and the NASD only penalize for failure to supervise. I think if you hire crooks you are responsible for the harm they cause. Especially if you're hiring guys with previous disciplinary records.

I think I would require broker-dealers, when they get a new client, to reveal their disciplinary history, to disclose their records in other words, for the firm and for the client. I think you could come up with guidelines in this regard that would disclose seriously abusive past behavior. Clients would be given an early warning if they chose to go forward with the relationship.

You should also outlaw binding arbitration agreements. That's where the customer signs away his right to go to a court of law if he's been taken advantage of. Industry-sponsored arbitration is not a fair substitute for your day in court.

You need a statutory definition of insider trading. I worked on the insider trading bill and we had a definition—but it was ultimately shot down. The fear is that if you define it, crooks will find a way around it. The result is the courts are deciding what insider trading is instead of the legislature.

I'd define market manipulation. There isn't anything in the 1934 Act that clearly defines what it is, and I'd make it easier to prove. And I'd consider granting customers a cooling off period. That is, if you've been sold a product—a transaction initiated by a broker—and you decide within, say, three days, that you've changed your mind, I think you ought to have the right to rescind. They recently passed a law like this in Georgia for certain low-priced securities.

If regulators and legislators would do some of what I've suggested, you'd start to have the kind of professional environment that would lessen fraud and abuse not only in the penny stock area but on Wall Street as well. People sometimes forget that some of the same tactics used in penny stocks can be applied to wider markets—it's too bad, but it happens.

■ LORENZO FORMATO

Lorenzo Formato is a former broker and penny stock operator who pleaded guilty to several federal felonies in connection with his previous activities. He has served time for his offenses and is part of the Federal Witness Protection Program. He testified with a modified microphone to alter his voice at congressional hearings before Congressman Edward Markey's (D-Mass) Committee on Energy and Commerce, House Tele-communications and Finance Subcommittee late in 1989: What follows is drawn from that testimony.

I never graduated from high school though I did receive a high school diploma. I went into the auto body business and it was then a fellow classmate of mine came to my auto body shop to have his car repaired. It was a new car and I was kind of in shock he was driving such a new car. I asked him how he was able to afford this car and he told me he was a stock broker. I had no idea what a stock broker was. I didn't know what stocks were.

I asked him if he could take me to where he works, and I went with him that day in my work clothes to his office, which was Mayflower Securities in Hackensack, New Jersey, and I went into his office in my work clothes to his boss, knocked on his boss' door and said if this guy can do whatever he is doing to buy that car, I can do it better, and his boss gave me the job.

What I did, I took a job as a night guard, and I studied the questions for the broker's exam that were given at the time. I was able to arrange to get a copy of the tests and I memorized all the answers to all the questions. I went and took the exam to become a registered representative or what we know as a stockbroker, and I passed that exam.

During the time that I was memorizing those questions I worked at Mayflower Securities using another registered representative's name and cold-calling people from a phone booth.

What I did was I listened to some of the salesmen who were in the office and I formed my own cold-call pitch by taking pieces of everyone's statements, and I became quite good at it. I used to call people from 8 A.M. until sometimes 11 P.M., seven days a week. I became a one-man firm by having so many clients. I didn't know what the hell I was doing in the brokerage business but I had so many clients I could just pick up a telephone and sell anything I wanted to sell to these people.

It was shortly after that I went to First Jersey Securities. The president of First Jersey was Bob Brennan. Bob Brennan knew how to treat his good salesmen well. Bob Brennan was, in my opinion, one of the smartest men that ever entered the over-the-counter brokers' industry as far as being able to manipulate stocks and manipulate people. I was a good salesman. I had trips to the Bahamas with my family paid by Brennan. I met other top salesmen.

I left the securities industry for a brief period of time and in 1977 I opened up a brokerage firm in New Jersey called A. L. Williamson & Co. I want to point out during all of this time, from the time of A. L. Williamson to the time I came to jail I was involved with organized crime.

The reason I was involved with those people in organized crime was so that when I would go and do one of these stock manipulations or one of these stock frauds or I wanted to successfully make a market in this stock without anyone else in the business getting involved and trying to undercut me or short one of my stocks, I needed the protection and I needed the strength of organized crime and they needed me.

I used to laugh at the SEC. I used to laugh at the Bureau of Securities. You know, new people in the business are all afraid of state regulators and the SEC. But it doesn't take someone very long to realize that the SEC does not have the power or the funds to go after stock fraud experts, and they are only a civil arm of the justice system. Criminal references must be made which are very rarely made. If they are made, you must then have a criminal system, justice system, that can go out and successfully indict and convict stock fraud experts, which is very difficult to do.

I wasn't afraid of the Justice Department. I viewed the brokerage industry as white-collar crime, and if you did get in trouble or you did get indicted, in most cases you would be handed a light sentence, probation, maybe a year at some nice, fancy camp somewhere.

I was indicted on Laser Arms stock fraud by the Federal Bureau of Investigations and the District of New Jersey. They were able to obtain wiretaps. I did in fact go to jail on Laser Arms stock fraud. But Laser Arms stock fraud is just one fraud of thousands and thousands of frauds that are taking place every single day. The over-the-counter (OTC) market is controlled by organized crime. The OTC market is controlled by people like myself, stock promoters, stockbrokers who go out, raise millions and millions and millions of dollars for themselves and for organized crime to feed themselves.

There are OTC companies that are legitimate companies that start out with legitimate financing but once the stock gets in the hands of the trader or the promoter or the stockbroker, it then becomes a manipulation. It can start out legitimate, but once it starts trading, it becomes manipulative. What I am saying is that every stock that I know of in the OTC industry that is being traded today is being manipulated in one form or another.

It's virtually impossible for an individual who does have a legitimate company to go to a small OTC brokerage firm and take his company public without him having to give away half of his company, without him having to give away a big chunk of the money that is raised for his company. It's an industry that is controlled by a small circle of people.

You cannot become a successful stock promoter. You cannot give in to this circle, and this circle dominates by fear and power. We not only tell stockbrokers what to sell, we tell them what price to sell the stocks for. We tell them whether to go up or whether to go down.

When I ran the company and I was chief executive also of that company, I had a machine in my office. It wasn't a brokerage firm. But I had a Nasdaq machine, and I was able to get it. And I could sit there, and I checked the price of my stock and the price of other stocks, and I could pick up a telephone from my office at Worldwide Ventures and tell my leading brokerage firms to move up a quarter, move up ahead a point, move down.

I would know if there was a blocked stock that was out there. I would tell them drop down half a buck and then move the market back up. These are things that I was able to do, because I had the power and I wielded the fear of organized crime behind me.

I have several recommendations. One of the recommendations would be promoters or consultants should be licensed, much like a registered representative or a stockbroker. They should have at least five year's experience in the business before they can apply for a promoter's license.

Security violators should not be allowed to act as a promoter or a consultant. All over-the-counter brokerage firms should be required to have a minimum of $1 million bond, and each registered representative should be bonded.

I think that the net capital requirements for the OTC brokerage firms should be raised from $30,000 to $300,000. Over-the-counter firms should be required to send a financial statement of their firm and what experience the registered representative has before they can open up an account and make a trade.

The customer should have to fill out a suitability statement showing annual income and net worth. Based on that, a scale can be used to see how much money, if any, the customer can afford to lose.

Blind pools should not be allowed to continue. Blind pools were set up for promoters and for owners of brokerage firms and for organized crime. A blind pool is the promoter's dream.

I have traveled and conducted stock manipulations all over the United States. I am sure we are all aware of the headlines regarding insider trading. In the total scope of things, insider trading doesn't even scratch the surface of the thousands and thousands of investors being hurt by stock manipulators like myself. The most important tool needed to tear down their house of fraud and convict these people who committed these acts of fraud with complete disregard, not only to the investing public but to the whole justice system, is dollars.

8

■■■

COMMODITIES FRAUD

"All through the 1980s they educated each other, and now they'll be with us for a long time."

■ MIKE VARGON

Mike Vargon is general counsel for the state securities agency of New Mexico. Along with Royce Griffin, he worked on a special project to rewrite and stiffen New Mexico's securities rules.

Out here we get a lot of commodity fraud. That's where the crooked operators seem to be moving in general. Away from stocks. Into commodities. That's the next great wave, and the states have been somewhat suspicious of the Commodities Futures Trading Commission (CFTC) in this regard. Basically the feeling was they tended to step in on the side of the target—and then they would tell the state to get out.

The trouble is that now there are so many of these guys. All through the 1980s they educated each other, and now they'll be with us for a long time. If they get chased out of penny stocks, they move right into bank-financed precious metals where there's no registration, no licensing as a precious metal dealer.

There's a group of banks who specialize in financing consumer precious metal deals known as bank-financed precious metal transactions. The beauty of it is that I, the dealer, don't have to have any money. I call you and say in these troubled times with a mere $2,000 down you can control $10,000 gold. If you agree, I send you the loan document from the bank, and you send in the check. The loan is executed, and the gold is deposited in your name, but in the process the dealer takes a big chunk out of the deal as a commission. Meanwhile, the bank is taking a large chunk in interest every month. For you to make a profit gold is going to have to move up a lot to overcome your commission and interest payments.

These kinds of activities fall right between the SEC and CFTC jurisdiction. The only group regulating this area with any effectiveness are the states.

Then there's the so-called dirt pile gold scams. The FBI indicted George Anderson for a number of schemes he put together like that. He had a buddy named Lloyd Sharp. They would sell you delayed delivery contracts for delivery of gold—you gave them $5,000 now and in nine months they would give you back $250 an ounce, a price which is too good to be true. Suddenly you're getting gold at $250 when its price is in the range of $350 to $400.

Of course they take the money and nobody sees the gold. That's the whole trick. Whatever it takes to get you to part with your money is what they will try to say, and then they'll have a variety of reasons, for a while, as to why you haven't gotten your gold after nine months. Sometimes what will happen is that state agencies will issue cease and desist orders—and that will be used as a reason why the gold won't be delivered. In other words, they'll blame the government for non-fulfillment of their scam. Sometimes they'll even be bold enough to put it right in the contract. It'll be right in there in small print that the delivery date in a delayed contract can be extended due to acts of God or government.

There's another kind of scam. We got a phone call that some of these types were having a meeting. This outfit was called Success Marketing. They were out of Florida, and they had a pitch saying if you sign up and agree to buy $400 worth of American gold eagle coins and get two other people to buy also, then you can put $100 down for $300 worth of coins.

We indicted this guy and slapped a cease and desist order on his outfit. This kind of thing is much like the Glenn Turner Dare to Be Great campaigns. You remember Glenn Turner. In the 1970s he did this thing where you paid a certain amount of money to come in at a certain level in his program, and then you'd receive these tapes that told you how to sell tapes to others who dared to be great. So nothing was really being sold except the opportunity to learn to sell more of the cassettes that would tell you how to sell more. That was determined to be a securities fraud. So many people have made so much money. The SEC and the NASD, they weren't really effective until the end of the 1980s. That was like closing the door after the horses had gotten out.

It's interesting if you look at the NASD board of governors. You can see a lot of penny stock guys represented all the way through the local and regional chapters. James Padgett, for instance, is former general counsel is on the District Business Conduct Committee of the NASD. Padgett was fined $2 million by the NASD.

9
■ ■ ■

LIMITED PARTNERSHIPS

"About $100 billion was lost to fraud."

■ SCOTT MILLER

Scott Miller, an idiosyncratic and controversial student of limited part-
nerships since the late 1950s, is known for taking a grim view of
partnerships. He claims he was, during the 1980s, the first and perhaps
the only truly independent analyst of limited partnerships. He does
not mince words about the product: "It was a $200 billion rip off."

It's difficult to get a true handle on how much limited partnerships
product was sold. Most people think it was about $100 billion. But
the true amount of limited partnerships, mostly in real estate, is closer
to $200 billion from 1973 through 1988. Of that $200 billion, maybe
ten percent of the investors will get their money back. That's not
profit, mind you. That's just breaking even. More than half, about
$100 billion was lost to fraud.

I've testified and consulted in a lot of litigation involving limited
partnership fraud, as an expert witness. I've also supplied due diligence
reports for more than 200 of the smaller brokerage firms that sold
partnerships to customers. I researched partnerships and issued a verdict
in my reports as to whether the facts are what the general partners
maintain they were and whether the partnerships were legitimate investment vehicles.

Very few partnerships qualified and the limited partnerships industry has all but disappeared. In fact, right now in the early 1990s, I'd say it's about dead. The salesmen are out of business and all the suckers have gone broke. That's not surprising given the quality of the product sold in the 1980s.

Back in the early 1980s, volume in partnerships doubled from one year to the next. I thought that was pretty incredible, but brokers and investors weren't looking at the limited partnerships too closely. I think I was one of the few to do in-depth analysis and I think I was one of the few researchers in the industry with a securities and real-estate background.

When the first real-estate partnerships appeared in the late 1950s and early 1960s, I started my research out of curiosity. I was like a taste-tester in a closet—I read the offerings for amusement. I read literally hundreds of them through the 1970s, then I made a business of it in the 1980s when broker-dealers asked for formal due diligence reports.

Brokers started selling more and more partnerships in the 1970s. When stockbrokers' commissions were deregulated, on Mayday—May 1, 1975—the partnership business went into orbit. After Mayday, the wirehouses would have gone broke but for limited partnerships with their high up-front fees. Limited partnerships saved the wirehouses, the big retail brokerages on Wall Street that sell product to consumers across the country. From the mid-1970s to the mid-1980s, limited partnerships provided the bulk of the profit for retail stock brokers. The records make the point.

Broker-dealers were supposed to get informed opinions—do their due diligence—before they marketed partnerships to clients. The honest and competent ones sought the best advice they could get, and I gave sophisticated, accurate analysis to the few who wanted the truth.

I got my first assignment for a written due diligence report from a west coast retail brokerage firm in 1980. I was then surprised to discover no one provided in-depth due diligence on limited partnerships. I called around to investigate the state-of-the-art but was surprised to learn how little analysis was available on limited partnerships. I collected limited partnership due diligence opinions from the bigger Wall Street firms. They were adolescent. They never caught onto or explained the tricky deals. If they did, they marketed them anyway.

The 1986 tax act killed limited partnerships, but tax reform was not responsible for the billions of fraud that was sold before. The limited partnerships industry tends to blame tax reform for all of its troubles.

In fact, every real-estate professional in the country knew in advance that tax reform was coming. So what did the syndicators do? They flooded the market. Their overbuilding aggravated the inevitable downturn. The limited partnership industry blames tax reform for the failure of real-estate partnerships, but fraud was the real reason limited partnerships failed. Syndicators knew investors had no possible way to get a reasonable return on their investments. The same syndicators now blame tax reform for their fraud.

Overbuilding. That's the real reason real estate went down, but it is not the reason most limited partnerships failed.

Shearson made a big mistake in 1985 with the purchase of Balcor Co., a company specializing in limited partnership products. After Shearson bought Balcor, management put pressure on brokers to sell the Balcor deals. Balcor became a factory, churning out real-estate investments that Shearson brokers sold regardless of their low quality. The Balcor purchase marked a low point for Shearson and the securities industry.

Late 1983, *Forbes* magazine contacted me to research an article on realty syndications. I explained how limited partnerships were a big scam, and they listened to me. They wrote the article, and it made quite a splash. I was quoted, and the article made me famous with syndicators.

Howard Rudnitsky—the author and a senior editor at *Forbes*— explained how tax laws caused bad deals to sell. Highly leveraged tax deals—which offered the illusion of a great return—were more attractive than sensible deals. The riskier the deal was, the greater the promised tax shelter, the more it sold.

Why? Because the old tax laws allowed investors to take tax losses on three to four times their actual investment. They had leverage. Limited partners put up a very small portion of the total investment—say 20 percent. Then they took write-offs, in case of losses, on 100 percent of the investment. So the more the limited partnership lost, the better.

Rudnitsky's article contributed to changes in tax laws. Late in 1984, congress passed tax legislation that slowed the tax shelter industry down just a little. It cut down some of the leverage and deductions in the deals.

It was not until the tax reform of 1986 that the laws became effective. The limited partnerships kept on selling. It was incredible to me, and I said so.

It was sad that the crooks could get away with the blatant frauds. Many were big syndicators. There hasn't been a criminal investigation for one out of every 1,000 partnership frauds. Prudential and other large broker-dealers settle their fraud suits for less than ten cents on the dollar, and there are other crooks ripping off the victims. Lawyers bring suits on behalf of partnership investors and then settle for small sums that pay big fees.

The broker-dealer firms can't be sued on the same partnership after a class action settlement, so lawyers make their fees and the broker-dealers get off cheaply. The limited partnerships get very little.

Now the Supreme Court's 1987 decision ruled that investors can't sue for fraud after three years from a sale. That was the best present possible for crooked syndicators because investors cannot know how fraudulent their investment is in only three years. Most limited partnerships were scams. Like Ponzis, they pay dividends while promoting new investors. Syndicators can easily keep their frauds going long enough— more than three years—to get home free. The new ruling on the statute of limitations was the worst possible thing to happen to millions of victims. The crooked syndicators won't go away either. They'll find new things, whatever is hot: oil, gas.

In the land of the blind, the one-eyed man is king. I'm one of the few freelancers in the due diligence business. Few others in the limited partnership business either knew what was going on or had the guts to say anything. I was extraordinarily outspoken and I still am, but very few paid attention.

■ FORMER SHEARSON BROKER

I remember how important the sale of limited partnerships were to Shearson even in the early 1980s. A good part of Shearson's training for new brokers was dedicated to reinforcing sales practices having to do with the successful marketing of public and private partnerships.

Shearson had a thoroughly convincing indoctrination for its newest sales-members. They flew fledgling brokers to one of three locations across the country and put the raw recruits through a crash course in securities salesmanship. I attended training in the Los Angeles area, one of three such Shearson training centers at the time—the others were in Chicago and New York.

We were put up in Century City, in nice condos there. Two to a room. It was pleasant, but in retrospect it was a joke. You knew you were there to learn how to make a lot of money, and maybe to make clients a lot of money too. So you tended to work hard, mornings and evenings and even weekends.

Just about every day, Shearson executives flew in to give important presentations on a variety of products. Limited partnerships received special attention because Shearson executives thought such products were a good way for young brokers to build a book, but I think there was another reason—new brokers might be more apt to sell shaky deals without question when they first began their Shearson careers.

Brokers were told that they were doing themselves a favor by selling private partnerships. We were told not to waste their time trying to figure out whether or not the partnerships would fly. We'd come to a big firm just so we wouldn't have to worry about things like due diligence.

Around that time Shearson was purchased by American Express Co.. They'd tell you: "We have the little blue [American Express] box now," and you should use it on correspondence and to reinforce the idea that American Express was somehow involved in the due diligence process.

Over and over they'd tell you the job of a broker was to sell the deal, not understand it. They made it clear we were not investment bankers. Recruits were given a variety of effective sales tools to help them in our mission. Perhaps the most successful aid in selling limited partnerships was the product profile. The product profile was for internal use only—the warning was printed that way on the front cover because the customer was supposed to learn about the limited partnership from the prospectus, the government document that spelled out in detail what the risks were of buying a limited partnership. The firm-supplied product profiles on the other hand were full of black-and-white and color glossy photos of the project being planned and described both the financing and the possible rewards of investing in the partnership in very positive terms. Yet the print on the profile could be easily whited-out so a broker could easily send it to a customer. Alternatively, brokers brought in clients and with a certain mysterious flair revealed the product profile with the *internal use only* still printed on. "I can't give it to you but maybe I can make you a photocopy of some of it," the broker might tell the customer. He'd feel like a big shot, like you're doing him a favor.

Finally the customer was ready to buy, and the broker would bring out the prospectus of the actual deal. Brokers often tried to make the final sale of a large limited partnership investment in person so that they didn't have to mail the prospectus to the customer—and risk getting it carefully read.

"The sign up sheets are in the back of this prospectus and you'll have to sign it," the broker might say. The sign up sheet would then be ripped out of the back of the prospectus. After the customer signed, the broker would hand over the rest of the prospectus saying, "Here, keep this in your files. Legally, I have to supply you with this."

Sometimes the broker might try to make a joke out of it, poking fun at the idea of SEC "boilerplate" language. And the customer might agree: "Oh, I know. All that risk stuff."

In the early and mid-1980s, some of the younger brokers at Shearson and other Wall Street firms, big and small, made a living selling almost nothing but limited partnerships. Brokers at Shearson were especially attracted to the partnerships because the gross commission on each one was so large. Each week brokers would get a big pile of new offerings including a sales sheet. The sales sheet would be made up of comments about hot products from different areas of the firm. One sheet would talk about stocks that were coming to market. Another would talk about bonds. A third would talk about especially promising limited partnerships. Later on the product profiles would be mailed to the offices. They were always labeled for internal use only. But they'd send five or ten to each broker, and they were always available in bulk for the asking if it were a public deal.

I didn't sell a great many partnerships during the time I was at Shearson; I never understood how such partnerships could prosper when 20% of the money raised was skimmed off the top by the general partner, by sales commissions for the broker and for the firm, and by a variety of other fees. It also seemed to me that with some of the more highly leveraged deals of the mid-1980s, there might be a lot of back taxes to pay if the deals failed.

But most brokers sold a lot of limited partnerships. The wholesalers would walk around like cockroaches—looking for an open door. You could say some of the most successful wholesalers were the Balcor agents.

Balcor was a company Shearson acquired in the early 1980s and finally shut down in the late 1980s when it became clear that the whole market was collapsing. But in 1983, brokers were suddenly saying: "Hey, if you want to put someone in a safe situation where they're not going to hit a home run but you won't have to worry about risk, you've got to try Balcor. This stuff is safe as a CD."

In the early 1980s the Balcor Man was always a welcome sight. First the branch manager would come by your office and tell you about a meeting in the conference room after the close of the market. You'd go in and sit down and in would come a spiffy guy in a pin-stripe suit with bundles of mailers and advertising slicks. He'd hand them across the room till everyone had a package and he'd say: "I'm so-and-so from Balcor. I've got a way that will make you rich but will let you sleep at night knowing your client has a safe return."

This was a great pitch to make because that was what everybody wanted. I've met hundreds, no thousands of brokers and less than five percent will willfully screw their clients. Those are the guys you see in Denver and New Jersey, the penny stock guys. So, you listened to what the guy from Balcor had to say. And you believed it. Balcor did not have schmucks working for them. They were very polished people. You could tell they knew what they were talking about. The guy would point out: "We don't try to hit a home run. We don't swing for the fences but we consistently hit singles and doubles." Then he'd start going through the sales material and you'd eat it up.

At the end of the meeting the guy would make a proposal to the branch manager. He would say: "I'll come back here in two weeks and make a presentation to your guys' clients." He'd do it like a challenge. He'd say that if the guys would guarantee five or ten clients apiece, he'd spring for a room and for refreshments at a hotel or whatever. He'd make a presentation and sell the clients. All the guys would have to do at the end of the night is sign up new clients for the Balcor program. Branch managers are made for things like that. After the Balcor guy would leave you'd spend time thinking of ways— three or four ways—to get people into the room for the Balcor sales pitch.

Well, the big night would finally come. All the brokers would show up at the hotel or whatever, usually a place like a Hyatt or a Mariott or something, and you'd stand around with name tags waiting for your clients to show up. There would be a secretary behind a desk, and she'd question the client: "Tell me who invited you?"

She'd point you out and then you'd make small talk with the client and try to find out how much they were worth. After a while you'd go into the conference or meeting room and there'd be a nice spread, wine and cheese or whatever. The guy from Balcor would be there too, and he'd be more laid back than he was at the branch meeting.

When everybody was sitting down he'd go into a ten- or fifteen-minute speech about his involvement with Balcor and real estate and then he'd pitch the value of real estate in general. You'd have a slide show too, showing some nice Balcor projects and talking about Balcor's stringent criteria. Then after everyone was hyped on real estate and Balcor, he'd explain how until recently you had to be a millionaire to invest in limited partnerships. But now, thanks to the new rules, anybody could participate. Usually there was a $5,000 dollar minimum—or $2,000 if you were using your IRA. After a little bit more of this you could tell that everybody in the room was starting to be sold. The Balcor guy would wind up: "Have an informative evening. The people who invited you tonight are in the back of the room. Go have a glass of wine and talk to your Shearson financial consultant." Probably nine out of ten wanted to buy. It was kind of a slam dunk.

But then a year or two later, when these things started sucking wind, it wasn't nearly so easy. People would call you up and you'd have to explain these weren't liquid investments. I didn't do much in the way of limited partnerships. But I put my clients into some Balcor product. I never thought anybody would have a complaint on those things. I went for the safest ones. But even some of those didn't work out.

I wasn't surprised when Balcor went belly up. I know Shearson tried to save it, but there was nothing to save. They're going to be paying for that one for a long time.

10

■ ■ ■

JUNK BONDS

*"**B**anks should be allowed to fail."*

■ JIM GRANT

Jim Grant's twice-monthly publication, Grant's Interest Rate Observer, is read by issuers, underwriters, and others in the securities industry who seek perspectives about where the economy is headed.

I was on the staff of *Barron's* from 1975 to 1983 when I left to found *Grant's*. It was then a Federal Reserve-centered world, and I thought my understanding of Treasury bonds would be valuable. But I came to see there were things more important—like the evolution of credit, and of private credit creation, and the dynamics of booms and busts.

In 1984, I had dinner with a couple of hedge-fund investors, a couple of people who had done a lot of thinking about junk bonds. They had this lurid story to tell about Drexel, and this strange fellow Milken, and this club or daisy chain of investors. I got hold of some of the junk-bond documents, and I came to the conclusion there was something wrong. In other words, it seemed to me that Milken was manipulating the buyers and sellers of his bonds to prop up their prices.

And as the boom of the 1980s continued, I came to understand a notion that has been propounded before—that during a boom, credit deteriorates while the psychology of lenders becomes hardened around the notion things will get better and better. You get a deterioration of standards.

I kept waiting for the bubble to burst. Many people made a lot of money by not subscribing to *Grant's* in 1984, 1985, 1986. What was lunatic became more so. What was unsavory became more objectionable. In the 1920s, there was the same type of credit decay. In the 1980s, everybody and his brother could get a loan.

I had a full head of indignation about what was going on at Drexel. I think Milken is a guilty man, but he's not the criminal that his most bitter enemies make him out to be. I think more interesting than the case against him is his role in the evolution of working out of the credit cycle.

I think every generation, or every other generation, has to go through this. In the wake of the 1920s crack up, securities laws were implemented.

People thought, if disclosure was honest and frank, that would be enough, but nobody reads the prospectuses. What mega-bull markets are all about is the urge to make something from nothing. It happens every so often.

It's a very humbling set of facts. Regulators anticipated trouble. They set up this intricate web of regulations, and what happens is what always happens. You probably can't protect people from themselves.

In the 1980s, deregulation went only so far. The asset side of the banking system's balance sheet was deregulated, but there wasn't the freedom for our financial institutions, on the whole, to fail. Deregulation didn't go far enough. It sounds hard-hearted, but I think banks should be allowed to fail. It's a coarse and violent way of policing lenders. Even with the big bank runs in the past, people recouped almost 100 cents on the dollar in many cases. What about now? It's going to cost taxpayers what, $500 billion, to bail out savings and loan customers?

If the lesson people draw from this current cycle is that free markets are destructive, then you'll see the same mistakes perpetuated in the future. Of course if there are no regulations people will still crack up. But what we have now is neither socialism nor capitalism. It's a twilight. I'd choose individual responsibility.

11

■ ■ ■

ARBITRATION

"The arbitration process . . . is supervised by the industry itself. . . . [That's] akin to letting the foxes run the henhouse."

■ THEODORE EPPENSTEIN

In 1987 the Supreme Court ruled that customers who sign arbitration agreements with securities firms are bound by them and must submit to arbitration if they have grievances.

Lawyer Theodore Eppenstein argued against this ruling in the Supreme Court. Such a decision, he says, threatens individual investors who have a basic right to expect fair dealing from the firms they do business with—and their constitutional right to a trial by jury.

In every contract there is an implied covenant of good faith and fair dealing. I believe the Supreme Court washed its hands of investor litigation not because of legal issues but because of cost—the Court feared too many angry investors can clog up the court system even more than it is already. But it's not an issue that can be easily resolved, and it's not an issue that's going to go away.

The lack of alternatives for investors faced with mounting investment losses is one of the more startling aspects of our economic and legal system. While investing by its nature deals with risk, most fair-minded individuals whether or not they work in the securities industry would probably agree that where the investor has not been well-informed beforehand, or where the investor has been bilked, legal recourse is not an unreasonable alternative.

Unfortunately, in this country, the alternatives of court are not always available. Because of the Supreme Court ruling, many of Wall Street's biggest retail brokerage firms have made signing arbitration agreements virtually mandatory.

The arbitration process for the most part is supervised by the industry itself—the NYSE, the American Stock Exchange or the NASD. Many investors perceive this to be akin to letting the foxes run the henhouse.

But in addition to Supreme Court-mandated arbitration, the unwary investor will face other difficulties. The average investor should be very careful about his choice of a lawyer because of the high level of experience necessary to pursue white-collar fraud in the arbitration arena.

The financial shenanigans of some brokers even at Wall Street's biggest firms, combined with the decisions of the nation's highest court, have made investing, and its aftermath, more treacherous. In 1991, the Supreme Court set a national standard for securities fraud in which the small investor has only three years or less to learn about the fraud and to legally pursue. Yet, to take one example, because of concealment, you may not have the ability to find out for more than the statutory period that your limited partnership has gone sour, and by then it's too late. There are firms peddling financial products that are not so hot. It's a wise investor who remembers that.

12

■■■

INSIDER TRADING

"More competition might help."

■ HARRY FIRST

Harry First is a professor specializing in white-collar crime at the University of New York School of Law.

The argument throughout the 1980s concerning insider trading was that it was a victimless crime and therefore not something especially heinous. The argument was important only because insider trading in the 1980s was such a highly charged issue.

Some felt SEC commissioner Shad was making an issue out of insider trading because Shad moved public attention away from the corporate governance issues of the 1970s. There's also sentiment that insider trading is not as terrible a crime as some of the more ordinary kinds of chicanery, penny stock crime, that kind of thing.

There was an argument, for instance, that insider trading by people with information actually helps bring that information efficiently to the market.

The other argument is that to the extent firms in the financial industry like law firms and brokerages believe their employees should not trade on inside information because it adversely affects their business—that is, to the extent the firms will police their employees—we don't need criminal law because of free market incentives. Law firms, for instance, make substantial efforts to police insider trading.

In the end, I don't have any quarrel with the emphasis on insider trading in the 1980s. Though I wouldn't have ended the concern for management integrity that the SEC had in the 1970s.

And when you look at the $100 million or more that someone like insider-trader Boesky accumulated, it doesn't seem to me that the economic value of his insider trading could possibly be worth $100 million. If insider trading were a legitimate market function, then the reward would be in line with other profits garnered in the marketplace. Boesky's profits seem out of line, which leads me to believe that insider trading gives insiders an edge that is more than economic.

We've lived with the federal law against fraud without definition, and I think we can live with a nebulous insider trading law. There's something to be said for the fact that if you define it, smart people will find a way around it.

More competition in the markets might help too. If only a few professionals have access to this information, that's certainly going to result in abuse. Regulatory capture is another consideration. The SEC used to have a reputation as one of the best of the enforcement agencies. The hope is that government will eventually set up a structure that will allow the free markets to operate more efficiently.

13

■ ■ ■

AUTOMATION

"Automation makes fraud more difficult."

■ WILLIAM BROKA

William Broka is vice president, trading and market services, at the National Association of Securities Dealers. An NASD "lifer," with 20 years' service, he faces the task of marketing the NASD's new trading services to the brokers and dealers it serves.

The SEC has launched a whole group of reforms aimed at making the financial markets fairer to investors. This includes various penny stock reforms. We anticipated the SEC's intention to make more disclosure available in some markets with our own automation efforts.

Automation makes fraud more difficult because prices become available in real time on electronic systems. You can see prices on your computer. That's what we're trying to do with penny stocks, through our OTCFD bulletin board, to make the prices available right away.

We're examining doing the same kind of thing in the junk bond market, making prices available through a NASD bond network. We even looked at putting limited partnership prices on our Nasdaq automated system in the early 1980s. The dealers who use our services didn't see much of a need for those prices though. Putting these services on a system creates an automated audit trail as well. You can then track a security electronically.

By allowing firms to make penny stock prices current, we think we'll encourage honesty in the market, give everyone better access to real-time information and help buyers and sellers make their decisions better. It may not eliminate manipulation, but it will make it less likely to happen.

We recently enhanced the OTC bulletin board service and made it more receptive for the traders using our system. At the present time, you can't execute trades on the system. That's why we call it a bulletin board. It simply shows you indications of dealers' interest in buying or selling certain stocks.

The SEC still has to define what a penny stock is. But once you define exactly what constitutes a penny stock, we can enhance this system in other ways such as providing transaction and volume information. Currently it's up and running, and people use it, but the SEC has yet to make some of the definitive statements we need to expand usage.

What we put on our automated bulletin board is a group of so-called pink sheet stocks, but there are other kinds of sheets as well. The yellow sheets are bond sheets. The white sheets are equity and bonds.

The SEC has also asked us to take a look at a fixed income trading system—junk bonds. Treasury asked some committees of ours to examine the issue as well. So we've done a prototype and we're still looking at how we'd offer it. Dealers would provide prices, of course, just the way they do for all the other securities our members trade.

14

■ ■ ■

MARKET STRUCTURE

"Of course the underwriters who had enjoyed the highly profitable advantage of a small oligopoly opposed the legislation."

■ WILLIAM PROXMIRE

William Proxmire's long and distinguished congressional career ended in an effort to tear down the Glass-Steagall rule that separated the banking and securities industry. He was ultimately defeated by the powerful congressman, John Dingell (D-Mich.). Dingell's father, also an important congressman, helped write and pass some of the original securities legislation. Proxmire supplied the following statement on his legislation.

The Glass-Steagall prohibition against commercial banks underwriting corporate securities was a congressional response to the widespread bank failures of the great depression. In fact the failures then, as now, were caused by a combination of excessive lending to high-risk businesses and grossly inadequate bank capital capable of absorbing the losses generated by widespread bankruptcies of business and household borrowers.

The process of underwriting or raising capital for business was not in fact risky in the great depression and it is not risky now. New underwriters have failed throughout American economic history. In fact the underwriter holds the securities that he underwrites for a very short time—usually a few weeks. The underwriter simply serves as a funnel between investors and the firms that require the capital.

Commercial banks are ideally qualified as underwriters. By their nature they have the professional know-how to appraise the soundness of borrowers, the availability of investment capital and the price in terms of interest rate or dividend commitment necessary to secure the desired capital. Supplying capital is the banks' business.

As chairman of the Senate Banking Committee in 1987, I surveyed banks, the chief financial officers of leading American corporations—the Fortune 500—governors, and mayors, who also constituted major users of investment capital, and leaders in the commercial and residential real-estate industry.

I also solicited the opinion of all three of the federal bank regulators. Specifically I requested and received on-the-record testimony before the Senate Banking Committee from the chairman of the Federal Reserve Board which regulates state member banks, the chairman of the Federal Deposit Insurance Corporations that regulates state non-member banks and the Comptroller of the Currency in the Treasury Department who regulates national banks. All testified in favor of the proposed legislation without reservation.

These are the experts who have been given the responsibility for safeguarding our commercial banks and preventing bank failures. They are also the officials who bear the brunt of criticism when the banks they regulate fail.

The support from all of these groups, corporate as well as government officials, was overwhelmingly in favor of repealing Glass-Steagall. Without exception they enthusiastically favored permitting banks to underwrite securities with three specific safeguards written into the law to prevent any risk to our banks.

The safeguards provided in the proposed legislation required these protections for underwriting banks:

First, the underwriting was required to be conducted by separate bank affiliates. The underwriting affiliate could not be owned by the bank itself. It could be owned by the holding company that also owned the bank. By this device any problems that developed for the underwriter could not affect the soundness of the affiliated bank. Secondly, the bank could not lend any funds to its underwriting affiliate. The affiliate was required to raise its own capital and fully bear any liability it developed. Finally, the bank was prohibited from buying any of the securities issued by its underwriting affiliate. None of these safeguards was regarded by banks, regulators or the community that required capital as compromising their interests in any way.

The overwhelming support for this legislation was reflected in the vote supporting it, both in the Senate Banking Committee and on the floor of the Senate itself. The banking committee reported the legislation to the floor of the Senate by a resounding eighteen to two vote, The Senate passed the legislation by a smashing ninety-four to two.

Of course the underwriters who with the exclusion of banks had enjoyed the highly profitable advantage of a small oligopoly opposed the legislation. In practice a small handful of lead underwriters are assured of hefty noncompetitive underwriting margins. Result: American industry and 250 million Americans pay the price in a higher cost of capital. This constitutes still another handicap in American competition with our vigorous international economic rivals in Europe and Asia.

How could congressman Dingell, whose father had been a House leader in helping to enact the original Glass-Steagall act, block legislation that enjoyed this overwhelming support?

Congressman Dingell does not serve on the House Banking Committee. He does, however, chair the House committee that has jurisdiction over a minor aspect of the bill. This enabled him to block the legislation in the House although it had overwhelming support in the House Banking Committee and by House leadership.

The bill died in the closing days of the 1988 session. That year I retired.

■ GEORGE JENSEN

George Jensen, founder of American Film Technologies—an energetic entrepreneur and former broker—discovered a novel way of bringing his company public: He did it himself. Featured in Inc. *magazine for this feat, Jensen calls his deal "unique" but in the same breath adds: "there's more of this to come."*

Our initial public offering for AFT raised $3.5 million. And we took in most of the money before the crash of 1987 and the rest just afterward. The price went from one to two dollars during the first day of trading.

But I think our success is a measure of our technology. We had developed a revolutionary film colorization technology and also what we call paperless animation that reduces costs and speeds up the process of imaging for video and film. We'd been successful raising money before we went public. I raised about $3 million through a private placement from about 250 investors to get our company off the ground in March of 1987.

But I knew I couldn't go through that again so I decided the way to move ahead was through an initial public offering. I'd been a stockbroker for Smith, Barney & Co. for seven years, so I knew some of the ins and outs—I knew it would be rough.

We really feel we're pioneers. We did our private placement, a primary and secondary offering, all without an investment banker. I don't think that's ever been done before. We raised $10 million altogether.

We couldn't attract enough investment capital because we did not have enough films or customers at the time. Now we're one of the fastest growing companies in America.

We're a great confidence builder for other entrepreneurial enterprises. Wall Street might do 300 initial public offerings (IPO) in a year but there are several times that many worth going public. An investment banker ideally likes to see a company in the black, but most young, growth companies can't get there—and it's more risk than Wall Street is willing to take. So there's a massive void to fill.

The void used to be filled by venture capital companies, but they've pulled in their horns. In the 1990s it's gotten worse. There's a pool of venture capital out there, but now instead of a third of it going into the early-stage deals, almost nothing does.

What happened was penny stock houses spoiled the market. They gave public financing for early-stage business a bad name, and now the rest of Wall Street is afraid to get involved. They're afraid to fill the niche.

I think to some degree it's the fault of the regulators. They should have insured that the public marketplace for growing companies was not subject to massive manipulation, but during the 1980s that's just what seemed to happen. That's just too bad. The capital formation process needs all the help it can get. I'm not sure it's getting the right kind of care. Look, we listed on the Philadelphia Stock Exchange; but they waived three of their rules for listing us. Today, the SEC will not let the Philadelphia Exchange waive any of their listing requirements.

My perspective is the regulators should be punishing the crooks, not the companies. If the markets are being abused, the regulators shouldn't be imposing more rules; they should be enforcing the ones already on the books.

Let young companies have a legitimate trading market. Why do you have to mandate that a company has to be in the black before it can list? Spell out the risk in the prospectus—in this country there is a large pool of wealthy investors who like taking a businessman's risk, so long as they're comfortable with management and understand that risk.

Either Wall Street and Washington will respond to these needs or there may be more deals like mine to come.

■ ■ ■

WHAT I LEARNED

In this section, industry observers have examined problems of the retail financial industry with various products marketed by the big brokers, including mutual funds, closed-end funds, junk bonds, and limited partnerships. In each of these instances, during certain time periods, products were massively marketed, using all of Wall Street's muscle, even when it was apparent these instruments were flawed.

One way to ameliorate the problem of overselling would be to diminish the tremendous sales clout that Wall Street's biggest retail firms have nationally and internationally. There are several ways to do this. Former Senator Proxmire wants to break up Wall Street's franchise by tearing down Glass-Steagall and letting more players into the game. I'm aware that Proxmire is concerned with making investment banking more efficient, not with adjusting Wall Street's retail sales practices. But I happen to think that anything that would introduce competition to Wall Street could aid the consumer by fragmenting the Street's marketing clout.

Automation might also help since Wall Street thrives on consumer ignorance of the prices of investment instruments. If enough prices are generated soon enough in new markets, and if prices are continually refined and more widely disseminated for established instruments, it is possible that an informed consumer could make better buying and selling decisions. Additionally, as Jensen points out, automation can help issuers sell shares in their efforts without going through Wall Street at all. This would certainly diminish Wall Street's marketing power. And if properly regulated, this kind of automated effort might open up a new source of funding for entrepreneurs through investment-banking trading nets.

The SEC itself has taken steps to give investors more information about small stocks by approving wider disclosure rules for the OTC and penny stock market. The agency backed the NASD in requiring OTC brokers to report trades within 90 seconds after execution. Under the new rules, real-time information on over 1,000 less active stocks will be available to investors.

The action taken in the spring of 1992 also exempted about 5,000 Nasdaq stocks from the SEC's new penny stock rules—derived from 1990 congressional action. About 6,000 instruments fall under the new and stricter congressional guidelines that mandate a broker must provide the investor with disclosure documents before proceeding with a transaction. Brokers must also tell customers how much they are making in commissions and what the stock quote is currently.

Other tough rules weren't implemented: Brokers won't have to tell customers whether or not they're making a market in the stock they're selling, for instance; though penny stock houses who want to manipulate an issue would find it difficult without making a market in the issue in question.

More than automation, in the retail marketplace better regulation is a cure. Perhaps Nasaa's idea of merit regulation, of sniffing out trumped up investments, is not such a bad idea in this context.

It is important that we have as fair and honest a marketplace as possible for individual investors in this country. Financial fraud breeds human misery and dissatisfaction with the marketplace. A less abusive way of selling financial instruments would probably lead to a more vibrant and energetic society. It would help cement the gains of market economies in the last decade.

If our current system of selling securities begins to offer the public international opportunities in a big way, investors may face more trouble, not less. The SEC has taken steps in the right direction; but securities fraud, like at least one other ancient profession, is a resilient vice. By firmly resisting the most obvious and fundamental ways to clean up the market—through merit regulation or by agency representation—the SEC ended up launching yet another 150 pages of regulations at the low end of the securities markets. And the chances are that crooks will sooner or later see their way round the new regulations; they have before.

Additionally, by avoiding a serious discussion about the professional and ethical issues of some of Wall Street's most prestigious firms, the SEC and congress promote the idea that there is no other way for securities to be marketed than under the present system.

The SEC, congress, the industry itself, could insist that salesmen take a greater responsibility for the products they sell. A more serious ethical framework for brokers to inhabit would be a good start, as Royce Griffin points out.

Of course, it's possible that mutual fund deregulation, if it actually comes to fruition, will encourage the growth of true fee-based agency brokerage—which might in turn lead to the establishment of a truly professional financial planning industry. But rather than wait for the market itself to generate a true class of securities professionals, regulators and congress should consider ways to stimulate such a movement. The big securities firms wouldn't like it, but investors probably would. Now is the time to open up Wall Street's retail franchise, insist on more price automation and sensible, hard-nosed regulation of the consumer securities market.

PART TWO

■ ■ ■

THE EVOLUTION OF CURRENT MARKET DIFFICULTIES

■ ■ ■

The preceding section of this book covered retail investment issues with which most consumers have at least some passing familiarity. In this second section, I have dealt with the extremely complex history of our ever-expanding financial industry—and how in the opinion of some (number me among them)—that history led to the 1987 stock market crash and subsequent stock market "volatility." These are murkier waters; most of the interviews in this section assume some working knowledge of our domestic financial industry and its history. I have tried, therefore, to give readers unfamiliar with its background a thumbnail sketch, which begins below. The reader may also take advantage of the glossary at the back of the book.

In 1987 the stock market moved down some 600 points in two sessions, and the country's credit underpinning was, at least momentarily, in some danger of coming undone. Wall Street executives and industry commissions later on explained the downward move as a compressed correction, aggravated by program trading. But the danger was real that the credit underpinnings of the nation could have collapsed along with the market.

Yet, for a few of Wall Street's more history-conscious observers, the stresses and strains that nearly fractured the Big Board had been building for nearly 30 years. An SEC Special Study of Securities Markets in 1963 predicted that the comfortable relationship between investors and physical stock exchanges would gradually be undermined by various forms of automated trading that bypassed traditional stock trading venues. What the study could not foresee was the rise of new kinds of financial instruments like options and futures, and also the rise of institutional investing—fueled by the enormous amounts of money in public and corporate pension plans—with attendant massive buying and selling power.

Institutional trading increasingly dominated the financial markets. By the late 1980s, 55 percent of all trades on the Big Board were on behalf of institutions—mostly money managers trading in turn on behalf of pension plans and mutual funds. These factors—computerized trading, new financial instruments, and massive institutional leverage— came together to exacerbate the downward move of the NYSE in October of 1987.

It's hard not to look back and come to the conclusion that big money, big politics, and big regulation have propped up the current structure despite evident dangers. Throughout the 1960s the Big Board fought against the Special Study and a band of "third market" off-exchange traders who wanted to trade NYSE-listed equities without bringing the order to the floor of the Exchange. It fought the deregulation of commissions that resulted in Mayday, and was, in fact, aided by the SEC in its struggle. Securities lawyer, Joel Seligman, author of a well-known history of the SEC, *The Transformation of Wall Street,* has written the handling of the fixed rates issue in the 1960s did more to sully the historic reputation of the agency than almost any other issue. During this period "the SEC actually acted like a champion of non-competition."

In 1975, as part of a comprehensive securities reform package, congress actually mandated the development of a nationwide electronic trading system. But the NYSE, with the help of a reluctant SEC, managed to impose a series of rudimentary electronic links between the nation's physical exchanges and some large firms.

By 1980 the NYSE had been fighting to preserve its special place in the corporate body of American capitalism for nearly 20 years. Its executives had fought rearguard actions against almost every major change proposed in the securities industry. Its specialists had once gone so far, late one night, to take axes to the first real electronic systems installed on the Exchange floor. But while those involved with the NYSE fought to maintain the status quo, the world beyond the NYSE kept evolving.

To understand the gradual, inexorable shift that occurred around the NYSE despite its best efforts, it is important to remember that the Big Board actually has several constituencies. The first, and perhaps most powerful, at least historically, is the specialist—who has an obligation to buy and sell shares in certain stocks—and floor brokerage community. The NYSE, and its policies, are to some degree controlled by the specialists, especially, because of their electoral clout. At the NYSE, the chairman is subject to a floor vote for board election. John Phelan, a former Marine and chairman of the Big Board during the 1980s, came from the specialist ranks himself.

Other constituencies include the Wall Street member firms and the institutions for whom they trade. Throughout the last 30 years, these groups have at times shown a common front and at times turned on each other as the argument over automation has evolved. In the 1970s a fundamental change began to take shape as technology became feasible to use for investing purposes.

Institutions, mostly so-called money managers—the buy side—and Wall Street firms, the sell side (because institutions, in simpler days, purchased securities brokers sold), were quick to adapt. Rudimentary programs, lists of trades, were bought and sold with the aid of mainframe computers as professional investors groped toward a more disciplined form of investing.

By the early 1980s, the pressure on the Big Board to facilitate some kind of efficient electronic utility was intense. The result was an upgrade of the NYSE's automated DOT linkage to SuperDot, an automated trading utility that connected the Big Board's specialist posts to firms that wished to send buy and sell orders to the floor of the Exchange. The SuperDot trading linkage, combined with the increased use of program trading, put pressure on the specialists in charge of maintaining an orderly market. These specialists were, ideally, supposed to move trading in their stocks up and down by eighths; fulfilling part of a specialist's mandate to buy and sell stock, as necessary, to maintain an orderly ascent and descent of prices.

But program trading, combined with the SuperDot order routing utility, began to overwhelm the specialist system in the 1980s. Massive quantities of orders to buy and sell poured in. Specialists, often small businessmen with modest capital, did not have the wherewithall to support the market in the face of such massive trading.

The advent of the options and futures rocked the world of the Big Board. For a while, in the 1970s, it tried to build an options business of its own. In the 1980s it set up its not-too-successful New York Futures Exchange (NYFE) to trade a variant of McGraw-Hill Inc.'s Standard & Poor's futures contract. But neither options nor futures products took root in New York because the Big Board's business, defined by culture and history, was stock trading. The Big Board's inability to move away from its heavily regulated and attractive—at least for participants—specialist's system, combined with new products from Chicago's open-outcry futures system, helped worsen the 1987 crash.

The nation's biggest Exchange had failed to keep pace with its customers' technological progress. The NYSE had mechanized portions of its order-entry and back-office procedures. But the Exchange had not addressed the central issue of its specialist system, nor how to offer program traders automated execution.

The lack of sufficient automation on the floor of the Big Board was only a symptom of a larger systemic difficulty. And this had to do with the immense money-making leverage that automation had bestowed on Wall Street. Glass-Steagall, in the 1930s, had separated Wall Street from commercial banking for two main reasons: to avoid conflicts of interest between banking and risky stock-brokering and -dealing activities; and to pool deal volume and business among a small group of Wall Street firms. The smaller the group, the easier to supervise and control from a regulatory point of view.

In the 1960s and 1970s, with the rise of institutional investing power, well-capitalized Wall Street firms began to buy and sell huge blocks of stocks. Institutional investing was abetted by pension plan collection of assets. The addition of computers gave Wall Street firms the ability to more efficiently trade these blocks. The addition of options and futures markets gave firms and institutions even more ways of combining investments to generate less risky profits. The combination of volume, automation, and new markets meant that certain Wall Street firms were not only seeing enormous amounts of securities, but also they were also able to act quickly on the information on several fronts. In the mid-1980s, the stock market began to jump around in a worrisome way.

More disturbingly, there was growing concern within the industry, especially among at least some institutional investors, that Wall Street was abusing its privileged position. Firms were using the information—or so some suspected—gained from customers to electronically place orders ahead of the trade. Some firms may even have been attempting to artificially induce volatility from which they could profit. A variety of financial products helped make such activities possible; increased order flow facilitated market moves, and computers allowed Wall Street to make the calculations that could result in profits.

Industry observers say that the information that moved markets was acquired by Wall Street firms and passed along to hedge funds. The Wall Street firms gained market information from the institutions trading with them. If an institution was about to sell or buy a big block of stock, word gradually began to travel among Wall Street's pilot fish—its hedge funds and proprietary traders. The situation was fueled by a process known as client facilitation.

Because of regulations still apparently on the books, Wall Street firms could bid for a "package trade"—a program trade, in reality— proposed by an institution. It worked like this: The institution would ask firms to bid for a certain trade. The successful bidder would become a partner in the trade by virtue of ceding commission in return for a share of the profits. Apparently, the firm could then begin to legally "frontrun" the transaction. If a big block of stock XYZ was about to be dropped on the market, the firm might choose to go short on the stock in advance. Then, when the time came to make the trade, the firm's traders would sell the stock down "sloppy" making sure that everyone in the market knew about it. This increased chances that the market would react in the expected way: Others would sell XYZ, and the firm would profit mightily from its short positions.

The preceding example is quite rudimentary. A sophisticated package trade included positions in the options and futures market that would also benefit from the expected market movement. The firm might even trigger some index arbitrage strategies, as they were moving the market, simply to confuse the issue.

There is no academic evidence, nor any good regulatory evidence, that index arbitrage, per se, causes severe market fluctuations: It may aggravate them and it may be part of the process, but it is not the single root cause. Hundreds of articles, several SEC studies, and numerous industry-generated studies indiscriminately attributed 1980s market moves in main to index arbitrage. As certain investors and economists such as Nobel prize-winner Merton Miller have pointed out, the process of buying in one market while selling in another is bound, ultimately, to be a stabilizing influence. Such misleading explanations, abetted by the SEC, possibly for political purposes, did no one in the public, or even the financial industry, any service.

But index arbitrage was a convenient whipping boy in the 1980s. This pleased Wall Street's old guard, which wanted to do away with computerized trading altogether if it could. This also didn't especially bother the big firms involved with program trading, since areas that could involve the real sources of market manipulation—package trading and esoteric forms of options market manipulation—were never dealt with, and hardly discussed. Outside of a few stories in *BusinessWeek* and *Institutional Investor,* the issue simply did not receive much widespread scrutiny.

The real key to the success of package trading, at least in the 1980s, was not necessarily the sloppy selling of packages by Wall Street firms alone. "Hedge funds" played a role too. Hedge funds were developed back in the 1950s partially as the result of an influential magazine article that predicted it might be possible to hedge one investment in the equity market against another to protect investments. Originally, hedge funds might be long one stock and short a stock with similar characteristics to insure they would not lose much if the market made a big move up or down. Later, as derivative instruments became available, hedgers began to use a variety of those instruments to set up their portfolios.

Hedgers are the financial industry's black hole. Privately run, investing private money, with a bent toward technology and quantitative investment techniques, these firms are secretive and often intensely profitable. Because they use Wall Street's biggest firms as their brokers, and because they trade in some size, information about institutional order flow tended to trickle from Wall Street firms to the most active hedge shops. Such a pattern, in fact, is evidenced in the cooperation of Boesky with Milken, for instance. Boesky traded with Milken; in return he received inside information and facilitated some of Milken's market rigging.

It is easy to make up conspiracy theories about Wall Street. And the truth is never clear-cut. Yet there probably existed in the 1980s, and exists today, a free and easy flow of information among proprietary trading firms and large Wall Street firms over the direction in which the market is headed—both generally and even in certain market sectors. This kind of information, not available to the general public, nor to the large public funds, aggravated market conditions in the 1980s and continues to play a role in generating profits domestically and internationally for the industry's largest players.

The Evolution of the NYSE and Automated Investing

The NYSE structure is rooted in a franchise erected 200 years ago, the "Buttonwood" pact. According to Big Board information, New York stockbrokers pledged to collect a minimum commission on all sales of public stock and to "give preference to each other" in their negotiations.

Over the next few decades, the NYSE proved itself the most aggressive of a group of city exchanges. What it could not swallow, it tried to shut down. Early in the 1800s, according to at least one version of Wall Street's history, the NYSE was still a formal auction market, holding a stock roll call several times a day during which investors would bid for securities lots. Meanwhile, uptown, a group of brokers had made the discovery that continuous stock trading, rather than one roll call a day, generated more commissions. Money and personnel were gravitating toward the uptown exchange until the NYSE brought those brokers into the fold as what later became specialists—traders responsible for the liquidity of certain assigned issues. The NYSE switched to continuous trading and never looked back.

This evolution is noteworthy if only because it would seem to indicate the Big Board's specialist system evolved from competitive pressures. The NYSE has been trying to document the benefits of its system—both its specialists and continuous trading—ever since.

In the mid-1800s, the nation was expanding westward, and Wall Street helped raise the funds that fueled the boom. The telegraph, and Wall Street's use of it to take stock orders from distant localities, further increased the power of the biggest banking firms and of the NYSE itself. Wall Street's largest brokerages are still called "wirehouses," hearkening back to that first serious surge of public orders.

In the 1920s, almost from the beginning of the bull market in 1922, volume and stock prices moved up at an astonishing rate. By 1925 the value of all NYSE listed stocks was around $25 billion, and by 1929 that figure had jumped to nearly $100 billion. And close to 20 million Americans owned some kind of stock, up from between 500,000 and 2 million before the war.

The 1929 crash sparked increased regulation of the financial industry. Glass-Steagall separated commercial banking from underwriting and selling public securities issues; the Securities Act of 1933 and the Securities Exchange Act of 1934 were aimed at curing manipulation and speculation within the public securities markets. The 1934 Act led to the creation of the SEC as an independent agency designed to regulate brokers and dealers and mandated public disclosure about publicly traded issues. Additionally, the 1934 Act gave government the power to set limits on the amount of credit Wall Street could offer institutional and private investors.

The framers of the 1930s securities regulations realized that the cost of government regulation of the fledgling securities industry would be prohibitive without industry cooperation. As a result, the SEC gradually reached a series of agreements with industry self-regulatory organizations (SROs), whereby exchanges such as the Big Board and the Curb—the American Stock Exchange—would be responsible for the behavior of their own members. States also retained regulatory powers through Nasaa.

After the tumultuous 1920s, the country was willing enough to ignore Wall Street: The Depression and the World War damped speculative fervor. The SEC meanwhile gained a reputation as a successful and honest regulator. The 1940s and 1950s were relatively calm years for the SEC, according to SEC historian Seligman; under President Dwight Eisenhower, the Commission's role was diminished while the industry's self-regulatory exchange organizations were encouraged to play a larger role.

Starting in the 1960s, however, the SEC returned to the public eye courtesy of the controversial Special Study of Securities Markets. By the late 1960s, two electronic networks had been devised to take advantage of the study's predictions: One was called Institutional Network (Instinet) and the other Automated Execution (AutEx). Both AutEx and Instinet were intended to let institutional investors and Wall Street firms tell each other about blocks of stock to be bought or sold.

The 1963 Special Study was comprehensive and objective: It pointed out unfairnesses in such fundamental NYSE practices as floor trading, odd lots, and short sales. But some of the study's strongest salvos were reserved for fixed commissions. The study made the point that commission rates were simply set by the highest possible price the market could bear, not on the basis of costs to dealers. Costs were adjusted to rates, not the other way round; and such a massive revenue stream led to equally massive problems. Lacking any reason to compete, the securities industry had grown increasingly complacent and inefficient.

The Special Study said that self-regulation had been an effective method of market discipline. But it questioned the ability of the Big Board to evolve. Despite the controversy generated by the Special Study, the NYSE was at the peak of its prestige during the 1960s and considered a much superior exchange to the splintered markets of Europe. The NYSE's dominance was actually built around two specific anti-competitive regulations: Fixed commissions for the services of Wall Street's brokers, and Rule 390, then called 394, which mandated Big Board member firms not do NYSE business away from the floor.

Things got worse with the so-called "paper crunch" of the 1960s that put a number of well-known firms out of business. The reasons for the difficulties were all too clear: Better technology had increased the number of investors in the market, but the methods used by firms to trade and clear stock transactions had failed to keep pace. Numerous firms simply drowned in a flood of orders as the 1960s bull market thundered. At one point the NYSE was regularly closing on Wednesdays to try to keep up with the order flow. The NYSE was also engaged in bitter dispute with various industry players, including Don Weedon of third-market maker Weeden & Co. Weeden's relentless attack on the Big Board's trading monopoly would eventually help lead to Mayday. In 1970, in an article entitled "The Gambling Game That Wall Street Plays," *BusinessWeek* was able to total up the toll of the industry's stance. "An unprecedented shortage of capital in the symbolic center of capitalism, Wall Street, has forced some 150 U.S.brokerage houses into liquidation, including a half dozen major member firms."

The paper crunch of the late 1960s combined with the bear market of the 1970s to break down the rickety capital structure of the industry. *BusinessWeek* referred to Wall Street as a "self-regulating monopoly . . . a rather precarious franchise" and added the situation had raised doubt about the whole system for buying and selling stocks.

In spring of 1971, the SEC issued its Institutional Investor Study Report stating, "the evolution of the securities markets has been . . . distorted by barriers to competition." The SEC and the industry were trying to address the problem of "give-backs" and other kinds of soft-dollar inducements to keep institutional business on the Big Board. The fixed commission rule was a barrier according to the SEC. The way the NYSE did business needed to be changed. The SEC called for a strong, central market network, saying it was a major goal and ideal of the securities markets.

Eventually, the industry's paper-crunch problems began to be resolved by automated systems for back-office processing. In 1972 the Securities Industry Automation Corp. (SIAC) made its debut. SIAC, partially owned by the NYSE, partially owned by the American Exchange, introduced automated systems that gradually unraveled the paper crunch. One of the most important systems introduced by SIAC was the Designated Order Turnaround (DOT) System that allowed small orders to be transmitted electronically from firms to the floor of the NYSE. In the early 1980s, at the behest, partially, of Morgan Stanley & Co. (which wanted to funnel program trades quickly to the floor of the Exchange), the Big Board expanded the system's speed and capacity and called the upgraded version SuperDot. Most regional exchanges now have versions of such systems.

While the paper crunch was gradually alleviated, the issues it presented were not easily disposed of. Between 1971 and 1975, an almost ceaseless flow of congressional studies took aim at the most important issues the Commission was dealing with: fixed commissions and a national market system. Finally, on January 23, 1975, after rejecting a flurry of last minute compromises, the SEC voted to terminate all fixed commission rates charged to nonmembers as of May 1, 1975.

The SEC also recommended the implementation of a national market system in 1975—one in which competing market makers might well replace the NYSE specialist network. The creation of Nasdaq and the success of its electronic quote network were possibly the most compelling arguments of all for a continuing evolution of national market linkages. In 1975 the promise of a Nasdaq network inspired Washington regulators to what passed for visionary thinking. Just possibly, by doing away with the NYSE's Rule 394 and by linking different marketplaces with the new electronic, computerized technology, a truly national market could be created.

Of course, it didn't happen. Rule 394—renamed 390—was never entirely removed by the SEC. Even today Wall Street firms are barred from making a market in most of the Big Board stocks they broker. Meanwhile, an SEC Advisory Committee on the Implementation of a Central Market System met for more than a year to try to work one out without success. The SEC solicited outside perspectives. They received more than 15 separate proposals on ways to build a national market network. The ideas of a team composed of market visionaries Junius

Peake, Morris Mendelson, and R. T. Williams received the most attention; these three called for implementing a fully workable national market linkage in stages over 10 to 15 years.

The paper was eventually presented to the national market committee. It caused a stir not only because of its thoroughness but because its presenters spent most of the day with the committee explaining their views. The national media picked up on the story. Peake and Mendelson—along with various versions of their theories of industry automation—became familiar throughout the industry. According to Mendelson, the real breakthrough of the automated system lay not in its computers but in its theory of "price and time priority." The idea was that the system would be rigorously fair, selecting buyers and sellers on a first-come, first-served basis.

Despite the publicity they received, the effect the men had on the committee was not overwhelming. And the committee's difficulty in reaching a consensus was taken as proof by the industry that it was impossible to define what a national market system was or how to implement it. With the committee in disarray, the Big Board was able to suggest a plan that fulfilled the barest minimum of congress's mandate. "We were able to come up with enough to satisfy the SEC," recalls one top NYSE executive.

What eventually satisfied the SEC was a consolidated tape, a composite quotation system, and the so-called Intermarket Trading System (ITS) that allowed customers to gain so-called best-price advantages from exchanges around the country. While in theory ITS provided the best possible stock price for customers, in fact it did not. In part this is because retail firms still cannot compete with specialists to make a market in stocks listed on the NYSE prior to 1979. And NYSE specialists cannot compete with Nasdaq market makers. ITS doesn't provide much competition and to unbiased observers it's not exactly state of the art.

ITS was not the only electronic experiment to promise more than it delivered. The Cincinnati Stock Exchange, the nation's first fully automated exchange, founded in part by the famous third-market maker Weeden & Co., also came to grief as Weeden began to experience financial difficulties.

With the help of Merrill Lynch and the SEC, the Exchange was salvaged, but again came to grief when Merrill Lynch pulled out. By then it had become obvious Merrill's presence—inspired by then chairman Donald Regan—was at least partially aimed at the NYSE: By participating in the Cincinnati experiment, Regan had thrown a good scare into NYSE, which was staunchly refusing to automate. But once the Big Board began to automate some of its functions, Cincinnati's apparent usefulness as electronic bait came to an end. The nation's first all-electronic system struggled along, nearly going under and becoming a nonfactor through the 1980s. It was finally purchased by the Chicago Board of Options Exchange (CBOE).

The deregulation of Mayday, coupled with a lack of oversight and enforcement in the 1980s, caused problems for the securities industry. But Mayday's influence on competition in the brokerage industry was complicated by an obscure pact in 1982 between two top securities regulators—Philip Johnson and John Shad.

Both these men had just been tapped to be the nation's most powerful regulators in their chosen areas: Shad in securities through the SEC and Johnson in commodities through the Commodities Futures Trading Commission. CFTC responsibilities, since its inception in 1974, included direct surveillance of futures market and enforcement, oversight of futures trading SROs, and approval of futures contracts. Once his accord with Shad had been reached, CFTC chairman Johnson, a commodities lawyer, sprang into action and released a pent-up flood of financial futures contracts.

In a popular Washington, D.C. watering-hole, The Monocle, these two government executives made a deal to give oversight of most financial futures to the Commodities Futures Trading Commission; the SEC received responsibility for the regulation of stock options though not options on futures. Thus, the SEC was stripped of the ability to oversee and enforce the single most dynamic arena of investment growth in the United States in the 1980s—the financial futures industry.

The Evolution of Derivatives

There are two kinds of exchange-based stock derivative products currently operating in the United States: options and futures. Options allow investors the right to buy or sell an asset or instrument at a given "strike price." Futures confer an obligation for the investor to buy or sell at a certain time and price. Call options allow the investor to buy at certain times and price; put options allow the investor the same right to sell. Futures are dealt in contracts to buy or sell a certain amount of a commodity or financial instrument at a specific price, to be delivered at a specific time in the future. In the 1990s, derivatives have travelled off-exchange to be applied by Wall Street in ever-more customized formats as hedges for individual, institutional transactions. The Chicago derivatives exchanges are fighting this trend.

The CBOE, once a subsidiary of the Chicago Board of Trade (CBOT), pioneered options trading in the early 1970s by standardizing contracts and by fixing expiration months and the times of strike prices. Today, options are traded in several ways on U.S exchanges. The Pacific Stock Exchange and the CBOE use market makers to insure liquidity; the Philadelphia Stock Exchange, the American, and New York use specialists.

Exchange-traded options flourished in the late 1970s and into the 1980s despite the competition from financial futures. But as the 1980s evolved, the preference of the industry's powerful institutional investors tipped toward financial futures, especially stock index futures, because of the ability to trade an index instead of an individual instrument.

The first organized futures exchange, the CBOT, was formed in 1848. Today, 16 domestic exchanges are authorized to trade futures contracts; only about 1 percent of the futures contracts are now settled via delivery of the underlying product. Trading, standardized as to month of expiration, quantity, and quality, takes place in the "pit" between floor brokers, representing customers' orders and locals, the floor traders trading for themselves.

Futures contracts on financial instruments such as interest rates and bonds were developed on various commodities exchanges in the early 1970s. Stock index futures create the obligation to receive or deliver the equivalent, in cash, of a certain group, or portfolio, of stocks.

One of the exchanges most aggressive in pursuing such instruments was the Chicago Mercantile Exchange (CME), or Merc, which was eager to find new products to compete with its larger rival, the Board of Trade. On August 15, 1971, then-President Richard Nixon allowed the dollar to float in value against other currencies around the world. Nixon had effectively abrogated the famous Bretton Woods Agreement of 1944 that in part linked U.S. currency to the gold standard. The Merc struck: It launched a currency contract to allow investors to lock in specific currency rates much as farmers and merchants had once wished to lock in grain prices. It decided to create a separate exchange with a catchy if not grandiose name: the International Monetary Market (IMM).

The IMM was in part the brainchild of an energetic and mercurial lawyer-turned-commodity-trader, Leo Melamed. Melamed had been the CME chairman throughout the early 1970s before stepping down. The convenient availability of the IMM as a separate exchange rejuvenated Melamed's position. He became chairman of the IMM after its formation in 1972.

By 1975 trading was active in many of the IMM's currency futures contracts. The CBOT, alerted by Melamed's successful efforts, had also moved to create various financial contracts, including, ultimately, fixed income and Government National Mortgage Association securities contracts, which trade today on the CBOT in enormous amounts.

In 1976 Melamed began a campaign to merge the IMM back into the larger exchange to prevent a separation of Mercantile Exchange and IMM activities. This was already happening, as the older brokers were starting to sell their monetary market seats, creating a division between those who held commodity-trading seats and those who held money-market seats.

Melamed stopped testing his popularity with the members in the mid-1970s, when the board created a title for him of special counsel. Additionally, because the title of special counsel seemed eventually not to reflect the extent of Melamed's role in the Merc's rush to greatness, the board voted him another title in the mid-1980s—chairman of the executive committee. By the time Melamed received his second title from grateful executives, the Merc was trading one of its most successful contracts, the S&P 500 Stock Price Index Future.

Stock futures had been backed by such luminaries as the Nobel prize-winning economist Milton Friedman, who was aware such a product had been in the works back in 1927 before the Depression put a stop to it. But until the early 1980s, when the Shad-Johnson accord went into effect, the Merc and other futures exchanges had been prevented from initiating them.

Stock index futures are based on the weighted average of stocks represented in the index; they were almost an immediate hit with institutional investors, especially those who were broadly invested in the S&P 500. Since the performance of the Standard & Poor's 500 was the gauge by which institutional performance was based, most institutions using quantitative trading techniques were interested in tracking the index in as many markets as possible.

The Merc S&P 500 Index soon became the most popular stock index futures contract, accounting for some 80 percent of the volume before the end of the 1980s. Melamed and other Merc executives helped build a new industry in the futures market. But it was soon apparent that the new market was having an unforeseen effect on the stock market. This was because institutional investors used the new products to hedge equity investments and ran massive amounts of money back and forth between the two markets.

Such trading was a natural outgrowth of the tendency for the market to be dominated by bigger and bigger investors—pension plans and money managers. Between 1955 and 1980, the NYSE found the holding of its listed stock by selected institutions grew tremendously, to nearly half—and more than half of all trading done on the NYSE was on behalf of institutions. The combination of institutional customers, computers, and the swelling international scene that connected stock and bond markets around the world radically shifted the investment scene. By 1987 more than $150 billion would be invested in various computerized trading strategies, both domestically and abroad. And due to various trading strategies, including index arbitrage and portfolio insurance, the market would be gyrating wildly.

The Growth of Institutional Trading

The volume of orders flowing back and forth between the Merc and the NYSE increased rapidly in the 1980s. Institutions, flush with pension-plan cash—alongside most public pension plans—had begun to use index investing strategies in a big way. The use of portfolio insurance, in which institutions sold index futures rather than cash as the market went down in order to be able to reinvest in an up move, gave the biggest players an unfortunate sense of comfort.

The use of indexed investing was, like derivatives themselves, the outgrowth of a long-term evolution—as crisply traced in a recent book, *Capital Ideas,* by Peter Bernstein. Since the 1930s, financial observers, mostly obscure professorial types, had been groping toward mathematically rational forms of investment. There was the Random Walk theory, for instance, postulating that market prices moved by chance and that to try to predict price moves was foolish, if not downright foolhardy. And the theory of the efficient market: An investor might momentarily find a profitable chink in the market's armor, but others would soon follow and the momentary inefficiency would be erased. Finally, securities theorists like William Sharpe began to pose perhaps the largest question of all: Can anyone truly beat the market?

By "the market" Sharpe meant the entire market. Professional investors spoke of beating the market, but by this they really meant one market average or another. No one had actually envisioned winning out over the entire market: That was all there was to invest in; it couldn't be done. From this insight gradually emerged the view that indexing of wide-ranging portfolios of stock was a way to keep up with—join—the broad current of market prices since you couldn't beat them.

In the 1970s there was an explosion of quantitative strategies, mathematical methods of investing through indexes. Mainframe computers churned out lists of stocks to be bought and sold. At Salomon Brothers, the top traders shouted for the "programs" early in the morning so they'd be ready to trade at the market's opening. On the West Coast, San Francisco's oldest bank Wells Fargo & Co. began to experiment with programs, offering lists of stocks to brokerage houses, which then bid on the right to buy or sell them—package trades, in other words. Since transaction cost reduction is a major goal of quantitative and passive trading, Wells Fargo now makes up to 90 percent of certain trades internally, swapping lists among its $100 billion worth of portfolios.

Dean LeBaron's East Coast Batterymarch Inc. also experimented with program trading, asking Wall Street firms to electronically transmit indications of interest which would then be filled by its stock lists. Today, one of Batterymarch's top traders, Evan Schulman, is involved with broker First Boston to build a national "best price" order-routing system. The evolution of quantitative trading, combined with increasing computer power, is changing big-time investing. Lists of buy and sell orders are beginning to meet and greet in ways—and in derivative markets—that would have been incomprehensible to yesterday's traders and investors. In the 1980s these changes, while evident to industry professionals, were misunderstood by the public, misreported by the media and all too often ignored or misdiagnosed by regulators and politicians.

Mayday and the unfixing of commissions, in dropping the commission price for large players, helped stimulate the feverish trading; the 1980s derivative markets really got things hopping, as managers started to use programs to switch their funds between derivative and cash positions. The original problems were noticed during the so-called "triple-witching hours"—four Fridays a year when index futures, index options, and equity options were settled. Stock prices, it was thought, would move rapidly up and down as index arbitrageurs—those who hedged their speculative positions in options and futures with stock investments—tried to adjust their stock market purchases to reflect the latest configurations of their Chicago positions. All through 1986, the NYSE and the Chicago exchanges tried to figure out how to handle the triple-witching volatility. Finally, the Merc agreed to switch its stock index futures settlements to the early morning, thus taking off some of the pressure on the stock market.

Portfolio insurance trading techniques loomed large in NYSE chairman Phelan's meltdown nightmare. Since portfolio insurance strategies called for the disciplined selling of stock futures to compensate for declines in the equity or "cash" market, the result was to put more pressure on the underlying equities: The more futures that were sold, the more the futures market went down. That meant equity investors, eyeing the futures market to see where stock prices would eventually be, observed increased price-erosion and sold more stock.

Stock index arbitrage, according to some, lay at the root of the problem. Some funds had to stay invested in the stock market no matter what; that was how they had been designed. But fund managers, or so the theory went, often bounced their portfolios between the equity futures market and the stock market to exploit the pricing differences between the two markets. When portfolio insurance was combined with stock index arbitrage, the resultant pressures fed volatility and set off computerized limit orders that fueled selling. The market could drop straight down 100 points, and no human hand would ever be involved.

On September 11 and 12, 1986, the Dow Jones Industrial Average dropped 120 points, or almost 7 percent. Late in January of 1987, the Dow dropped another 115 points in an hour.

What the preceding explanation lacked, however, was a triggering event, for which at least one persuasive former top options trader and passionate market observer has an explanation. Morris Propp, who has been interviewed by *Barron's* and appeared before Markey's subcommittee to explain his insights, is convinced that one of the major problems facing the market is implementation of cash settlement and the manipulation it fosters in the derivative markets. According to Propp, the small size of the options industry, combined with cash settlement in options and futures, provides a built-in mechanism for manipulation affecting the stock market.

After blaming market instability on index arbitrage in several complicated studies, the SEC finally pointed to the options market as a major player in market instability. In the 1987 crash, institutions hedged using the futures markets—and portfolio insurance—but in the early 1990s the big managers hedged with options. Wall Street took the other side of hedge, but, in covering, the firms moved the market down.

In the mid-1980s the mechanisms for market moves were perhaps not so clear-cut. But the results were just as obvious. To counteract what was going wrong, Phelan quietly began to implement a safety net whereby trading would be halted on over 1,000 stocks if computer-aided selling dropped the market more than 25 percent.

Phelan was not alone in his efforts to stem market volatility. In Washington, Markey's subcommittee held several hearings on the subject, the first one late in 1986. Markey's hearings did not cause much of a stir. And Washington's regulatory agencies apparently remained calm in the face of increasing stock-market price fluctuation.

The SEC, still under Shad's woozy regime, was equally hamstrung. The SEC's internal culture had shifted: Its staff had been picked and promoted for their free-market viewpoints, its bureaucracy shaped to promote efficiency of issuance but not to investigate possible market distortions.

The combination of a lack of oversight, computer trading strategies, new derivative instruments, and 30 years of inconclusive physical exchange deregulation was finally going to catch up to the industry and the administration. In late October, program trading spun out of control. Hundreds of millions of shares were sold: On October 19, the market began its descent.

The Crash

On Bloody Monday, October 19, 1987, the market was pounded down 300 points in the morning and 500 by the close of trading. The 1987 crash has been documented in a number of books, including Tim Mertz' *Black Monday,* and Avner Arbel and Albert Kaff's *Crash,* from which some of the following is drawn.

On Tuesday, with the market down again toward mid-morning, Phelan placed "warning" calls about the market to Jerry Corrigan, the chairman of the New York Federal Reserve; Howard Baker, chief of staff at the White House; and David Ruder, chairman of the SEC. Phelan had the same message for each: He had a fallback plan—but if the market fell another 300 or 400 points "we'll have to close."

Such a meltdown had already been foreshadowed by a 114-point swing on January 23, 1987. "At some point you are going to have a first class catastrophe," Phelan warned in an article in the securities trade magazine *IDD*. Top securities executives like Alan Greenberg, chief executive of Bear Stearns & Co., called warnings like the ones Phelan issued in 1987 "totally ridiculous." Many in the industry shared Greenberg's philosophy on the matter: "Don't fix things that aren't broken."

The move actually began on Wednesday, October 14. That's when a trade deficit figure of $15 instead of $30 billion was announced, and Japanese Treasury investors began to sell. The bond market bounced down in heavy selling; the Dow gave up 95 points that day. On Friday, October 16, options expired and the Dow lost more than 100 points in a single session—the sixth highest percentage decline since the end of World War II. The move erased about $145 billion worth of equity capital from the value of America's largest corporations. But for the entire week, the sagging Dow had actually given up double that. Worries about the declining prices of bonds worldwide coupled with a continued decline of the dollar and a rise in interest rates had Wall Street on edge.

On Sunday and on into early Monday, Tokyo's Nikkei Index began to fall. It fell 620 points in all, for a total downturn of 2.3 percent. Other stock exchanges around the world were hit even harder. In Chicago, early in the morning, the futures traders calculated the values of their portfolios based on Friday's stale numbers, and the selling started again when the S&P pit opened. Speculators took a look at the numbers emanating from Chicago and decided that the market must be headed emphatically lower. Buyers took a look at the numbers and stayed out of the market. NYSE specialists, hit with thousands of sell offers, found no one waiting to buy at any price. The Big Board choked on the volume and the size of the downturn.

On Tuesday morning, the market reacted more favorably. But after moving up 200 points early, the market resumed its downward course. Between 10:00 and 12:00 the Dow gave back the entire gain plus another 30 points. Though not many were aware of it at the time, the actual numbers reflected by the Merc's futures index showed that the Dow actually touched bottom around 1,400, some 400 points less than where it would finally close. By then it seemed as if the Dow would drop past 1,700. Portfolio insurance had proved unworkable:

Faced with such astounding market drops, fund managers had panicked and sold stocks themselves rather than the futures contracts.

As the Mercantile Exchange S&P index plunged, Melamed and Phelan spoke by phone. "We don't want to close," Phelan told the CME chief. But the Big Board chairman seemed to indicate it was something he would have to consider unless the situation changed. (Today, NYSE spokesmen deny that Phelan ever seriously considered closing the Exchange.)

Melamed was with trusted associates, some of the men who had helped him build the Merc: president Bill Brodsky and Merc Chairman Jack Sandner. The three men knew that the CBOE option market had been shut down and that the American Stock Exchange had stopped trading options on the Major Market Index(MMI), events that Melamed later termed frightening.

The Merc executives told Phelan they would have to talk to the executive committee, which was meeting in emergency session, and would then get back to him about their own plans. Soon, Melamed stood near the pit while an exchange staffer read a brief but historic statement through an electronic bullhorn. For the first time ever, the pit was officially closed. (Later *The Wall Street Journal*'s Metz would request the text of the message and a Merc spokesman would say it had been mislaid.)

The closing of the S&P pit left only one futures index running, the CBOT's MMI. Like Melamed, the CBOT's Karsten "Cash" Mahlmann and his staff had been in touch with Phelan throughout the morning. Since the MMI is made up of only 20 major stocks, Mahlmann had staffers calling around the country to determine how many of the stocks in the index were actually still trading. And when it became apparent that 17 of the 20 were still trading on one exchange or another in various parts of the country, Mahlmann knew he could keep the MMI open.

In a 1989 interview before he left the CBOT, Mahlmann said he was not concerned with the selling pressure that Melamed maintains was a factor in his decision to close. (What would have happened if the MMI had closed? "Thank God we don't have to think about it," he said.) Soon after the closing of the CME's S&P pit, CBOT officials called Phelan to tell him that the MMI would remain open. And shortly after that call everything changed, and the market began to move back up.

None of the nation's top financial market executives involved have ever admitted that the scenario that now occurred was in any way planned. But the blizzard of studies, reports, and books written about the 1987 crash would seem to indicate that in some sense the Chicago markets, along with New York institutions, traders, and specialists may have acted in concert to defuse the crisis. Possibly it was serendipity: the decision of the CBOT to remain open, the decision of Melamed to close the Merc, Phelan's continuing indecision. But it is also possible that as the pieces of the puzzle fell together, the disparate players came together in at least a partially planned, hasty salvage attempt, as author Metz has maintained. Certain NYSE specialists bought "sloppy" in New York, ignoring sell orders, purchasing the 13 largest MMI stocks, gradually forcing the market higher.

It was easier after the closing of the S&P index. The MMI, much smaller and therefore easier to manipulate, was the only available stock-futures index. In the short minutes that followed, millions of dollars poured into the index as the futures traders for the various big Wall Street firms bid up MMI contracts much as they had at the CME. Only here there were not so many voracious local traders ready to stem the bull's stampede.

With fewer stock futures to buy and fewer local traders available to short contracts, the rally picked up pace. In time investors and even regulators and legislators would tend to downplay the single scariest fact to emerge from the 1987 crash: The fate of the most successful economic system in the world had hung on a slim index of rarely traded stock futures and the ragged determination of a few small businessmen to manipulate the market until it started back up. "It was no miracle," Phelan would say later. "Markets turn."

Yet Phelan would later tell the well-known business commentator Adam Smith in his book, *The Roaring 80s,* that if the markets had not turned, "major firms could have failed. Banks that loaned to the major firms could have been in trouble. You never know where the dominoes stop."

Aftermath

In the immediate aftermath of the crash, the securities industry did what it did best. It attacked symptoms while bemoaning causes. Fundamental money managers blamed "rocket scientists," the quants with computers, and manufactured elaborate conspiracy theories. New York blamed Chicago and vice-versa. Regulators sided with their respective industries. Washington politicians were suspicious but timid. Hearings occurred with great frequency.

Eventually, the Chicago exchanges imposed daily price limits on the movement of financial futures. The New York exchanges proposed restrictions on certain kinds of computerized trading. Because New York was the more powerful media market, much coverage was focused on how to rein in Chicago "speculators."

Chicago traders, not quite so well versed in press relations, fought back as best they could. It was true, they agreed, that it was easier to purchase large amounts of product on the futures exchange than in the stock market because the Chicago futures market extended more credit to buyers. But the market also demanded surety bonds and pulled investors out of the market the same day if they could not meet margin calls.

The NYSE, said Chicago, did not demand that investors pay for stock they bought on margin for up to five days. And this meant that banks lending money to brokers, who in turn lent the money to investors, had no way of knowing for an entire working week how well investors who had borrowed money were doing. In the case of a crisis, like the crash of 1987, banks became increasingly leery of lending more money to investors and to members of the NYSE, including the specialists. These NYSE members who are responsible for keeping orderly markets in specific stocks came under attack from the banks who denied them capital to buy back stocks as the buyer of last resort, and then from regulators who accused the specialists of selling short—betting that stocks would move down, thus increasing selling pressure.

Chicago argued that it was the banks' leeriness to extend more credit—based on faulty NYSE margin requirements—that dried up buying capital and aggravated the downward spiral of October's selling pressure. According to Chicago's way of seeing things, it was only the announcement by the Federal Reserve offering additional credit to Wall Street firms, investors, and specialists that turned the situation around.

Since the crash was an overwhelming event, explanations tended to be simplistic or vague. Those who favored efficient market explanations—fundamental economic reasons for every kind of market move—had a difficult time with the historic downturn. The most well-publicized job—or at least the quickest job, was done by the

Brady commission, led by white-shoe Dillon, Read & Co. chief executive Nick Brady, which did not even try to address the crash using efficient market theories. Instead, the report implied the opposite: The crash had been the product of a classic, speculative-type bubble that had ballooned in the 1980s and, aggravated by program trading, had finally burst.

Brady was tapped to head the commission by his good friend, then-Vice President George Bush, who would later name Brady Secretary of the Treasury.

Brady's report singled out the "disengagement" of stocks, futures, and options as a single, critical event that set off the crash. In other words, instead of moving together as they usually did, the various markets had gone off in their own separate free-falls. Once the crash had become full-blown, the Big Board basically shut down and arbitrage became impossible. Selling pressure fueled downward momentum, eventually visiting all exchanges with nearly unstoppable downward momentum.

Brady criticized voluntary SuperDot halts, saying that the more slowly the NYSE executed trades, the more quickly the differences between the stock and futures market would develop into a 1987-type crash. The research favored making the SuperDot more available to smaller orders, increasing liquidity and decreasing volatility by breaking down volume among thousands of individual investors.

The report indicated that more capitalization for the specialists might not have helped the situation, at least to begin with. Instead, the report recommended that specific regulatory mechanisms be put into place: circuit breakers, price limits, volume limits, and trading halts. The report pointed up the disjunction between the futures stock indexes and the stock market and stated that one regulator should be in charge of similar products.

In addition to the Brady report, both Chicago and New York financial markets moved quickly to issue reports of their own. In Chicago, Melamed turned to an old friend and future Nobel Prize winner, the economist Merton Miller. Miller was one of the founders of modern arbitrage theory, the theory on which the stock index futures market had in part been built. Not surprisingly, the CME commission concluded there was absolutely no evidence that stock index futures trading—arbitrage—had caused the crash. (Though Miller privately does admit that the practice, because of the current market set-up, may have exacerbated the market's fall.)

The report pointed out that the so-called uptick rule, which allows short sales to be executed only at a price higher than that of the last differently priced trade preceding it, actually helped exacerbate selling pressure by concentrating it in Chicago. Additionally, the report said that because of the "30 percent" or Short-Short rule applying to mutual fund companies, many funds are reluctant to invest in futures. The profits of a single successful futures hedge could cause a fund's entire earnings to become subject to full taxation.

Even as Miller and his group raced to complete their report, the NYSE's hand-picked evaluator, former Attorney General Nicholas Katzenbach was putting the finishing touches on his, "An Overview of Program Trading and Its Impact on Current Trading Practices," which was released at the end of 1987. Katzenbach's report, perhaps the thinnest and simplest-sounding of the five major reports on the crash, nevertheless makes several conclusions that were present in the Brady report and some other, later reports as well.

According to Katzenbach, stock index arbitrage, to which some ascribed a leading role in the stock market crash, was not itself to blame. It was the interaction between the two markets as a result of stock index arbitrage that caused volatility and ultimately helped precipitate the crash. "To link closely two markets with such disparate standards defies common sense," Katzenbach wrote. "It can only help encourage trading speculation and lead investors to forget long term investment and concentrate on short term trading."

The Chicago exchanges, buttressed by the Miller report and protected by political muscle, fought against the imposition of outside regulations throughout 1988 and into 1989. With the help of the Reagan administration, which apparently did not want to see increased regulation, various bills aimed at the Chicago markets and its CFTC regulators were either stalled or defeated in both the House and Senate. At the same time, the CME and CBOT made sure they moved ahead with certain adjustments in tandem with New York.

In Washington the tension mirrored the postures of New York and Chicago. First of all there was the regulatory controversy between the CFTC and the SEC. In turn, the congressional committees running the regulators faced the prospect of squaring off in a long political battle over securities turf. The nation's two agricultural committees, one in the House and one in the Senate, had jurisdiction over the CFTC. The Senate Banking Committee and the House Energy and

Commerce Committee and its Telecommunications and Finance sub-committee watched over the SEC.

The agricultural committees also had a strong Illinois delegation to back them up in a time of struggle—one that included the powerful House Ways and Means Committee chairman, Dan Rostenkowski (D-Ill.). Facing off with Rostenkowski was the even more powerful House Energy and Commerce Committee under John Dingell (D-Mich.).

Leaders of the Chicago futures industry had always viewed Dingell with suspicion. At least some industry leaders were relatively sure Dingell's view, like those of his subcommittee's chairman, Markey, would reflect the position he had as a congressional boss of the SEC. He would come down hard on the side of the SEC in a turf fight: He would insist on more SEC jurisdiction over the markets.

The press picked up on the controversy. *Time* magazine wrote about "The War of Two Cities," an article Melamed later labeled "the worst piece of journalism I've ever seen from a responsible magazine."

In 1987 and 1988 alone, according to the *Washington Post,* the CME contributed nearly $300,000 to the coffers of congress. In addition to political action committee (PAC) money, the Chicago exchanges began flying legislators in for speaking engagements for which they retained cash honoraria, and also to meet with various exchange officials, for which the legislators received sums labeled as "appearance fees." In 1987 the Chicago Exchanges handed out nearly 50 sums of $1,000 and $2,000 to legislators, including now-Vice President Dan Quayle. Another top national politician, now-Senate Banking Committee Chairman Donald Riegle (D-Mich.), received nearly $30,000 in campaign and personal contributions from the exchanges.

The Futures Industry Association (FIA) was active after the crash too, hiring a lobbying firm and arranging to have representatives meet quickly with Brady after he had been appointed to head the task force to study the crash. Meanwhile, President Reagan, whose free-market bias gave him an instinctive sympathy for Chicago's perspective, eventually placed FIA general counsel Mary Schapiro on board the SEC as commissioner. It was a move widely thought to be aimed at then SEC chairman David Ruder's maverick policies and also designed to show Washington where the administration's sympathy lay.

More than six months after the stock market crash, the *Washington Post* reported that Melamed finally sat down at a formal breakfast peacemaking session with Phelan; Melamed had asked for the breakfast, but Phelan's presence was a tacit acknowledgment that the Big Board, too, needed to have a truce with its most crafty and powerful competitor. The two men had already met in Washington at the instigation of the SEC and CFTC not long after the crash. But this meeting was more important since it led to increased cooperation that allowed New York and Chicago to announce a wide array of actions that were being taken independently to defuse the possibility of another Big Board plunge. By early July of 1988, the two exchanges were able to announce an agreement to coordinate trading halts in the case of a major downward market move.

For the next three years, the markets stumbled along. The system was working, but barely. There were continued crashes, not so severe as 1987, but maybe that was only because there was less public money in the market and therefore less volume to trigger. There was, of course, the so-called mini-crash of 1989, which resulted in yet more studies and more finger pointing. Index arbitrage was trotted out as reason why program traders should be banned before they destroyed "our" market, as Bill O'Neil, publisher of *Investor's Business Daily,* put it.

The SEC, under Richard Breeden, made no bones about its intention to try to take authority away from the CFTC regarding stock index futures. Brady firmly supported Breeden in his quest, further politicizing what should have been—in a better world—an objective search for the truth. Other side-shows emerged. The NYSE heatedly defended its specialist system as a stabilizing influence. The Big Board even went so far as to convene a special Blue Ribbon panel to investigate the root causes of the market's instability. The panel, led by Roger Smith, then chief-executive of General Motors, released a report that was widely seen as a vindication of Wall Street's—and the Big Board's—views about program trading—that it exacerbated market moves. According to the panel, the solution was to "slow down the train."

After the release of the report, the NYSE took further steps to implement formal market stoppages and slowdowns. In the meantime, the Big Board made an announcement that spoke volumes about the real, underlying nature of the debate. It announced a ten-year plan to install an electronic after-hours trading network.

The Big Board, by its actions, not its press releases, had finally acknowledged that the world was changing and that automated execution systems were not only possible and practical, but even necessary.

Unfortunately, most cures for the crash of 1987 and for subsequent continued volatility were aimed at symptoms and not at the underlying causes. Politics and the complexity of what occurred prevented the various commissions from investigating one of the possible root causes of the market crash—options market manipulation. And reconstruction was further complicated by arguments involving the so-called benefits of a specialist system as opposed to a market-maker system. What all this boils down to is that in a liquid market where buyers and sellers meet to trade, someone ideally should have an affirmative obligation to make the trade. It is not clear, however, in the markets of the future, who or what this someone should be.

Perhaps in the electronic markets of tomorrow the someone will be the corporations that have an interest in supporting their own securities. Or perhaps it will be institutions that have a similar interest in securities where they have large interests. Quite possibly, in an environment where large chunks of indexed instruments are being bought and sold, the whole question about who should provide liquidity to the market will begin to fade—at least for heavily traded instruments. In time, debates over the efficacy of various forms of physical exchanges may even be settled by computer modeling. Donald Unruh, an electronic trading pioneer, has done some intriguing work in this area.

Right now, we have more immediate difficulties: In the opinion of sophisticated observers, a fragile stock market intimately related to an ever-expanding universe of other instruments—futures, options, OTC derivatives—is subject to continual market manipulation that still threatens the structure.

For Propp and some others the root cause of such manipulation lies in the mechanism of cash settlement: Yet derivatives markets and cash settlement aren't going away. Ironically, Propp—who would like to shut down such products—also believes he knows how such manipulation can be at least partially ameliorated. Currently, options are settled monthly, but there is no reason why options cash settlement couldn't be staggered, Propp points out. Futures cash settlement could be staggered, too, diminishing the impact—and manipulative possibilities—of many instruments settling together.

Additionally, it is possible that an increasing array of worldwide markets, worldwide players (including pension plans), increasingly diverse investment strategies, and more securities information will begin to disperse the most obvious kinds of repetitive volatility. Technology, properly utilized and widely available, can at least make manipulations harder by exposing them to the broadest possible professional audience.

Alternatively, as sophisticated market observers like financial writer Mayer have pointed out, international investing may bring more risks since capital flows and economic trends may flow in the same direction at the same time, exacerbating both booms and busts. One way to avoid this risk may be to deepen the market—allow more players into the game, allow more information to be disseminated to more buyers and sellers. And most important, allow those buyers and sellers to deal with one another in a relatively unstructured environment.

The idea that some dozen large firms will have access to worldwide trading information just as some six or so Wall Street firms had access to massive amounts of domestic trading information in the 1980s is disturbing. So much information concentrated in so few hands is a recipe for a fragile, uneasy marketplace. More regulation of fewer players is apt only to exacerbate the dilemma. The real answer is to open up the marketplace, make it more "robust" (in the current jargon), by allowing more buyers and sellers to deal directly with one another, using the electronic nets that are gradually evolving worldwide.

15

■■■

MARKET STRUCTURE

" The Society traders came down and became the specialists."

■ FRED RITTEREISER

Fred Rittereiser has been involved in electronic markets since the early 1970s and served as president of Instinet during the mid-1980s. Fred is the older brother of Robert Rittereiser, who took over the giant retail broker E. F. Hutton in the mid-1980s.

Fred and Bob are partners in Yorkville Associates Inc., a private management consulting firm specializing in financial services.

I'm a student of the industry. I've been involved in it all my professional life. I started in OTC equity block trading. I remember the national market system conferences the industry sponsored. I represented the NASD. Those conferences were mandated by the SEC and went on for four years. The SEC had to come up with a plan and didn't necessarily want to lead the process, so Harold Williams, then chairman of the SEC, told the industry to come up with a national market system.

The first meetings took place in 1974. That was the meeting of the 15-person Blue Ribbon Panel. The various exchanges, the self-regulatory organizations sent reps at the subcommittee level, and the subcommittees went on and on despite the dissolving of the Blue Ribbon Panel.

I was at an OTC market-maker and registered block trader in the 1970s; we used to do some program trading by phone, moving out large blocks of stock and buying other blocks of stock. We'd buy IBM and sell DEC at some kind of ratio. Buy 40,000, sell 60,000—equity program trading—according to some computer strategy. The idea was to beat the market—if the market moved up one point, you wanted to be in a stock that might move up two. It was kind of primitive. The institutional head trader, for instance, he would call and say "I have a program, a new program." We'd say, "What's the program?" "I want to buy so and so and sell so and so." That's how you started talking about a transaction that was the forefather of program trading in the 1980s.

The S&P futures changed everything. Once you developed the S&P futures, you had the capability to put together various algorithm that replicated movements in the marketplace.

The instability in the market during the late-1980s came about in part because exchange firms sold on downticks. The uptick rule, which stipulates that in a down market you can sell a share of stock only once the market has moved up an eighth of a point—that rule went out the window for the big firms selling blocks of stock in the 1980s. It was just like leverage—the big firms got around margin requirements in the 1980s because the margin rules had been set up for the individual investor. It was a no-action letter to Merrill Lynch from SEC in the mid-1980s that really set things off. Essentially the SEC ruled the big Wall Street firms could do what they wanted to in the futures market. They were exempt from stock market rules like the uptick rule, the margin rule. Now you could create all the shorts and longs you wanted to. There was no end to the amount of paper you could create, to the amount of leverage. Now the NYSE seems to have addressed the issues of selling on downticks by fining the big Wall Street firms involved.

The NYSE's problems haven't change much, at a fundamental level, since the 1970s. They basically have a very tough job with the specialists who have an affirmative obligation to buy and sell securities. They are given a charter, and it's very strict. In reality the only time the specialists make money is basically because they have the ability to open the market in the morning. They set their positions based on supply and demand so they open the market up long or short. That's because they know what's in the crowd and on their books, including the limit orders. If they have a lot of orders to buy or sell when the market hits a certain point, they can make the judgment the market in that stock is probably going to drift in that direction sooner or later.

The NYSE is still the dominant exchange. It knows how to survive as an institution. At one point in time in the late 1800s there were 14 so-called exchanges. But only one was a real threat, the Open Society of New York Brokers. The American was the Curb exchange, and it served the purposes of the NYSE because little companies could trade there until they were big enough for the Big Board. The Open Society was a different deal. It was formed back in the mid-1800s when the NYSE was still an auction market. In an auction there would be a roll call and brokers would bid for stock purchases. But the Open Society allowed continuous trading of stocks. And after a while the Open Society organized itself into trading positions with specialists just the way the Big Board is organized now. It was the Open Society that formed the approach of the modern exchange.

As more and more trading moved uptown because people liked the convenience of trading when they wanted to, the NYSE saw they would have to come to an understanding with the Open Society. Only they couldn't just swallow the Society and put it out of business. They had to cut a deal. When they merged, the NYSE went out of the roll-call business and into full-time, continuous trading. So the Society traders came down and became the specialists. They had the experience in open outcry. They knew how to move the stocks.

Now we're going to go back to auction markets. What we'll eventually end up with is a rolling electronic call system with continuous interactive trading. Specialists as we know them today will be replaced—or the function will evolve into some form of electronic dealer.

■ OLD HEDGE FUND OPERATOR

Alfred Jones founded the first hedge fund, A. W. Jones. The concept took a while to catch on. The first one was formed around 1950. And the second one was formed about 1962—Fairfield Partners in Fairfield Conn.

Jones interviewed successful investors, and having done these interviews, he thought, Well, why don't I look at this and see if there is any commonality or common thread that runs through them.

He found out the things these fellows were best at was picking stocks both long and short. The thing they were least good at was knowing which way the market was going. So it became clear to him that you should formulate an approach in which you could emphasize stock and deemphasize the market movement. It was a kind of modern portfolio management strategy. But no indexes. Only the stock market.

Jones decided to be long and short at all times. He considered this to be a conservative approach as long as you did it on a consistent basis. Also Jones decided he would not charge a fee for his services but would share in the profits of his clients. Most hedge funds are set up as partnerships with the manager serving as the general partner and the investors serving as limited partner.

Hedge fund was just Wall Street jargon. What Jones was running was an investment partnership using hedging techniques. But over time the hedge fund name was applied to Jones and all the other hedge funds coming along after him.

Of course, not every fund operated like Jones's. The ones that came after, and there were quite a number, may have been referred to as hedge funds even though some of them never sold short a stock. They did tend to charge a performance fee, however. So they elaborated on the compensation even if they didn't get the strategy right.

These days hedge funds hedge with puts and calls in the options market. There was an explosion of these funds when the market took off in the early 1980s.

■ DONALD REGAN

As chairman of Merrill Lynch, Donald Regan kept a high profile on Wall Street throughout the 1970s and into the 1980s. Arrogant, even dictatorial, Regan's reign at Merrill was a success. Many (including Regan) trace the decline of the powerful firm in the 1980s to Regan's departure for the White House, where he later served as Treasury Secretary.

During the 1970s and early 1980s, along with the Weeden brothers, Regan fought many of the battles for an electronic exchange. He was the first major Wall Street executive to argue for deregulated com-

missions. For a while Merrill even participated in the Weeden-supported electronic Cincinnati Stock Exchange before pulling out in 1983.

We would not have had the crash of 1987 if we had gone electronic early on. Program trading would have not been introduced. What you're doing with program trading is taking a bunch of stocks and trading them at a historic price on the stock market and in futures. As it stands now, the reason for the disparity is that those who have computers move faster than those who don't. An electronic system would have taken care of that disparity. It would have killed the inefficiency.

There should be an electronic marketplace. The floor trader is an anachronism. We participated with Weeden in the Cincinnati marketplace. The NYSE specialists were afraid, of course. Naturally they didn't want it—they guard their franchise jealously. But we had our electronic marketplace, and I still say that's the market of the future. Bond traders have an automated system. They trade with computers—they don't stand and scream at each other the way they do in Chicago.

If you go back and look at the Merrill Lynch experiment—if it had been utilized properly—by now we'd have sophisticated machines implanted. We'd have a sophisticated automated trading system, but the Big Board didn't want it. Floor traders and specialists outvoted the upstairs. Oh, they'll tell you that they don't have a monopoly, but the Exchange paid too much attention to its traders. When the chairman comes up for election he has to have over 600 votes and he has to get a majority of the brokers and specialists. If he doesn't, he's out on his ear.

Had I stayed at Treasury I think I would have spoken out more on program trading. I voluntarily went and testified before Markey's subcommittee. The floors of our major exchanges are still living in the past. Wall Street's analysts penalize companies who don't modernize— but the Street's exchanges are archaic,

I don't know any economic benefit derived from program trading. It doesn't even benefit the markets. The program traders have injected volatility and fear into the market. Individual investors know they are unable to compete with large mainframes and good software. They can't compete with big players who can trade in and out and push a stock in and out.

It's bad for the market, but that's the trading mentality. You get caught up in the mentality—you have to have that instinct. I would say it's a fever. And it infects top management also. The fever gets into the blood—now the market has been commoditized.

I don't think deregulation caused any of this. Mayday was a separate issue. We had to make underwriting and securities sales a business rather than a group of guys rigging rates. How can you practice closet capitalism and then expect everyone else to live or die by capitalism? Remember, at that point of time we had large institutions coming to the forefront: insurance companies, mutual funds, pension funds. They were getting cuts in rates by many under-the-table transactions. These things involved anything from entertainment to business to free services. It was a soft dollar business, it was simply to cut rates. If firms violated the rates they'd get fined. Wall Street thought the antidote for increased costs was more revenue and they kept ratcheting up the commission structure. What nonsense. It wasn't allowed in any other business. It made for built-in inefficiencies.

But it's true, as deregulation unfolded a lot of people and institutions became greedy and took advantage of situations. Additionally, there have been a lot of new instruments coming onto Wall Street—either to raise capital or to provide people with ways to invest capital, like these so-called bridge loans.

We should do away with Glass-Steagall. The Japanese are allowing banks to merge and go into securities business. Why is everybody protected under these cartel rules? What the hell happened to competition? There is no God-given right that Wall Street firms should all succeed.

■ ANDY KLEIN
_____

Andy Klein was director of market regulation for the Securities and Exchange Commission throughout the late 1970s. He faults the SEC for lack of courage in the 1970s and 1980s and hopes it is not too late for the nation's securities industry to regain the ground that has been lost.

The origins of the national market system were attributable to market fragmentation—trading in the same stocks in multiple markets—in a fixed commission rate environment and the pressures of big institutions on the fixed rate structure during the late 1960s and early 1970s.

There was significant congressional and SEC concern that more should be done to insure that customers of brokers could get best execution of their trades. As things were, there was little assurance that best execution was occurring—that is, if there was a better price in Boston, why was your broker getting a worse price by trading in New York? There also was a general feeling that there should be more competition between and among markets and market makers to produce the best price and add depth to the markets as a whole.

The debate over these issues really began under Bill Casey in the early 1970s, when he was chairman of the SEC. Most of the important work on the issues, however, was done under Ray Garrett, who served as chairman through the mid-1970s. It was Garrett who oversaw implementation of the consolidated tape, adoption of a rule requiring development of a composite quotation screen that would collect bids and offers from all markets so that anyone could see the best quotes, and the unfixing of consumer rates—developments that have transformed our trading markets. All of these steps were being pushed by the SEC well before passage of the Securities Act Amendments of 1975.

Although that law all but required deregulation of commissions, such deregulation was something that the SEC had already determined to do. The new law also effectively barred institutions from becoming members of an exchange and trading for their own accounts—a policy difficult to understand since exchange membership was sought by institutions solely to avoid fixed commissions, something that the same law eliminated. But the most important part of the legislation may have been the grant to the SEC of enhanced regulatory powers to facilitate creation of eight national market systems, a true central market. The powers given to the SEC to bring about a national market system were very broad, near plenary. It was enormous artillery against entrenched interests and the status quo.

The SEC set about fulfilling its mandate to create a national market system by addressing a host of anticompetitive barriers erected by the most powerful markets—those in New York. One extremely difficult issue was off-board trading rules of exchanges, which prevented firms from handling their customers' order in agency or principal trades off exchange. These rules stood in the way of true upstairs competition with the exchange by dealers who were members of those exchanges.

The SEC proposed eliminating these rules, allowing anybody to trade anywhere. Ultimately, however, the SEC settled for less than half a loaf, alleviating these rules to continue to apply to stocks listed on exchanges before 1981—that is, most of them. The Commission had better luck in bringing into being both the consolidated tape and the composite quotation system.

When Harold Williams took over as SEC chairman, he questioned how far the SEC should go in mandating a new kind of market system. Had he been more visionary and less risk-averse, perhaps the Commission would and could have done more to push the envelope in the national market system area. But Williams was troubled by the idea of breaking eggs to make the omelette. He was worried about the Commission's ability to make the kinds of judgment that an active national market system policy required. Wholesale elimination of off-board trading rules was never achieved and real competition to exchange markets never developed. In the end, though, the Commission deferred to the same forces whose clubiness and footdragging had caused congress to act in the first place: the New York exchanges and the broker-dealer establishment.

Chris Keith, the chief technology executive for the Big Board, became the point man for a compromise market linkage system known today as the Intermarket Trading System (ITS), a fairly elementary way of communicating orders between and among exchange floors. ITS was and remains a far cry from the consolidated limit order book and automatic order routing systems under study at the SEC at the time ITS was proposed.

By 1980 many of the pressures that had given rise to the national market system idea had dissipated. The SEC spent most of the 1980s working on the problems of split CFTC/SEC jurisdiction, derivative index products and market volatility issues related to the advent of futures trading based on securities.

Many blame former chairman Shad for losing the battle for authority over securities-related futures products in 1982, but that's not so. It was Garrett who gave that store away in 1973, distracted as he was by fixed rates, institutional membership on exchanges and the national market system. congress offered the SEC the job of regulating the futures market at that time, but Garrett didn't want to know from hog bellies. So congress set up the CFTC instead. He, like all regulators, was preoccupied by yesterday's problems.

I walked away from the SEC at the end of 1979 thinking that all that worry over market structure had been a bit of a waste. Why not just link up the markets with TVs at home and let customers buy securities products directly with a credit card? When I read that, in effect, Sears Roebuck & Co. is now selling such a trading method over home computers, I figured that the idea had finally been presented from the right quarter—the private sector. Good luck to such efforts.

16

■ ■ ■

Nasdaq

"We were the Rodney Dangerfield of securities markets."

■ GORDON MACKLIN

Energetic former NASD president, Gordon Macklin brought the modern Nasdaq marketplace into being against formidable odds. The American Stock Exchange fought for years to undermine the network, and the state regulatory bodies were not much more accommodating.

I happened to be a member of the NASD board representing district number nine (Ohio and Kentucky). Robert Haack was president of the NASD then—that was before he went to the NYSE. The board formed an automation subcommittee. They did a considerable amount of industry analysis including hiring professional consultants. Ultimately, they came up with specifications for an automated trading system. They got a bid from the Bunker Ramo corporation to build the system, and that's who they awarded it to. It was an ongoing project when I took over as NASD president from Robert Walbert, Haack's successor.

I'd been with a regional brokerage firm for twenty years, so I tended to think long-term. When I came on as president in the spring of 1970, I was thinking ten years. Since I had been a member of the long-range planning committee as well as the board, I was fully aware of all the background work that had led to the idea of Nasdaq. I had a good idea of what it would take to make the system a success. I knew it would be a long haul. We were the Rodney Dangerfield of securities markets, so to speak. We got no respect.

I had worked with emerging companies as a broker and investment banker. In retrospect, I've spent my life growing up with companies. So I was comfortable with the role, and with the mission—get Nasdaq up and operating and grow it into a real market.

The way the market worked back then—it was called the OTC —they gathered up the quotes every day by a bunch of messengers. These quotes were published on mimeographed sheets which happened to be pink in color. They were a guide to the dealers about price. The NASD had a rule that if you were a broker executing a customer order you had to check with three different market makers. That was the way the market worked—with once-a-day quotes and messenger services.

In the late SEC special study of securities markets in the 1960s, the NASD was asked to come up with a better system. That request plus the studies that followed led to the birth of the Nasdaq—the national automated quotation system. Instead of a physical exchange, we gave NASD brokers computer screens on which they could see stock prices, and make offers to buy or sell stock.

On February 8, 1971, the system commenced operation. It was a success—and it was immediately obvious we would need a place to clear trades as volume grew. That accelerated our efforts to construct a national clearing system for Nasdaq. It was quite a fight.

Later on, we spun off the clearance companies of NASD and merged our clearing corporations with those of the American Stock Exchange and the NYSE. That is today known as the National Securities Clearing Corp. The evolution is directly related to the growth of industry needs.

A lot of work and effort focused on the clearing effort to make Nasdaq viable. It was a long war—the exchanges were trying to throw sand in the gears for years.

Perhaps the biggest battle of all was when we decided to set up separate markets within Nasdaq. The Nasdaq list was a heterogeneous selection of companies including small, extremely speculative companies. When the SEC mandated more reporting in certain stocks and left it up to us which ones we were willing to pick, it became obvious here was a perfect opportunity to create an elite class of greater companies. We could take out the smaller ones—have them not trade under such stringent rules.

The 1987 crash was certainly a victory for John Phelan. He won the battle of public relations. He reacted quickly and started blaming the commodities and futures markets as well as Nasdaq. He grabbed the high ground and executed beautifully. The truth of it is there were problems in trading all equities.

■ NASD EMPLOYEE

The NASD has to make up its mind if it is an exchange, a regulator, or a trade organization representing brokers. Right now the organization wears three hats and all three are in conflict with each other.

On the TV commercials, Nasdaq's electronic market is built for the Next Hundred Years, but the Nasdaq system still mostly depends on phone contact. Instead of traders trading with each other on a floor, they trade with telephone. There's a screen there, but it's still mostly a passive kind of system—it's not truly interactive even though they keep upgrading the software.

There's points past which the NASD can't go. They can't set up a truly innovative system because that kind of trading network could threaten to put the NASD's own membership out of business.

How can an organization whose membership is made up entirely of brokers design innovative products to put its own membership out of business? That's the same problem the industry faces when it tries to regulate itself. These are issues the NASD doesn't have real answers to. At least not right now.

17

■■■

AUTOMATION

"People didn't want to hear how a good computer system would operate."

■ MORRIS MENDELSON

Along with Peake and Williams, Wharton finance professor Morris Mendelson wrote a paper on automated trading that was submitted to the SEC in the mid-1970s. The SEC was then trying to figure out how to implement a national market system. The Peake-Mendelson-Williams electronic trading proposal was seen by many as a basis on which to build such a network.

In 1969 I started thinking about computers and trading. I sat down and wrote a paper on what was wrong with the NYSE at the time. I showed it to a well-known professor of securities law. I'll never forget, he said, "If you publish this in an academic journal, no one will read it and that will be too bad."

I came up with a monograph called "From Automated Quotes to Automated Trading." I worked on it from 1969 to 1971, and it was published as one of a series of New York University bulletins in March 1972 by The New York University Institute of Finance there. Versions of the paper were incorporated into congressional hearings.

In 1975 I was working on a project on the future of the securities industry for the Stanford Research Institute. I was doing a lot of interviewing and I visited New York to meet Jay Peake—he was a big back-office guy, and he already had a reputation for problem-solving and tackling the paper crunch.

He had an office in a firm with a big clearing operation. He had left Shields by then. A year later he called me out of the blue. He said he wanted to write a paper on automating the market. The 1975 Act had called for the creation of a national market board to look into ways to create a national market system, and he had some ideas on the subject. By then he'd heard about the paper I'd written, and he thought we were thinking along the same lines. So he wanted to prepare a submission with me. We'd have more credibility together, he figured. We included Williams, who knew about technology and computers, so we had a complete team. Today Williams hasn't got the enthusiasm for the system that Jay and I do.

All this came about because the SEC announced they were undertaking this study in answer to the congressional mandate for a national market system. I have to say I was initially skeptical about Jay's proposition because of my earlier experience. We had dinner at a restaurant in Philadelphia. I don't charge for such consultations, but I insist on a good dinner. We talked. Peake told me what he was thinking about—and essentially it was a radical simplification of the paper I had written. Mine was just a lot more complex.

So we sat down and we wrote a paper together. We wrote it in about two weeks. It wasn't hard—we'd been thinking about these ideas for years. In its simplest form the paper made the argument that you could build a system that would allow traders to place orders on a screen. If the orders matched, they'd be executed instantly. If a buy or sell order was not matched it would sit there until someone took it out—in the order in which it appeared. Very simple. Not complicated at all. The underlying concept was price and time priority. The first order at a certain price got filled first.

We sent the paper off and it made a big splash. The SEC study group gave us the courtesy of a full day's interrogation, but I wasn't much impressed—the SEC staffers didn't understand what we were saying. I had the feeling that, being lawyers, they were frightened of the whole undertaking. They didn't understand what was going on and they didn't want to interfere.

No one in the study group ever acknowledged ours was the best plan, but the press picked up on it from the releases Jay and I sent out. The press made a big deal out of it—lots of articles. Plus, we were the only group who made a formal presentation—we requested it. They gave us the courtesy of listening to us for a whole day. We felt we'd done a good job but we hadn't convinced them.

The securities industry never wanted automated trading. It was a threat. The SEC was threatened too. They never understood the basic arguments for or against the ideas we proposed, and there were other issues that the industry didn't want to deal with. The second important part of the Mayday act was to get rid of the NYSE Rule 390. First the SEC proposed that Rule 390 be done away with entirely. Then they proposed the rule not apply for any stock listed after 1981.

In a sense, the idea of having a national market system was to get around the fragmentation of doing away with Rule 390. That was the proposed Rule 19c-3. I always thought what the industry ended up with in the late 1970s was a flawed compromise that insured nothing much would change.

The liquidity of the NYSE—it's competitive edge—may soon disappear. They haven't been moving fast enough. In May 1989, I attended an academic conference at the NYSE. People started spouting myths about how a market would work. They wouldn't give me the floor. They didn't want to hear how a good computer system would operate.

18

■ ■ ■

THE BIG BOARD

*" The view of marketplaces is flawed at the most
fundamental level."*

■ CHRISTOPHER KEITH

*Retired now, Christopher Keith was the "resident iconoclast" at the
NYSE for nearly 20 years. He is a small, animated man who lives
quietly with his wife in a large, breezy Manhattan apartment that
includes on its walls many of his daughter's paintings and, in broad
bookcases, a goodly number of tomes on literary and philosophical
subjects.*

At SIAC, the Big Board's automation subsidiary, I was Mr.
Fixit. Whenever a project had been run over by a beer truck, before
they gave it last rites they brought it to my office. One day it turned
out I had all the projects in one state or another of reconstruction
and so I was named head of development, though head of recovery
would have been more exact. It was only when I moved over to the
Exchange itself that I dwindled into an intellectual.

ITS was dreamed up in the days when the pressure for the national
market system was intense. Washington types were talking about a
centralized order switch routing shares to best market. One day Floyd
Brandow, a Milbank Tweed lawyer who was NYSE's outside counsel
and an exceedingly capable man, and I sat in an empty sixth floor
office and I outlined some of the technological alternatives to the
current Washington priorities. Floyd asked questions about each and

112

then pronounced: "Well I sort of like Alternate C." That's what we presented to my boss, Bob Hall, who also made an improvement or two.

Subsequently any of number of people played roles in bringing the creature ITS, the Intermarket Trading System, to life and could claim, I suppose with some merit, some parental credit, but ITS has remained to this day substantially Floyd's alternative C.

The basic idea was simplicity itself. Put a special quote machine on each Exchange floor to allow a floor broker to get a better price from another exchange, if available.

ITS has been disdained by some as being "only a compromise." It was a compromise of course, and compromises have always been disdained, particularly by those who have not bothered to think through the implications of not compromising. For one thing, it is alleged not to be a true best price mechanism, which is quite true, at least within price-priority sense.

But in the real world, the central problem of most system design relates to the handling of competing priorities. And acknowledging the legitimate entitlement of each of these priorities does not lead to system purity, which does not lead to beauty which does not satisfy the multitudes. One example is Steve Wunsch, and his electronic call market. In any marketplace, one competition between priorities is the one between the need for liquidity and the demand for continuous pricing.

Steve's breakthrough was to do away with the need for continuous pricing—which he did by fiat. He just declared there was no such need. That produced something wonderfully simple which promised to dispense, as by-product, with the entire securities industry as we know it. But why stop there I always wondered. Why not eliminate the need for banking service later than two in the afternoon, or before noon also by fiat. Then we could also dispense with the banking industry as we know it.

Another contention underlying the basic structure of markets is the one between a market's two underlying functions. A market is a transaction mechanism, which everyone seems to understand. But it is something else. It is also a price discovery mechanism, and this is an aspect few seem to understand though of the two it is the price discovery mechanism whose effect is the more ubiquitous, and continuous.

Now the system types encountered this priority dilemma and saw no dilemma. Peake, for example, just like Wunsch, solved the problem by doing away with one of the contenders. Peake did not declare by fiat that there was no need for a price discovery mechanism. The Peake-Mendelson model simply transferred that function, in its entirety, lock stock and barrel to the customer. The problem became wonderfully simple. Of course what qualified these customer with or without aid from a broker to make such pricing decisions—what the cost to them would be if they were wrong—how their interests could be protected against those with better or later information—were left unaddressed.

The whole public view of marketplaces is flawed at the most fundamental level. Outsiders tend to look at an exchange floor as having only one function, a factory producing transactions. But of course it is not just producing transactions; it is also arriving at consensus. That is to say, it is not just an executive; it is a legislature as well.

ITS was indeed a compromise, but it was rooted in the fact that it tried to effect a link between legislatures, and not just one between computers.

19

FINANCIAL FUTURES

"He pointed at me and he said, 'Son you don't do anything but work on those futures financial contracts.'"

■ MARK POWERS

Mark Powers helped create financial futures: first as the first chief economist of the Chicago Merc, and then as the first chief economist of the CFTC. Powers is one of the unsung power-brokers of the financial futures industry.

Producers have never liked futures, farmers do not like futures. Wall Street treats futures like something to trade—farmers believe that futures manipulate their price. But there is a need for futures, especially an efficient pricing mechanism.

What makes for the most efficient pricing mechanism is the most pricing points: the more points you have, the more liquidity and efficiency you have, because more buyers and sellers are contributing. The price is less liable to move from events extraneous to the legitimate price.

Farmers hedge too, even though they don't like the market. The trading-middlemen are the biggest hedgers, the big grain firms. So the futures market serves an important purpose.

The current explosion of futures products is the result of a number of trends that came together in the 1960s, 1970s, and 1980s. To begin with, the 1929 crash left us with a legacy of strict financial regulations for banks, insurance companies, and securities markets. These regulations gradually began to be relaxed in the 1960s under President Kennedy.

Another important historical milestone was the Russian launching of Sputnik and this country's initial determination to emphasize mathematics and engineering skills for children at school.

A result of this educational effort was a generation of young people comfortable with numbers and computer skills. These young people also experienced the Vietnam war and went through a series of events that led them to question authority and become receptive to new ways of doing things.

Something that hasn't been noticed, but is, I think, really important, is that in 1970 there was a corn blight that brought turmoil to the commodity markets. You also had President Lyndon Johnson upping the money supply to pay for the war and Great Society programs. After a while, people began to wonder how to price things. Eventually, you had Myron Scholes and Fisher Black coming out with their methodology for how you price contingent claims and rank alternatives. That meant people had tools to understand that prices weren't fixed, that investors could buy and sell financial instruments along a spectrum of prices. I think Scholes and Black will win Nobel prizes sometime.

Finally, you had Nixon taking us off the gold standard—letting the worth of our currency against other currencies be pegged by the market instead of fixed by government.

These trends all combined in the 1970s into a tremendous explosion of financial instruments. The CBOE began to trade. The Chicago Merc began to trade financial futures, and these trends continued into the 1980s where they became full-blown marketplaces with an enormous impact on how we do business.

From a purely historical perspective, there were a number of people who contributed to the growth of these markets. One obviously is Melamed. Leo always lands on his feet. He came on board the Merc around 1962. E. B. Harris was president of the Exchange then. I was doing my Ph.D. on the Chicago Merc and that's how I met Leo and the others. My thesis dealt with how commodity exchanges developed new products, and I focused on pork bellies since they were the first really new contracts to come along in decades.

The Merc used to trade onions, but back in 1960, after onions were banned, the Merc hit some really hard times. Some younger members began to think about the development of pork bellies as a replacement for onions. Nobody had ever traded meat before, but once John Wayne got interested in trading cattle, that made the whole idea more appealing.

So these young turks were the driving force, especially Steven Greenberg—he was chairman when they brought on the new commodities. Greenberg served from 1962 to 1966 and he really revived the Exchange along with Bill Katz and Bob O'Brien—they brought the Merc back to where the seats were selling for $30,000 and the Exchange was advertising nationwide.

Leo Melamed was a kindred spirit, a young turk too—very smart, very articulate and a good tactician. He was a lawyer, but he didn't want to be. I think he obviously found the trading fascinating. He became chairman in 1969 and 1970. Later he became chairman of the Merc's IMM, once it became clear the opportunity existed.

Leo was doing his own trading for his own account, so he didn't have to worry about customers. Most of the others had businesses to run. Leo had talent, and the time and desire to serve. Plus, there was a lot of prestige.

Dr. Milton Friedman is a great economist and also an important part of the story of financial futures. I don't believe he met Leo until the fall of 1971.

I met Dr. Friedman in 1966; I was in graduate school. He came to Wisconsin and lectured at some classes. He started to talk about money futures early in this century, and I found that fascinating—that there had been a move to start a stock futures trading in 1927, and that had gathered steam until 1929 when the crash killed it.

I was working on my dissertation on futures contracts, and I was also interested in new products. I thought about why other things— meat, for instance—was traded on a futures exchange. I knew about the Merc plan for livestock. I did my dissertation, and I got to know most of the key players in the process.

Then in the fall of 1969 the Merc called and said they wanted to be the first exchange to hire a full-time economist. Harris was president then. They wanted me to identify new products, to do research for the Exchange, and to try to develop a professional education effort—not a public relations effort, but a real drive to educate economists and other professionals about the futures market. Harris especially thought the financial arena and gold were possibilities for futures.

Shortly after I got there, I called Milton Friedman and I said to him, What do you think about trading money as a commodity? He said he liked the idea and offered suggestions.

A year-and-a-half later President Nixon gave us a gift. On August 15, 1971, he said we were essentially bankrupt with no ability to honor our gold commitment. And he put a price freeze in place. The next morning I went to Harris's office: he was on the phone to the regulators in Washington. By this time, you understand, the CBOT had announced they wouldn't open—if you have a price freeze you have no need of a futures market to predict prices, obviously. That was how they thought about it anyway.

But Harris wasn't going to settle for that. He kept pushing until he got the word that nothing in what Nixon had done would forbid the Exchange from opening. And then, I'll never forget it, he hung up the phone and said, "We are open for business." He pointed at me and he said, "Son you don't do anything but work on those futures financial contracts."

He and Leo immediately grasped what was happening—once Nixon had taken us off the gold standard, currency prices would start to fluctuate. Money-linked futures were suddenly the hottest idea around. I think even then no one thought the price freeze would last long, but the de-linking of gold—that was something else. That was going to stick. And we knew how to take advantage of it.

In late 1971 we held a press conference. I gave a paper and Milton's famous memo was handed out, the one that endorsed currency futures as an extension of the free market. I started working and writing rules and things. We opened for business in 1972. There were no regulations, by the way. We weren't regulated by any one, and it was only a question of writing and creating an exchange exactly the way we wanted. I came up with a lot of rules that are now common in all the exchanges trading financial futures. What I did was take commodities rules and apply them where I thought they worked. It was a tremendous opportunity, to create a market from scratch like that.

Eventually, Leo began to take over, as it became clear the IMM was an idea whose time had come. I was the main staff operating the office of IMM until late 1975 when I left for Washington and the CFTC. I had less contact with the Merc. Leo really put his imprint on it. He got behind the S&P contract in 1982. That was certainly his baby. The Merc's big success in the financial markets came when it got that exclusive contract with the S&P, because that is the bellwether measure that pension fund managers measure their success by.

I think the 1990s will be a time of consolidation. The 1990s will see new regulations and a certain slowing down of innovation. We already have considerably more re-regulation than people know.

I don't think this is necessarily bad, but it could have two consequences that could be negative. For one thing, the biggest players will probably move their activities off-shore to other countries to avoid re-regulation. This will mean a net loss of jobs and taxes here at home.

Additionally, regulations tend to stifle innovation, and therefore there may be more financial innovation overseas than here in the 1990s.

20

■ ■ ■

SHAD-JOHNSON

"We really just wanted to scratch an itch."

■ PHILIP JOHNSON

Philip Johnson is a trim, neat-looking man. You might not easily guess, on a first meeting, that he is perhaps the nation's preeminent futures lawyer, responsible for codifying the regulations of the entire commodities industry in several thick volumes published by Little, Brown & Co.

Just as important as this life's work, or even more so, was the 1982 deal that had its beginnings at The Monocle restaurant. Over lunch, Johnson and John Shad settled a debate over who would regulate stock index and other securities-related futures. Following that lunch at the famous congressional hangout, Johnson and Shad decided that the CFTC should have oversight over the products. Additionally, the two men agreed that futures and other such products should include cash-settlement—a critical part of what made stock index futures so successful—and so controversial.

I was managing editor of the *Yale Law Journal* and a lawyer in Chicago with Kirkland & Ellis for nearly 20 years. I represented the CBOT from 1966 to 1981. I was founding attorney for the National Futures Association. I advised on the formation of the CBOE.

I had just returned from Puerto Rico after writing my treatise on commodities regulation when I got a letter from the White House telling me I was being considered as the next chairman. I actually took office in June of 1981.

The first initiative of the accord between John Shad and myself came in the spring of 1981. At that time John had been confirmed as new chairman of SEC. I was still awaiting CFTC confirmation. I suggested to John at the time that we should sit down at some point. I wrote him a letter.

Once we were both in Washington and both confirmed, I contacted him for lunch in mid-summer, about July 1981. He had a favorite restaurant called The Monocle. It was nearby the SEC offices at the time. And so we made arrangements to have lunch there. It's a sort of all-purpose continental, all-American place. Very well known.

I instantly liked him. He was very courteous. He seemed low-key and no-nonsense. He didn't go to Washington to take pot shots at government officials. He had a specific agenda for his agency. He wanted to get the Edgar system up and running—to electronically disseminate new issue information.

At that time the SEC was arguing with the CFTC over certain products and some of the futures markets had challenged the SEC in court, but stock index futures were very much a question mark. I didn't know then they would become so big. John wasn't about to capitulate on the jurisdictional issue without discussions but he thought it was a distraction from some of the other things he wanted to do.

Since stock index futures have been very helpful in terms of the management of portfolios, I have no reservations today about it.

My view was that the CFTC was set up to regulate the futures industry. I didn't care if the industry was creating soybeans, cattle, or bonds. It's simple. The futures markets provide a hedging vehicle. The securities markets are regulated for capital formation purposes.

I suppose it depends on where you come from. I don't have any reason to rethink it. With cooperation among the agencies almost any problem can be solved.

The CFTC at the time was going through a reauthorization in 1982. We put the necessary sections in that bill. John put the necessary sections in his securities statute. Once it was enacted by congress there was no need to do anything else. Dingell's staff was not happy with the accord, but you don't intentionally keep wars going. The great strength of this agreement was that all members of congress had become so weary of this strife.

I don't think either John or I ever thought it would be such a big deal. We really just wanted to scratch an itch. This jurisdictional agreement has lasted longer than most marriages. If John has had a change of heart, that's his business. I do remember seeing him once at the office after I stepped down, and we were discussing triple-witching. He said, "Phil, did you ever think what we did would result in these kinds of things?"

John and I announced the agreement on Pearl Harbor Day, December 7, 1981. Later on people started referring to it as a second Pearl Harbor.

21

THE CFTC

"There were definitely skirmishes with the SEC. . . ."

■ SUSAN PHILLIPS

An economist, Susan Phillips served first as commissioner and then as chairman of the CFTC from 1981 to 1987. The CFTC's longest-lived chairman, Phillips had the good fortune to serve when John Shad was chairman of the SEC. Shad's business-oriented approach to regulatory affairs set the tone for a somewhat less-confrontational relationship between the two agencies during the early and mid-1980s.

I came to Washington in the mid-1970s from the University of Iowa where I was on the finance faculty. After my fellowship expired, I came back to the University of Iowa. I worked on a book with Dick Zecher called *The SEC and the Public Interest.* The thesis of the book was looking at the economics of regulation. We looked at the costs and benefits of a number of SEC regulations. We suggested that technology would drive regulation, not the other way around, and I think that's pretty much the way it has happened.

The book, along with my other research, and my previous experience in Washington helped me get the invitation by the Reagan administration to become a CFTC commissioner. I had experience and had studied regulation and financial markets, and it was clear that financial futures were becoming more and more important.

I went as a commissioner in November 1981 and served with Philip Johnson, who was chairman at that time. As an economist, I learned a great deal from him.

Johnson believed in hedging stock market risk and other commissioners did too.

There were some lawsuits holding up stock futures, and Phil and John Shad resolved that issue through their famous accord. The Shad-Johnson accord was approved about two weeks after I got back to Washington. I saw it as a pragmatic solution. I happen to think all futures and options products should be regulated by the CFTC, and that includes stock options now regulated by the SEC.

Another major issue was cash settlement. Commodity futures markets were originally set up with physical delivery of the product if the futures position is held through the day of settlement. Generally, in futures there is quarterly settlement, but with cash settlement, you can just deliver the cash equivalent of whatever it is you are trading—stocks, currencies, or bonds. That makes it a lot less difficult to trade these products. The first cash-settlement contract was Eurodollars, which was a CME contract.

After Phil went back to private practice, I became the chairman of the CFTC. There were definitely skirmishes with the SEC when I was there—in fact there was a major skirmish over how narrow a stock index could be for a futures contract.

In other areas at the CFTC, we did a lot of computerization and put into place audit trails and improved self-regulatory capabilities. I left in July of 1987 before the market crash, but I have to say when the market did crash, I felt the Agency was prepared to deal with it.

22

■ ■ ■

THE SEC

"Economics has a lot to say about the kinds of problems we were looking at."

■ CHARLES COX

Charles Cox was the SEC's first chief economist, arriving a little after Shad. Cox's reputation as a believer in deregulation helped him get the job. He later served as an SEC commissioner and, finally, before Ruder came on board, as acting chairman of the SEC.

If you know John Shad at all, you know he's a man of action and can't abide bureaucracy. He was very committed to an SEC that worked to protect investors. He simply said, "Let's evaluate what we're doing." He asked, "Is what we're doing increasing the costs for investors? What are the benefits and what are the costs?"

I was there as chief economist until I moved over to be a commissioner. Greg Jarrell joined us as chief economist and to replace me. I would say we had something in common, Greg, John, and I. It was the idea that economics has a lot to say about the kinds of problems we were looking at.

Shad was the main reason I went to the SEC. I didn't have any input into the Shad-Johnson accord but I was in favor of letting the markets work and getting on with the job.

I would say there are still executives at the SEC who are rather skeptical of the contributions economics can make to SEC market regulation. The SEC had 50 years as almost being completely a lawyer agency. I think it is changing. There is more attention paid to economic analysis. There's a higher-quality office there now.

I didn't believe markets alone should determine how the securities market would work. Obviously when your job is regulating securities markets you come to believe there is a role for government, but there are also limits. It's a delicate line.

If they ban stock index futures I think substitutes will be developed. But I can't tell you just what. One that springs readily to mind is trading futures and options overseas.

It's not a matter of shutting down financial futures and then we can nod off to sleep again. Information is so readily available and easily transmitted these days that it makes very little difference whether you are physically located in the United States or in some other country. You can set up markets and trade futures or derivatives from any geographic location.

■ COMBINED SOURCES, THE SEC

Shad wanted to change the way things were done in Washington at the SEC. The SEC's chief enforcer Stanley Sporkin, along with Harold Williams, had chased after corporations. Shad wanted to make the SEC a more efficient regulator for Wall Street. That was his interest.

Shad reversed or toned down some Sporkin policies. Now SEC staffers had to prove that there was culpability of some sort at the very top of a firm before bringing an action. It's safe to say that Shad gave Wall Street more breathing space than most other commissioners. He truly believed in the principal of self-regulation, and this was under Reagan. Shad was a big contributor of Reagan's and he was Reagan's fund-raiser in New York. In Washington he was very faithful to Reagan's deregulatory mandate.

Shad's attachment to Drexel was through Fred Josephs, chief executive of Drexel and former top executive at Hutton under Shad.

Shad's chief emphasis was on insider trading. But it's true, there were some who doubted just how serious he was about it. Boesky was only caught after insider trader Dennis Levine was exposed through an anonymous letter sent to Merrill Lynch. When Levine started talking he fingered several Wall Street executives including, most importantly, Boesky.

I don't think Shad ever believed that Drexel had in any systematic way violated securities regulations. But he was prepared to believe that Milken might have been sloppy, might have done some foolish things—deprived of proper oversight and supervision out there on the West Coast where he had his office.

In 1987, Shad left for the Netherlands where he took a position as the American ambassador. It's easy to say that Shad's emphasis on saving money, cutting staff, and self-regulation led to a variety of securities abuses in the 1980s. But if John had truly bucked the administration on these issues, the game would have carried on without him. He did the best job he was capable of.

■ CHARLES TRZCINKA

Charles Trzcinka, a professor of economics at the University of Buffalo, worked as a senior economist at the Security and Exchange Commission's office of economic analysis from 1987 to 1989. A spring 1982 article in The Wall Street Journal, *coming from a study of his at the SEC, may help lead to the deregulation of mutual funds.*

The SEC economists have never had any clout. The SEC is definitely a lawyers' agency. That was why John Shad was unsettling to the SEC, I think. He wasn't like the normal securities lawyer. He was more the Wall Street type, and he wanted economic advice. He thought the SEC should have connections with Wall Street that exceeded strictly regulatory and legalistic analysis.

He got frustrated with the level of economic expertise and brought in Cox as chief economist. Cox was a somewhat controversial choice because of arguments over his qualifications. Then Cox moved over to become a commissioner and Shad brought in Jarrell.

The big source of concern had to do with the advice of economists regarding SEC studies. SEC market reg. executives kept the economists out of the 1987 study on the market crash and it was the same story in 1989. These reports make assessments about strategies like index arbitrage, but economists have grave doubt that index arbitrage can trigger or significantly contribute to huge market drops.

Some of the conclusions the SEC reached in the 1980s about market drops may have more to do with the SEC expanding authority than with economics. For instance, if you maintain that index arbitrage destabilizes the market, then you have to argue for one regulator. So maybe you're making economic conclusions for bureaucratic reasons.

SEC executives tended not to believe the CFTC was a very good regulator. The idea was, if the SEC set the margins for futures, it could help dampen volatility, but it is also true that top people at the SEC tend to take jobs with law firms that have Wall Street clients. They have a financial interest in promoting the interests of Wall Street. You would have trouble uncovering evidence that the Wall Street establishment was pushing the SEC to cut off cheaper providers of financial services, like the Chicago markets, but it certainly is in Wall Street's interest to do so.

On the other hand, sincerely, I don't think anyone at the SEC ever saw themselves as an agent of Wall Street. But the SEC is Wall Street's regulatory body. And there is probably a degree of regulatory capture.

The SEC is a very interesting place for economists. But the issues have changed and the importance has changed.

■ A FORMER SEC EMPLOYEE

At the SEC, if you were not a lawyer you didn't count. It never failed.

Since this place is run by the Bar, you don't have highly qualified financial people with time to look at the documents they get. The Securities Act of 1934 is based on disclosure, not the merits of the deal. You must pass a certain standard to sell your securities publicly, but the act doesn't mandate good disclosure. Only disclosure. The SEC is just woefully unknowledgeable in the ways of modern finance.

For a while the staff didn't even have computers. It was like trying to fight World War II when Poland came out with the cavalry to fight the tanks. They would tell us to wait for Edgar: They were going to hook us all in electronically to everything. Well, Edgar was a priority of John Shad. They've been talking about Edgar for more than a decade.

The regulation business can be a good business for lawyers. It's a career path, not an agency. Some people aren't able to get into a law firm right away as law has become more and more competitive. So this is a little networking place. Lawyers with SEC experience can bill a lot of money.

Basically, the SEC has two major things it does. Disclosure, first of all. The Division of Corporation Finance looks at the 10Ks and 10Qs, prospectuses, proxy statements. The idea is to review at least some of these to insure they are providing accurate, complete information.

The other thing is enforcement. The Division of Enforcement gets the most publicity. It's the largest division because the regional offices are involved. There are nine regions. And people are about evenly split—1,000 here and 1,000 in regions.

Then there is the Division of Market Regulation. That is mainly involved with self-regulatory organizations and NASD oversight. Finally, there's the Division of Investment Management. That's in charge of regulating management companies and investment advisers. It watches over mutual funds and mutual fund prospectuses, open- and closed-end funds, disclosure of fees, that kind of thing.

The General Counsel's Office is a fifth area. It's not authorized to do criminal cases, only civil. They act as legal adviser and ultimate arbitrator. The enforcement function is the main justification for the SEC. If there was no enforcement, people wouldn't pay attention to the stuff.

The SEC reflects government philosophy. The government was regulatory minded in the 1960s and so was the SEC. In the 1970s the stock market was terrible and the main thing the SEC did was push through Mayday. In the late 1970s there was Sporkin looking at the corporations.

The SEC is supposed to be interested in consumer protection but that hasn't been a priority. In the 1980s I think there was a basic reluctance to want to acknowledge the workloads were getting out of hand.

Ruder came on board and created the penny stock task force. But what was that? It was three people, the head of the task force and two assistants. At least Ruder acknowledged it, the problems with staffing and morale.

What did it all add up to in the 1980s? You have to wonder if deregulation worked the way it was meant to. You have to say no sometime. You can't treat all people exactly the same.

23

■ ■ ■

New York Futures

"Speculation is a dirty word in New York."

■ CHARLES EPSTEIN

Charles Epstein was the managing director of marketing of the New York Futures Exchanges (NYFE) before being let go—apparently for questioning the SEC about its attitude toward futures contracts in a letter he wrote to the SEC's chairman, Richard Breeden.

The NYFE was created by the NYSE to compete with Chicago. It was incorporated in 1979 and started trading in early 1980, but it had fundamental flaws. They were trading contracts identical to those traded in Chicago. They had the idea that because the specialists were such good traders, that anything that the NYSE traded would be successful for the Exchange. They were wrong. The specialists came down to the floor of the NYFE and some of them lost a lot of money. They didn't like it.

Then there were the so-called Backgammon Days when the traders played backgammon on the floor while waiting for the Exchange to file to trade new contracts.

Phelan helped start the NYFE. It was actually former chairman Mil Battin's idea to diversify the stock exchange through a supermarket approach. The NYSE would offer everything, just like J. C. Penny, which Battin used to run. Stocks, futures, options, bonds. They wanted to diversify, but the fundamental problem—at least in futures—is that they don't have a pool of floor traders, of risk takers. You need speculation in futures—you need someone on the other side of the trade, but speculation is a dirty word in New York.

So the NYFE drifted. A seat that cost $30,000 in 1980 cost $200 by the end of the decade. And it was too bad, because some of the contracts traded on the NYFE had promise if the NYSE was really able to get behind the Exchange and give it some support, but competition was such a foreign concept to them. They started it to compete with Chicago, but they don't like what goes on in Chicago. So therefore they didn't like the futures trading which occurred on the NYFE much either. It's a kind of vicious circle and the NYFE got trapped inside.

24

■■■

THE CRASH

"There was a conspiracy in the broadest sense."

■ TIM METZ

Tim Metz's timely book Black Monday, *published a year after the 1987 stock crash, makes the important point that Big Board market-makers, with the approval of government, manipulated stocks to save the marketplace. Metz's perspective —despite his admiration for the NYSE's specialists—is a critical part of the market's debate; it shows how dangerous the situation in late 1987 really was.*

When the market crash came, I knew I had to write about it. I'd been in *The Wall Street Journal*'s market group for eight years. I really had the background to do it—I knew all the players.

I'm hoping history will be kind to my book. It was widely reviewed. The Big Board did a good job in defusing the so-called conspiracy theory, but there was a conspiracy in the broadest sense; not a malevolent conspiracy, but definitely an agreement to do everything possible to save the market.

First you have to understand some background. Once the S&P 500 futures index started booming in the 1980s, the big Wall Street firms like Salomon and Morgan Stanley started trying to move the index around. They did this by selling the index up or down in a very obvious "sloppy" way. They'd dress their trader in a different kind of coat or something and make sure everyone in the pit knew what they were doing. Whatever Salomon tried to do, Morgan tried to do the opposite of. They had some big wars, trying to establish dominance in the Merc S&P pit. Obviously, they wanted the locals, the other traders, to follow their lead. That created the price movement they needed. By the mid-1980s, Salomon had the upper hand.

Once you have created a disparity between the cash and futures markets, you can cash in—buy the futures, sell the stock, whatever. It's no accident that the market moves up and down and then somehow moves up right toward the close so everyone can take their profit. That's what's been happening in the early 1990s, that's what happened in the 1980s. Everybody's playing that game now. Index arbitrage itself doesn't cause market swings—rather it's the games the firms play to create the discount they need to arbitrage. That's why people say program trading moves the market.

The big firms see the order flow, they try to stay informed about where the order flow is headed. During the crash, for instance, Salomon traded ahead of the rally in the CBOT's stock index, the Major Market Index.

The crash actually began on Friday, October 16. That was the first day the Dow ever lost more than 100 points in a single session, but for the entire week the Dow gave up about double that.

On Monday, at the Chicago Merc, the opening call moved the major stock index futures down more than 20 points. In New York, things went nuts—there was no buying, only selling. What happened? The system got backed up. Nobody knew where the market was. In Chicago they were trading off of Friday's numbers.

The more the Chicago market moved down, the more selling pressure there was. Institutions sold, speculators sold, and then the NYSE specialists started selling short. It was so bad that by 10:30 A.M. one-third of the stocks making up the Dow still hadn't opened. The Dow supposedly had moved down 100 points in two hours, but actually it was about double that. By 11 A.M. volume had reached 150 million shares. By the end of the day the Dow had plunged 508 points, and about 23 percent of its value. The damage was worse at the Merc where stock index futures prices went down 30 percent. The most incredible thing of all was the volume—some 600 million shares altogether. It was a real Black Monday.

On Tuesday morning Phelan met with most of the leaders of Wall Street, the top guys from Salomon, Merrill, Morgan Stanley, and the other firms. They were all there. By then he'd already started his damage control. He'd been on TV the night before. What did he say? "It's the nearest thing to a meltdown I want to see."

You can only speculate what they talked about in the morning meeting, the Wall Street guys. You can bet they talked about closing the market though. One thing that helped, I think, was the Fed's Alan Greenspan that morning making it clear the nation's banking system would provide the necessary credit to insure the nation's commercial banks and Big Board specialists had enough cash to continue trading in the market.

The market went up some on that news, about 200 points, but then it broke big. Around 12 or 12:30 it was about as grim as it gets. You know Phelan wanted to close the market no matter what they say. He was calling everyone. One reason Melamed shut down the Chicago markets was because he thought the Big Board's closure was imminent—and then all the selling would be headed in his direction.

But there was another reason for Melamed to close down the Exchange. He was not only taking pressure off his own pit if the NYSE closed but he was also taking pressure off the Big Board. That's because the big institutional buyers looked first to the future's market to see which way the Dow was headed. And so long as it looked like program selling was going to beat the Dow down, nobody would step forward to buy.

Also the markets were terribly out of sync. Because the NYSE lagged in its trading reports so much, the futures markets stayed at a perpetual discount. Everybody would look to the futures and see that the pit was predicting lower prices on the NYSE, so nobody would buy.

The answer was to bid up the prices of the S&P futures, but there was too much volume. Wall Street spent a lot of money trying to do that. So they did something else instead.

This was the final fallback, the one Phelan mentioned. A reporter from the *New York Times* was there to interview Phelan, and he sat right outside of Phelan's office and every time the secretary placed another call for Phelan, he wrote it down. The first person to call was John Gutfreund, the head of Salomon Brothers. It might have been around noon. And there's a possibility that Gutfreund suggested to Phelan that the S&P 500 futures be shut down.

Anyway, after that call, Phelan made some other calls. He called Corrigan, the head of the New York Federal Reserve, and he called

Ruder, and he called Howard Baker, the White House chief of staff. He told Baker, "Howard, we're down to one fallback and if that doesn't work, then it's down another 500 points."

I believe Phelan wanted the White House to know exactly what was going on. Phelan knew he was going to do something grim. That's why he called all those people, every one of them. Later on he said he had felt the market would just have to trade its way out of the fall—but it wasn't the market trading, it was the specialists.

What they did was simple. First of all, Phelan must have said something like, "Leo, you've got to close. As long as people see a discount, we'll never get any buyers."

Once Melamed shut down the S&P pit, the only major futures index still trading was the CBOT's MMI. That's only 20 major stocks, and 17 of the 20 were still trading around the country. Melamed knew Mahlmann could keep the MMI open, and so did Phelan. It's not like these guys weren't talking or anything.

And once Melamed shut down the pit, some of the specialists got busy buying up the Dow in New York. The MMI contains a lot of Dow stocks, and it was at a 60-point discount, but 60 points equals one point on the S&P: that's why it didn't take much to move it. So they bought stock, not futures. Everybody thinks Wall Street bought the MMI directly, but they didn't.

I am absolutely positive: On Tuesday specialists bid up certain stocks on the Dow, the ones underlying the MMI in Chicago. It was all done in 13 stocks—that's what it took to push the MMI up in Chicago.

The fellows at the *Journal* had it reversed. They implied the buying in the MMI was driving the market in New York, but it was the specialists buying on the floor of the Exchange that broke the crash. The *Journal* won a Pulitzer prize largely for its brilliant retrospective on the events on that day, which their story called "Terrible Tuesday," even though the MMI inference was incorrect.

I went and got the trading activity for the day. It was right there. It was all done in 13 Dow stocks. What would you think it would take to push GE up $1.00 in a normal day—how many shares? During that half-hour, they didn't have to buy more than 100 to 1,000 shares of each stock to push the price up $1.00, believe it or not. And this in the face of the heaviest selling pressure in history!

That's what turned the market. When I asked Phelan, he said, "Markets turn." And I added in my book, "Or are turned."

Later on, when my book came out, it was reviewed by some major magazines—and the New York Stock Exchange denied my central contention, that the market was turned by Phelan and the specialists. But I was in a cab with one of the fellows from Big Board public relations, and he was enjoying the roasting I was getting at the time. He told me, "Tim, you didn't expect us to admit it, did you?"

If the market had collapsed it would have been a much bigger catastrophe. Anything secured by a financial security would have been in default. How the hell would you have sorted it out? You would have had a major credit crisis. It was a scary time.

The trouble is, not much has changed. They're still playing games. They've tried to protect the markets by adding in collars and such. That means the market can't move down as quickly, but the trouble is, there's already a bias toward moving markets up rather than down because of the SEC uptick rule for short sellers.

So now we have a market that was, in the early 1990s, out of touch with reality. The market's hit 3000. Outside it looks like a Depression.

I'm not sure what you can do. The genie is out of the bottle. Computers are here to stay and so is indexing. One thing to do, surely, is open up the industry. Automated systems and regulation to make the securities industry more competitive might make it harder to move the market. You can't go back, anyhow.

You'd think there would be more significant comment on these issues. When I was at the *Journal* in the 1960s, it wasn't such a big deal to be there, but after the 1970s and Watergate you started getting all these resumes from Harvard and Yale. Reporting was suddenly glamorous. So then you ended up with the sons interviewing their fathers on Wall Street. That's what I think. It's a class thing. Old-time business reporters tended to be skeptical because they were from a different class than the people they covered. In the 1980s, that wasn't true anymore. I think some skepticism was lost.

And it's true there's the problem of who's supporting the business press. When the crash happened, the editor of *The Wall Street Journal*, Norman Pearlstine, wasn't in New York. He was in France, making speeches to advertisers. Things have changed.

25

▄▄▄

CASH SETTLEMENT

*"**I** believe our markets are controlled."*

■ MORRIS PROPP

Morris Propp has been a vocal critic of cash settlement. He came to Wall Street in 1972 as an ex-aerospace engineer with a strong mathematics background and a Harvard MBA. Options arbitrage became his specialty and with the help of an original mathematical model for option evaluation, he became one of the largest proprietary traders of listed options.

Propp eventually retired from options trading, in part because he felt that bigger players were controlling short-term market swings and profiting from concurrent option positions.

Propp testified before the House Telecommunications and Finance sub-committee and was later the subject of a Barron's *article. The observations below are based on conversations and unpublished essays.*

My firm actively bought and sold options on the basis of fair value. We traded 10,000 contracts per day, every day, and were quite profitable. I continued to be a major trader on all listed options exchanges until the early 1980s when position limits expanded and John Shad's new SEC sent a clear message that markets were being deregulated.

Traders knew that takeovers were all preceded by unusually heavy option activity and that the SEC was sleeping through it all. Occasionally this new SEC would come down on a small-fry, a secretary or blue-collar worker, who had made $20,000 on illegally obtained information, but it was obvious the arbs at the major firms with the so-called Chinese walls were getting away with murder.

Of course this had an impact on the effectiveness of any option evaluation system that relied upon the assumption of market randomness. In the new, unregulated takeover environment, positioning options was like walking through a minefield.

But there was worse to come. In 1982 John Shad co-sponsored the Shad-Johnson Accord that rang the death-knell for fair equity markets because it introduced cash settlement. This broke the bank at Wall Street. Cash settlement simply means that at expiration, options and futures turn to cash at whatever price the underlying index dictates.

Disposal of cash settlement instruments is simplicity itself. They just disappear, but make no mistake, there is no free lunch here. Cash settlement instruments affect the market with great complexity. It is hard to imagine any legitimate product or security where buying and selling in unlimited quantity doesn't have an impact on price, but this is exactly what we have with our new cash settled derivative instruments at expiration.

In normal markets, which do not settle for cash, unwinding positions will work to stabilize, to return markets to states of equilibrium. Short-covering buyers don't want to drive prices up and liquidating sellers don't want to drive the market down. Every participant in a fair market has an incentive to maintain stability. In a fair market, creation of volatility and market movement is expensive and risky business since there is no guarantee of an exit.

In a fair market, a single entity, even one with unlimited resources, cannot create its own profit. Certainly one could buy up the entire capitalization of a company or, for that matter, the total supply of silver, driving the price to absurd levels. On a mark-to-market basis, that entity would show handsome gains, but when the time comes to sell, to create the profit, unless circumstances or the perception of others has changed, liquidating the position will drive the price back down, probably to where it began.

Cash settlement changes that picture. It provides both the means to orchestrate volatility and the assurance of unlimited liquidity at exit points.

In July 1986 the noted mathematician, Fischer Black, now an associate of Goldman, Sachs published his important article, "Noise" in *The Journal of Finance*. Black contends that the vast majority of market participants base decisions on noise, not information. What someone is convinced is information is probably noise because it has already been discounted by the marketplace. With so many noise traders, anyone with real information can profit. Black suggests seeking out and investing in costly information to harvest the noise traders.

Black doesn't tell us how to find real information. Ivan Boesky found an effective way—one with severe drawbacks. Many money managers argue that legitimate research is often overwhelmed by overall market volatility.

Our securities industry takes space travel and genetic engineering for granted yet still takes "random walk" and "no one is bigger than the market" seriously. This is in spite of repeated evidence that markets, even for government Treasury notes, can be controlled.

Consider the rhetoric of index arbitrage. We understand the theory. High-speed computers allow operators to transact in massive size in three markets simultaneously, to make a profit.

As a trader who has looked for riskless dollars in related markets for twenty years, I do not believe that index arbitrage exists as it is commonly described, except under rare and extreme conditions.

Transaction risk is simply too high. Theoretical studies of index arbitrage do not focus on the enormity of transaction risk relative to profit potential. One such study, "A Primer on Program Trading and Stock Price Volatility," by Duffee, Kupiec, and White, Federal Reserve System researchers, goes so far as to suggest that "institutional investors may at least partially profit from a short-term increase in intra-day volatility through their ability to profit from index arbitrage." Apparently these researchers believe that there is some tooth-fairy handing out money to investors simultaneously on two exchanges.

In reality, major firms involved in so-called index arbitrage play other games entirely. First, rather than entering orders that can be executed simultaneously in different markets against random participants—which true arbitrage requires—major players simply leg into positions or front-run the market. When the leg is closed, same day, who's to observe that no legitimate arbitrage ever took place, that no opportunity for true arbitrage ever existed?

A second form of so-called index arbitrage that does take place is the quasi-legal pre-arranged, pre-packaged transaction between two parties. One party is locked into a small profit, the other into a small loss.

Now why would anyone be interested in taking the loss side of a riskless pre-packaged S&P future versus a stock basket position? The answer is that the cash settled future versus a stock basket is in itself a highly complex hybrid security with substantial theoretical and practical value of its own to an entity powerful enough to move markets—a major market manipulator group specifically. This hybrid is a fundamental cornerstone and principal driver of the existing market control mechanism yet it is never discussed, never analyzed.

I suggest that major market moves at or near options/futures expiration are fueled by the unwinding of options/futures versus stock basket hybrids. These may have been established at a small loss initially but they are instrumental in driving a market move of predetermined magnitude, direction and timing as they are unwound. This is self-generated inside information shared by a handful of operators who position themselves accordingly in index options.

It should be clear that if any group can induce an index to a pre-set level at settlement with near certainty, that entity has enough information to trade "cash settled" index options and futures profitably against anyone else. The financial trade-off appears to be the cost of moving the market versus the amount which can be harvested from noise traders.

Volatility seems to get all the attention, especially after major market breaks. Traders know that market operators make the most money fastest in volatile markets. Public traders, the noise traders, are drawn to volatility, liquidity and leverage.

Since I believe our markets are controlled, I likewise believe that volatility can also be controlled, contained or expanded through the same process.

The upshot of regulatory reality is that congress has sent a loud and clear message that they will not tolerate manipulation with excessive volatility. Thus if the operators persist with extreme volatility, they run the risk that the cash settlement mechanism will be properly scrutinized—and then inevitably challenged and shut down.

A proper analysis of cash settlement should treat periodic extremes in volatility as the symptom, not the problem. When volatility recedes temporarily we should not construe this as a sign of restored market health or soundness.

After the market mini-crash in October 1989 I stated to congress that I expected volatility to be minimal for the immediate future because the operators would lay low.

I also told congress to expect a spate of new volatility studies from the regular hack academicians at the various sponsored research centers. The SEC and congress treat proffered volatility studies by the mercenaries with great respect. We should understand that professors, like lawyers and accountants, enjoy the finer things in life. Just as lawyers argue points of view they may personally reject, we now have doctors, scientists, and professors who are paid to take public stances on issues.

Confusion is a key characteristic of our new markets. Is it not one of the great enigmas of modern finance that with so much written by so many experts, the intelligent investor is still confused about derivatives, how they work and interact or why we have them in the first place?

On several occasions I expressed surprise that no theoretical work had been done on the cash settlement subject. In October 1990 the economist at a major exchange asked me to review a new paper by Praveen Kumar and Duane Seppi of Carnegie Mellon entitled "Futures Manipulation with Cash Settlement."

Eagerly I began the paper only to find that Kumar and Seppi had used two assumptions that prejudiced their study.

Their first assumption was that no single manipulator group exists in these markets and that "manipulators" are simply competing "noise traders" (they cite Fischer Black's article) who do not act in concert or coordinate with one another. Their second assumption was that cash settlement is "de facto the normal settlement mechanism" for all futures contracts "since only 3% of all [standard] futures contracts take delivery."

Academia's first attempt at analysis of cash settlement was alarming and I wrote the authors pointing out that a study to determine whether manipulation exists should not begin with the assumption that all manipulators are uninformed noise traders. I pointed out, in the context of Black's article, that the only significant manipulator is one who can be distinguished from noise traders by the ability to move prices to creative consistent profits—or achieve other specialized objectives—in an otherwise fair market.

I stressed that they had no basis for any initial assumption that a manipulator group did not exist and rather, the importance and ultimate value of their study was the determination that such a manipulator group or mechanism could or could not exist uniquely in cash settled markets.

As to their second specious assumption that all futures markets are de facto cash settled, I explained that ownership of a conventional futures contract, settled in its underlying physical, is the exact financial equivalent to ownership of that physical, except that delivery is postponed. The owner of that contract has the identical financial risks that he would have owning the physical itself. The fact that owners of conventional futures contracts rarely take delivery does not alter this principle. More, unwinding the arbitrage between physical and future has no destabilizing impact on the market. The holder of the physical, a farmer for example, delivers against a maturing short future.

In the conventional futures markets, the residual position, the three percent, is considered by many to be the raison d'etre of those markets in the first place. Delivery does not destabilize the market, it is the market.

Consider and contrast the "cash settled" index futures markets. Here too an arbitrage opportunity exists between futures and underlying stock baskets. But here is a marked difference that completely escaped Kumar and Seppi. To close the arbitrage risklessly, the entire stock basket must be unwound precisely at the settlement bell at expiration.

Thus, if a participant is short stock versus long futures, closing the position out risklessly means market-on-bell repurchase of short stocks. Any higher prices paid for stock is equally offset by higher proceeds from the "cash settled" future and there certainly is no financial incentive to tread carefully on the market.

Quite the contrary. A manipulator group unwinding such a position might want to creative as much disruption as possible (or as would escape the notice of sleepy regulators), especially if they were net long futures or equivalents, the cash settled index options.

The Kumar-Seppi study relies on an initial assumption that no manipulation exists to arrive at the mathematical conclusion that the cash settlement feature of the derivative instruments has no material impact on markets. The study shoots itself in the foot. False assumptions leading to false conclusions are a hallmark of many of the studies on derivative products.

Wall Street's message to the small investor has been: Don't try to understand what's going on, it's done with computers. Just place your bets. This is unacceptable and regulators are duty-bound to understand the impact that cash settlement has on the markets.

A last point: Nearly everyone agrees, as do I, that separating the expiration of S&P futures from the afternoon CBOE's OEX and SPX options expiration has reduced triple-witching-day volatility.

The NYSE has taken the position that since moving futures settlement to the opening has reduced volatility, moving options expiration to the opening will further reduce volatility.

Yet index options and S&P futures are all interchangeable parts of the same whole on expiration day. Moving a large portion of the combined open interest to morning settlement has effectively diluted the expiration event. To move option settlement to the morning would mean the event would reconcentrate open interest.

I liken the NYSE's logic to the following analogy: A dog and a cat live in the same small apartment and fight incessantly. Their master decides to keep the cat locked in the bedroom and the fighting stops except for hisses and growls. The owner concludes that if moving the cat to the bedroom has had such good effect, imagine how peaceful it would be if he also moves the dog into the bedroom!

I would also suggest that there is little magical about morning versus afternoon settlement except that the Big Board specialists can usurp much of the CBOE market-maker potency. Whether this is beneficial to the public is unclear.

What has had a beneficial impact on volatility is reducing the enormity of the expiration event by splitting up open interest at expiration into two smaller events.

Further separating or staggering the expiration of the various cash-settled derivative-instrument open interests might further decrease overall expiration volatility, in the long run.

Creation of market volatility is expensive. So long as there is a big payoff it remains worthwhile for dominant market operators. Make the payoffs smaller and the game will change.

The evidence that groups act together to influence various markets is convincing. There is no sin in being right or smart or a good market-timer, but there are limits to the credibility of frequency of coincidence.

I believe that changes can be made to reduce market volatility and to reduce manipulation. I likewise believe that any group with the wherewithal to manipulate has the wherewithal to create or contain volatility over the short term, thereby embarrassing the successful advocates of meaningful change by making that change initially backfire.

The more activity in cash settled derivative instruments, and the more such products become available, the farther away investors and traders are drawn from primary markets where companies look for capital. Let's get our priorities straight. Let's understand cash settlement. I say get rid of it and get back to basics.

26

■■■

BRADY COMMISSION

"Certainly there are organizations set up for front-running."

■ BOB KIRBY

Bob Kirby, chief investment officer of $20 billion Capital Guardian Trust, was one of the members of the Brady commission that was set up to investigate the 1987 stock market crash. Along with other members of that influential committee, Kirby had access to confidential information from the NYSE that was destroyed—as per agreement—after the investigation ran its course.

Front-running takes on disguises so broad and varied you can hardly believe it. And it happens in some of the finest and most honorable firms around. I don't mean to imply that what is happening is illegal. The laws aren't on the books, necessarily.

But certainly there are organizations set up for front-running. The hedge funds guys cooperate with Wall Street firms. I'm still not certain I know anything, but the woods are full of spies and everybody can hear the drums.

I mean, if you ask a guy running a portfolio, you find over and over that he's been picked off. The trade at a certain price that should have been his has suddenly moved up. Someone has taken the shares you want to buy. Or dumped them right after you buy.

I never asked Nick Brady how he selected me, but I always admired him from his position as chairman of Dillon Read, which is a fine Wall Street firm. I suspect my appointment was partly geographical since I'm based in California. He called me up on the phone. We had to work very fast and very hard. We used to jump around the country to meet. Every Monday morning I got on a plane. We would meet Tuesday, Wednesday and Thursday. We did the very best we could, but there were so many areas we just couldn't get into. Options were one area I'm still foggy about.

But what finally emerged was clear enough in my own mind. The 1987 crash was kicked off by program trading and by that damn strategy of portfolio insurance. What happened was that everybody knew what the overhangs were—where the big institutions would have to sell because of their portfolio insurance strategies. Everybody knew the mathematics, in other words, so everybody knew what was coming, and that put more pressure on the market except for those players who were smart enough to be on the other side.

Wall Street was on the other side and so were some of the hedge funds. There were no clear-cut sides, it's never so clear as the media likes to portray it.

Chicago, New York, everybody is mixed up in it. It's an internecine kind of war, the way these things always are; but, for public consumption I think the NYSE pointed fingers at Chicago. Phelan was very good that way. The NYSE exists to serve its members. They had a great incentive not to give us price information. We never did get information about when trades actually took place. The best we could get from the Big Board was information about when the trades hit the floor, but from there until the order was executed might have been several hours during that time.

Of course it confused the public, but Phelan had a job to do. You don't want to be blamed for something like the crash. The White House had to get involved before the Depository Trust Company would disgorge the names of the players involved with the largest orders during the crash. When you found out they were some of the most responsible institutions in our country, it made you want to go lie down for a moment.

Does this all concern me? Yes. It's been going on for so long, and it's so hard to prove, and it's so dangerous, that I think we have to keep the pressure up. Ultimately, one single regulator has to have power over both the cash and the future markets to take control of this thing. Logically that should be the SEC. I think we're heading in that direction, and I hope we continue that way as fast as possible. We don't have any time to waste.

27

PROGRAM TRADING

*"**I**f the SEC wanted to shut down program trading, they'd simply do away with hedged executions that don't happen simultaneously."*

■ VICTOR SPERANDEO

He's a solidly built man with a thick head of black hair he brushes nervously while he watches the electronic numbers flicker on the consoles in front of him. He'll trade anything—options, futures stocks, bonds—and his opinions are sought by such publications as Barron's. *Through the 1980s, he was one of a few successful big-time day-traders (in three separate markets: options, futures, stocks) in an industry that shakes out entrepreneurs with its intraday swings. These days Victor Sperandeo trades in New Jersey instead of New York—at least partially as a tax protest.*

The market tanked in 1987 and then again in 1989 during the "mini-crash" when the market went down 190 points on one Friday afternoon, but there've been other, smaller drops since then.

Morgan Stanley created much of what I call "the games." I give them a lot of credit, they're creative, and they've made a lot of money. They put on these huge positions and unwound them at appropriate moments for their own accounts and customers who are their partners.

Others call this package trading. It's also called customer facilitation. In other words, say a customer wants to sell out $1 billion worth of stock. Well, the big Wall Street firms will bid for that business. The money-manager will usually initiate a request for a bid. The firm will

147

offer to split the profits with the big institutions fifty-fifty. The firm will want the business so badly sometimes that it will guarantee to eat any loss.

What the firm can do is take that position and sell futures and buy index puts, then sell the stocks down sloppy. Others know they're selling that billion dollar position in ABC and XYZ corporations. But before they sell, they may execute index arbitrage programs to confuse the issue. What they're doing is setting up the futures market for their $1 billion sell program. They over-hedge by selling more than the position they're selling so as to reap large rewards as the execution takes place.

But the biggest advantage of all is that the firm will know when the program ends. The firm selling moves the market down, and since only the firm knows exactly when the trade will end, the firm has an advantage on the up side as well. When the market stops moving down artificially, it will start to bounce back. If you buy ahead of the bounce-back you can make money on the up side as well.

This is also called client facilitation and it is perfectly legal. That's because the firm is in the trade with the client. He's part of the client's deal. It all sounds like front-running, but it isn't because of this technicality.

If the SEC wanted to shut down program trading, they'd simply do away with hedged executions that don't happen simultaneously. It's not very complex. This business is complicated—but the big ideas tend to develop gradually. If you observe, you can see the pattern. That's what I do all day long. I watch. I watch and trade.

The market started booming in 1982, but programs didn't really get going until 1985. If you read my *Barron's* interview in 1983, I basically said that block traders would do well because they could hedge their positions.

But 1986 was when the Wall Street firms began to put these programs into serious use. I've had dealings with most of the major firms involved with these programs.

There's no morality involved in program trading. No good or bad. Traders have adapted to the environment and pursued what profitable areas have been opened up to them. The things they have been involved in are things that anybody would have been involved in in similar situations. Block traders are going to hedge their positions and make money any way they can.

28

■■■

POLITICS

"So long as it's the policy of the American government to sell treasury bonds through Nomura, they aren't going to go after that firm."

■ JOHN FITZGIBBON

John Fitzgibbon's 30-year career on Wall Street included stints as a broker, investment adviser and stock trader. It ultimately brought him in contact with the Japanese's most powerful securities firm, Nomura Securities, where he served as a vice president for its American subsidiary. What he saw at Nomura became the subject of his book, Deceitful Practices. *The book documents how the largest securities firm in the world routinely flouted American regulations, staffing offices with unlicensed personnel and dealing in unregistered securities.*

According to *Economist* magazine, a Nomura Japanese executive I refer to as "Vinegar" Andy Saitoh in my book, is next in line to be president. I worked directly for him for a while in New York when he was head of institutional sales in this country. The reason he is in line for the presidency of Nomura is that he is considered Mr. Clean. He was not involved in any of the Japanese scandals that were reported over there in 1991 involving Nomura and kickbacks illegally paid to clients to compensate them for losses.

But in my book, Saitoh is directly involved in stock market rigging, illegal sales practices, violations of the securities acts of 1933 and 1934, NASD rules of fair practice and supervising unregistered salesmen

149

selling unregistered securities. I witnessed all this myself. I can document it, and there are other former Nomura employees who can too.

When this book was not yet published, some friends of mine encouraged me to go to the regulatory authorities with what I had seen and documented. I decided they were right. So I went to the SEC with some of the allegations in the book. This was in the late 1970s. I spoke to Michael Gregg, now in charge of compliance at Dean Witter. He was then deputy director of enforcement for the SEC, and he told me they knew all about it—that Nomura had been selling unregistered paper in the U.S. even though SEC wouldn't give them clearance. I asked, if he knew why Nomura had not been disciplined, and he said the State Department asked the SEC to cease and desist.

I finally spoke to John Dingell's office. He's the man ultimately in charge of SEC oversight. I gave Dingell's staff a copy of my manuscript. Later, the investigators came to the house and I spoke to them, so I knew they had started their investigation. I could tell they had not bothered to learn the complexities of the SEC securities laws. However, they did travel all over the place to resort areas in Miami, Washington, everywhere. That was on Dingell's side. I never did find out how it turned out. I guess it just died.

In June of 1989 I wrote to Dingell and said a vice president of Nomura, a fellow I'd gotten to know while researching my book, was willing to testify that Nomura was guilty of bookkeeping rules, net capital violation, and other violations all aimed at securing a primary dealer position back in 1986. In response to my letter, I was informed that Dingell had asked Ruder to look into the matter and get back to him in mid-August.

I didn't hear any more about it until late summer when somebody from a major business magazine called me up with the full contents of my letter in front of them. Thank God it was a reporter I knew. They didn't do anything with the letter, but they confirmed it had been leaked by Dingell's office directly to this magazine.

In early October I got a call out of the blue from the SEC; they had my letter, too, since Dingell had sent it to them. I blasted them. I told them my letter had been leaked and asked why I should cooperate further. The SEC staffer apologized and backed off. I told him to go back to Dingell's oversight committee; they knew everything I had to say, even if they were leaking it all over the place.

In November I received a Xerox copy from Dingell's office. That's all it was, just a Xeroxed reply to Dingell's request for an investigation. It read: "The [SEC's] New York regional office has conducted a thorough inquiry into Mr. Fitzgibbon's complaints. Based on information received to date the staff has determined there is no basis for pursuing this matter further. In this regard it is noteworthy Mr. Fitzgibbons refused to cooperate regarding this inquiry."

This is the kicker. In July of 1990 Nomura Securities signed an NYSE consent without admitting or denying guilt, taking a censure and $180,000 fine for six securities violations, including the net capital violation which I'd brought to the attention of Dingell. This was the same complaint the SEC determined there was "no basis" for. Now I have contempt for the SEC. Respect is earned, they haven't earned my respect.

What it comes down to is this. Nomura supports the public debt. It sells our Treasuries to the Japanese public. The Feds won't lift a finger for the enforcement of our regulations until that changes. So long as it's the policy of the American government to sell treasury bonds through Nomura, they aren't going to go after that firm.

■ NANCY SMITH

Nancy Smith was a chief aide to the House Subcommittee on Tele-communications and Agriculture in the 1980s. Hard-working and savvy, Smith looks more like a bright college student on sabbatical than one of the more powerful players in securities regulation—and a young woman who had a considerable impact on modernizing regulations of the American marketplace.

In 1974 congress created the CFTC to oversee the futures markets. And then in 1981, stock index futures were invented. These new products created a regulatory dilemma—were they futures, to be regulated by the CFTC or were they securities, to be regulated by the SEC? The chairmen of both regulatory bodies, Philip Johnson at the CFTC and John Shad at the SEC, settled the matter in an accord which was adopted by congress and signed into law. The result was that the

CFTC regulated stock index futures and options on such futures, and the SEC regulated stock index options.

The accord set the parameters for the jurisdictional split that exists today. Unfortunately, at the time of the accord, no one predicted the overwhelming influence that stock index futures would subsequently have on the stock market through futures-related program trading strategies.

Chairman Markey of the Telecommunications and Finance Subcommittee did call hearings to examine the impacts of such program trading before the October 19, 1987 market crash. And Markey did send a letter expressing concern about the intense volatility created by such trading in the week before the crash. However, it took the crash, and its aftermath, to prod the Administration into a detailed investigation, through the appointment of the Brady commission, to look into the trading strategies that produced the largest market decline in the Dow's history. The Brady commission provided striking evidence for a realignment of regulatory jurisdiction so that stock index futures and stocks would be brought under a single regulator.

In 1988, chairman Markey introduced legislation to bring stock index future under the jurisdiction of the SEC. But the legislation languished. It took the mini-crash of October 1989 to reignite interest in passing the reforms identified as a result of the 1987 crash. Although the Stock Market Reform Act of 1990 did not include a transfer of jurisdiction regarding stock index futures, it did provide the SEC with the tools necessary to more effectively regulate our markets and, hopefully, to prevent market crashes of the magnitude of 1987 and 1989. Most significantly, the Act gave the SEC the authority to regulate program trading strategies which produce unnecessary and excessive levels of stock market volatility.

In 1991, chairman Markey managed a number of securities bills which strengthened the hand of regulators in battling securities fraud. These bills included a measure which gave the SEC enhanced enforcement authority and the power to assess civil remedies. And finally, Markey successfully authored and passed into law reforms of the penny stock market which resulted in increased protections for investors that have been routinely victimized in that market. The passage of all these securities laws in 1991 prompted chairman Richard Breeden of the SEC to declare that such far-reaching reforms of our securities markets had not been seen since the 1940s.

Enacting radical market restructuring legislation such as Glass-Steagall is still debatable. There are a lot of very smart people who don't believe that we should give our banks new speculative securities powers when the banks are at their weakest. I believe that you have to grant such powers incrementally and as the banking industry demonstrates its resolve to handle such powers responsibly. We shouldn't have the U. S. taxpayers finance a radical new experiment. Such powers should be handed out with a great deal of caution.

I think the legislation that we did get passed was long overdue. It greatly strengthened the hand of the SEC to aggressively pursue fraud. But it is impossible to fashion a regulatory system which successfully attacks all sources of abuse in the system. For instance, take compensation. That's the basic way the industry motivates people and we have to fashion sensible regulation to compensate for a structure that encourages conflicts of interest.

An enhanced electronic audit trail would help to detect some kinds of market fraud, but there are some markets where such audit trails are lacking. It took the crash of 1987 and the mini-crash of 1988 for legislators and regulators to start putting in place some of the reforms and information-sharing agreements between the various markets to police the markets effectively. There's always a lag between market innovation and effective regulation.

Fundamental structural reforms in the regulation of the securities, futures and financial services industry will in some cases only take place when we institute reforms in our campaign finance laws. Whether it is health care or any other issue that pits entrenched special interests against the need for reform, the fundamental barrier to progress is how we fund our legislators' political campaigns. Unfortunately, it often takes a catastrophic event to overcome the power of the special interests.

■ LAWRENCE HAAS

Journalist Lawrence Haas writes for the National Journal in Washington D.C., and is also the author of a book, Running on Empty: Bush, Congress, and the Politics of a Bankrupt Government. *The book traces the failure of congress and the Bush administration to grapple with the budget deficit in the first year of the Bush administration. Subsequently, an agreement was reached in late 1990.*

Right now, in Washington, the administration is trying to update both the supervision and activities of financial institutions so that they match the activities of their counterparts in other nations. That means banks ought to be allowed to provide more services, maybe even the kind of services currently forbidden by Glass-Steagall. Of course, that's not going to happen easily, as Senator Proxmire found out.

It's not just a battle of regulators and politicians, it's also a battle between the special interests who have much to gain or lose as a result of this gigantic overhaul. We've got a huge battle between banks, real-estate interests, insurance companies and securities firms over who ought to do what, and even which regulator ought to be in charge of supervising what products.

We have created a system of government in which interest groups are allowed an open door in the corridors of government. Any voter can go see his or her representative, but if a representative of a major interest group wants to see someone, the door opens a lot quicker.

Since we have private financing of campaigns, members of congress are dependent on private donations, and many of the donations come from special interests who see government as a powerful factor in their industries. We came to this system gradually, as government in Washington grew since the 1930s and became a larger part of people's lives. As government grew, it created more programs. The more programs, the more opportunities for private interests to manipulate and expand those programs.

Keep in mind that before the New Deal, government comprised less than five percent of the gross national product. Today it's almost 25 percent, a quarter of the GNP.

Once a benefit is enshrined, it's almost impossible to get it off the books. Washington is out of touch, but in other ways it is too in-touch. Voters at home don't want their elected representatives to cut spending—I don't know if a change in the structure and bureaucracy of government can fix that—but there's no question that there are small programs that the public as a whole does not care about.

I'm not sure if a cure for our deficit problem can come in the absence of a change in public opinion—the public does not want to accept the medicine. In poll after poll, the public says do something about the deficit, but the public also says don't raise my taxes, and don't cut every major area of spending.

Public financing might be one answer to our problems. If we had public financing instead of private financing, then private interest groups wouldn't have so much clout with politicians, but I don't think the chances are great that we'll get public financing: we have never had it. Matching funds were a step in the right direction, but we ought to go farther.

■ A PROGRAM TRADER

The problem is not program trading. The problem is the way the system interacts. For one thing, 25 percent of total U.S. corporate assets are represented by the pension plans. Upwards of three quarters of a trillion dollars is managed among the top fifty institutional money managers. About one trillion dollars are represented among the top one hundred public and private investment plans in the United States.

Everybody has an axe to grind. The money managers, for instance, come in two flavors: The old-fashioned active money managers try to invest their portfolios in individual kinds of products and equities, and they're quite upset about the newer breed of passive managers who depend on Wall Street for program trading strategies, or who index their funds to the performance of the market.

So the active money managers have an axe to grind. They have to justify the performance of their funds. I don't know about their individual performance, but I know active fund mangers have had a bad record generally during the 1980s. There's just too much money to invest these days without some kind of program or indexing strategy.

To justify their lousy performance, these managers blame program trading. So that's one battle—between active managers who say the market is rigged and want to see all derivative products shut down and the passive managers who are making use of the products and derivative strategies.

What are the regulators doing in the meantime? The regulators are playing to congress because they are concerned about losing their power base. So their reaction is determined not by the reality of what is occurring in the marketplace but by what congress thinks about that reality. And congress gets its feedback from special interest groups and from its constituents—many of whom have no idea of what is occurring in the marketplace or the true forces that have been generated.

The constituents that congress is hearing from have been getting their information from Wall Street's most prestigious and vocal leaders. People like Phelan and the current Big Board chairman, William Donaldson.

But the exchanges are playing to the regulators because they want to maintain their monopolies. The public is confused because it does not see the agendas behind what's being said. For instance, the NYSE spent the first part of the 1980s trying to get rid of market volatility and the last part of the 1980s blaming the volatility on Chicago. That's like shooting the messenger.

What about Wall Street? The Wall Street firms make money through computerized program trading strategies so they like the way the system is. Most importantly they like regulations because regulations create volatility and inspire public confidence all at once.

But the volatility stems from lack of price information and control of the information flow.

The system is essentially rigid and needs to be deregulated, not regulated more—which is what's happening now.

No single entity in the whole equation has any self-interest invested in pushing for deregulation. Wall Street enjoys a certain amount of regulation. Regulators thrive on it, obviously. The exchanges are products of it. The money managers—passive and active—are also products of regulation and would probably like more, not less.

The only group that might actively push for deregulation is Corporate America, but they have no vested interest in seeing the situation resolved since they are not in the business of intermediation.

Everybody else has some interest in supporting the status quo, but the status quo means fewer and fewer players with more and more money. And more money means more power, and more ability to control the markets.

I don't think these trends are going to be reversed quickly. I fear for the future of our capital markets structure, I really do. A blow-up in a truly interlinked global marketplace would make 1987 look like peanuts.

29

■■■

THE MEDIA

"The entire country is routinely misinformed about the truth."

■ TED SMITH

An associate professor and director of graduate studies at the school of mass communications, Virginia Commonwealth University, Dr. Ted Smith has written or edited five books, including The Vanishing Economy, *an analysis of television news coverage of economic affairs, 1983–87.*

Journalists, and this includes business journalists, are not trained to evaluate research. They go in with a layman's understanding of what is actually driving the process. The press, including the business press, is concerned primarily with how it fares with consumers. Unless consumers demand truth, they won't get it.

The business press, in particular, functions as an adjunct of the business community. It functions only so far as key people will talk to it and validate what it's saying. It's just like the larger media covering government. Journalists, as a whole, are not so much liberal as statist, and that includes the business press.

The business press is a specialized press with a much higher level of expertise than in television news. In that sense it's more responsible and conservative, but it still has all the problems of being a closed profession unwilling to move ahead of the industry it's covering. What concerns me is that the entire country is routinely misinformed about the truth.

The media does not like to lay out stories that present a lot of basic information—you can't talk about trends that have roots in the past. Herd mentality is what takes over. The media do not encourage creativity, they do not encourage people to develop unique insights on things. Certain operating assumptions spread throughout all levels of the media. There are far more rewards for writing a false story that fits preconceptions than a true one that breaks those preconceptions. Journalists tend to go with the flow.

Where the problem is located is in the emergence of a closed and unitary press—that grew up gradually, but it really took hold in this century when journalism became a profession. Journalists came to a gentlemen's agreement not to attack each other. Before then you basically had a bunch of individual printers taking sides. Newspapers were extremely partisan, they were mouthpieces. The Federalist newspapers attacked the anti-Federalist newspapers.

Nowadays newspapers are supposed to be disseminators of impartial truth. So that's the one thing that needs to change—the principal unwritten rule that you don't go after other professional journalists. If journalists started going after each other, it would become clear very quickly that the general quality of coverage is very poor—if journalists really criticized the media content it would be devastating to the media. You would have a huge sorting out.

None of this was planned, but what you were getting from the 1830s on, once you had mass circulation, were pressures to be populist—and sensationalistic. Newspapers had been players in the conflict of ideas, but they gradually became observers, tending to reproduce the debate, not participate.

One problem is that journalism has become more or less a unitary profession; it is autonomous, and answerable to no one outside the profession. Journalists have emerged as a sort of closed elite who are biased in a certain way—especially when it comes to the economy. They get to winnow who gets to be a journalist.

WHAT I LEARNED

In this section, industry observers have traced the evolution of the financial industry's sell side—its securities firms and exchanges—and the continuing struggle to gain a profit by dominating the nation's financial structure.

These observers have pointed out that the effort to control and dominate the markets, especially the equity and derivatives markets, has led to the invention of new products and the application of technology in some areas and its exclusion in others. There is certainly suspicion that the financial industry's struggle to maintain control of pricing information and stock dealing ultimately led to the destabilization of the stock market in October 1987. Many of these beliefs remain unproven. But a good number of financial industry observers seem to agree with former Brady commission member Kirby that "the woods are full of spies and everybody can hear the drums."

These issues still haven't been taken very seriously by some of the country's major news organizations. Perhaps, as media observer Ted Smith points out, the lack of a fractious press is at fault. Business publications, especially, tend to be trade vehicles writ large. The tone of many business articles, even today, that discuss the securities marketplace tend to be filled with descriptions of "rocket scientists" concocting wizardly products (derivatives are currently the flavor) that can be conceived of—and comprehended—only by the greatest financial minds. Alternatively, Wall Street's activities seem to be condemned as the antisocial products of greedy individuals. Both propositions are probably simplistic.

Confusion abounds. Perceptive but critical observers like Morris
Propp have grave doubts about much of the received wisdom of the
financial industry, communicated in less than complete detail by the
financial press. Observers like Propp—and there are others equally
concerned but less vocal—doubt most of the popular and harmless
explanations of why the stock market goes up and down (i.e., index
arbitrage), or even why certain instruments were invented and set up
in certain ways. And former industry executives like John Fitzgibbon
have seen for themselves how America's regulatory agencies refuse
to enforce the rules equally—and even deny and dissemble when confronted.

It's not hard to believe, after talking to these informed observers,
that something is wrong with our financial industry and its watchdogs.
If a small group of powerful firms on Wall Street can squeeze the
securities marketplace for their own benefit—and almost destabilize
the economy in the process—then some sort of serious, purposeful,
sustained reexamination needs to occur. The last section of this book
explores some of the trends in the nation's financial industry that may
provide the glimmerings of a solution to some of the problems our
markets are apparently facing.

By injecting new players into the industry, by opening up complex,
misunderstood instruments to public scrutiny, it is possible that capital
formation can be enhanced and markets made slightly less prone to
crashes. Booms and busts are one thing. Explosive downturns that
destabilize the underpinnings of a modern nation's credit structure are
another. As our equities and derivatives markets—never mind our bond
and foreign exchange markets—become increasingly international in
scope, these issues can only grow more important and worthy of the
closest possible scrutiny by concerned citizens.

What's probably most frightening of all is whether our current
system of government, with its entrenched interest groups and lobbying
dollars, can muster the will to make a purposeful and effective reexamination of the country's financial structure.

PART THREE

■ ■ ■

FREE MARKET SOLUTIONS

■ ■ ■

Worldwide trading nets, derivatives strategies, and international financial firms are changing the way the financial industry operates domestically and abroad. Exchanges themselves are offering new products and ways to trade them. Ultimately, an international market of some size will probably emerge in which the world's biggest investors will trade and settle among themselves. It may be that the more of these large players there are, the less they would conform to current buy-side/sell-side conventions, and the healthier and deeper the nation's—and ultimately the world's—markets might be. Regulators can help deepen international and domestic markets; by paying attention to serious clearing and settlement issues, regulators and industry officials can help alleviate any potential worldwide market disruptions.

Securities industry profitability in the United States tailed off in the late 1980s. In 1988, NYSE share volume dropped 15.5 percent. The United States went from over 98 percent of world trading in stock index futures to less than 55 percent in only three years.

What was the problem? A 1990 Office of Technology (OTA) *Electronic Bulls & Bears* report on the securities industry traced the evolution of automation and its collision with industry and regulatory interests over the years. The report recommended a reexamination of America's current market structure. The system's division of labor between banks and securities firms, rules like Rule 390 that artificially concentrate order flow at the Big Board all should be reviewed, the report said.

In the past, review has not led to action. In the 1970s, congress gave the SEC a mandate to create a national market system. What emerged was ITS, the rudimentary electronic bulletin board.

The need for more competition within the securities industry was debated in the 1970s and 1980s. Deregulation brought changes but did not affect the clout of the biggest firms. In the last decade, the industry's powerful marketing monopoly swung into action. Billions of dollars' worth of instruments with no pricing history and little available real-time pricing were marketed to consumers across the country.

The stock market crash of 1987 was at least partly the result of an imbalance of electronic power: Those with computers and the knowledge to use them overwhelmed the nation's old-fashioned physical exchanges. A lack of real-time pricing information left players without the knowledge of the market's whereabouts and aggravated the panic.

Following the crash, the NYSE and portions of the media blamed "program trading" and "speculation." Index arbitrage was pointed to as a culprit, and regulators along with the industry's New York bankers took aim at the Chicago financial futures markets. Program trading—strategies far more complex and varied than mere arbitrage—probably did have something to do with the crash. Wall Street firms and hedge funds may well have tried to trigger institutional portfolio insurance selling levels, thus setting off selling pressure that rapidly got out of control. In any case, the current way of doing business in our marketplace—a few brokers exposed to massive order flow rushing into rigid physical exchange mechanisms—is not working well no matter how profitable the "industry" becomes in its cyclical fashion.

To complicate the situation, the media has pitched in with books and articles that in some cases seem simplistic. Deregulation is often blamed for problems of the late 1980s, though there has not been much discussion about how deregulation collided with other regulations still on the books to increase stress on the system.

One recent popular business book, for instance, seems to suggest that the SEC needs a Democratic administration to run properly. Another says that the main achievement of the 1980s was incarcerating Michael Milken. Both these assumptions, even if accurate, seem to miss some important points. Yet they dovetail neatly with the mythology about our markets, our politicians, and our regulators that the country has maintained for most of this last century.

America's current belief structure about its marketplace was at least to some extent formed by the great crash of 1929, which devalued by half securities issued in that decade. Over the next 40 years numerous statutes emerged from the rubble and dealt with an astonishing array of domestic financial enterprise: The 1933 Act deals with the public offering of securities; the 1934 Act deals with exchanges and public utilities; the 1935 Act deals with trust indentures; the 1939 Act deals with investment companies; the 1940 Act deals with investment advisors and investors; and the 1978 Act deals with investors.

There may be some doubt of the efficacy of this deluge of regulation, yet America's postwar dominance was such that even under stringent regulatory control the country's financial markets and its economy, as a whole, boomed. As a result, several generations of Americans grew up secure in the belief that financial marketplaces were relatively static, that ways of raising capital and trading securities were predictable, and that regulation in place to insure overt "speculation" was effective and appropriate.

In the 1980s things changed. Americans found out that regulations when not enforced—or when forced to interact with a new, automated and commoditized environment—led to increased market instability. Meanwhile, a rising market generated increased financial fraud. Throughout the 1980s the SEC prosecuted stock-tipsters—insider traders—ultimately netting the biggest fish, Milken. The argument can probably be made, however, that the failure of between $50 and $100 billion worth of limited partnerships, $20 billion worth of penny stock scams, and $100 billion in failing limited partnerships may have done as much or even more to erode investor confidence than did insider trading.

Many of the country's most cherished economic beliefs have come under fire: Physical stock trading is reluctantly giving way to automation; equity markets are giving way to derivatives. The NYSE still accounts for about 83 percent of trading, but it's actually half that because many shares traded are block deals committed by professional traders, crossed by telephone, and then sent downstairs to the floor so that the information can be passed along through SIAC's automated utilities and put out on the electronic tapes.

In 1991, futures and options exchanges wheeled out new products, including such contracts as two-year Treasury notes, four-year interest rate swaps, three-year rate swaps, mark–yen cross-rate futures, and S&P 100 and S&P Midcap 400 stock indexes. The one product the NYSE offered to take advantage of program trading, preconstructed baskets of stock, was removed from the market in late 1991. Equity trading is not evolving. Derivatives trading is.

Nearly a decade ago, a few institutional investors began swapping stocks; now electronic trading accounts for 20 to 30 million shares a day. California-based Wells Fargo, with nearly $104 billion under management, does many trades internally, swapping securities between its own portfolios and significantly lowering transactions costs.

Client facilitation, the idea of helping an institution or corporation buy or sell a massive block of securities, is a costly service that some of the country's biggest firms, including Morgan Stanley, have abandoned or are in the process of abandoning.

Meanwhile, corporations are starting to trade with other corporations, as *BusinessWeek* pointed out late in 1990, buying securities from issuers and bypassing Wall Street altogether. Firms like Exxon, General Motors, and others sometimes market their commercial paper themselves. IBM has set up the IBM Money Market Account available to shareholders or anyone with $2,500 to invest. Some companies are also directly selling longer-term debt to investors.

What may be even more significant than corporate participation in the markets is the idea that pension funds and large investors could take a more active role in the investing of their own assets.

In the industry's current structure and operation, observers can begin to glimpse the future. Quantitative investing, new over-the-counter and exchange-traded instruments utilized by a broad array of international traders through a variety of electronic nets—these trends will tend to blur national boundaries and current perceptions, in this country anyway, of what constitutes a broker, a dealer, a bank, or a fund.

This evolution is occurring. Domestically, the danger is that politicians and regulators will step in to stop it, to shore up the very parts of the system that are the most fragile and the most likely to be swept away first. Likely candidates: the nation's physical exchanges and rigid buy-side/sell-side structure.

The urge to return to simpler times is always strong. Left-wing environmentalists want a less complex, less polluting society. Right-wing conservatives want to restore traditional values they say were present in this country earlier this century. Those who would return the financial industry to the past are an especially broad and vocal group of regulators, legislators, bankers, and market participants. Their arguments are convincing or at least appealing. Once Wall Street was a place where private firms acted as responsible agents for their clients, where hostile takeovers, junk bonds, electronic trading, futures and options derivatives and other kinds of complex, evolving on-and-off exchange instruments did not exist, for good reason. Markets were a useful invention, necessary for price generation; investing for the "long term" was responsible; trading in and out of the market was to be frowned on as speculation. And speculation was something that had got the nation into trouble in the 1920s.

But the 1980s made some of the preceding perceptions, no matter how attractive, obsolete. The nation's financial markets can go back, as some have argued, but the cost will be great, and the result will simply move investment away from this country to other parts of the globe.

It is simple to rail against speculation, to put crooked insider traders in jail, to damn 1980s greed, to demand that markets perform worthwhile services. It takes a peculiar kind of hardheaded courage to welcome a freed-up market. Free markets are prone to wide swings, and to abuse by powerful, greedy participants. Free markets, in fact, are sloppy, distasteful environments where seemingly crass know-nothings can quickly become rich. But free markets are also places where jobs are created, where economies are fueled. Vibrant free markets, freely accessible, are a powerful force for change and for growth. The trends point in their direction.

Domestic Automation

Most domestic automated securities execution systems now fit into two categories (though that's starting to change). On the one hand are real-time order-matching systems, which bring together buy and sell orders when they reach the same price, taking into account the time the order was placed, and sometimes the size. The other kind of common system—often referred to as a "black box" since no one sees inside—crosses large blocks of buy and sell orders at specific intervals, usually once a day or several times a week, depending on volume. These are called, naturally enough, crossing networks.

Current domestic automated exchanges partake of both these types of systems. A list would include Reuter's American-based Instinet real-time order-matching system and crossing network; Jefferies's ITG's real-time system, Quantex, and its crossing network, Posit; Wunsch's electronic auction system; Bernard Madoff's automated trading system; and the Small Order Execution, Soes, facility of the Nasdaq system.

Other automated systems include Thomson Financial Inc.'s AutEx system and the NASD's new penny stock utility. But such systems often do not offer any comprehensive automated routing or execution function: They are, or have been, basically bulletin boards, ways for buyers and sellers to see, by electronic screens, what kind of interest exists in certain securities. To execute a trade, the buyer or seller picks up the phone.

Even with Rule 390 still in place, such systems are stealing volume from the Big Board. In 1991, overall average daily volume on Instinet was nearly 10 million shares, while trading on its Crossing Network constituted another 2 million shares. Average daily volume on Jefferies' Posit was more than 3 million, according to an internal SEC study. Meanwhile, Bernard Madoff's firm, with its automated trading facility, traded 9 million shares, or roughly 10 percent of the NYSE's average volume of 194 million shares traded. Madoff's volume might be considerably decreased if Rule 390 were done away with and brokers had more choices about where to send orders.)

Among major markets, the NASD's electronic system Nasdaq is the most advanced. But until recently its mechanized stock matching networks, like Soes, and another execution system for larger orders, were rarely used. Traders and market makers using the system prefer to handle most trades by telephone. Most would acknowledge that the NASD is still a telephone-based market absolutely dominated, by regulation and structure, by the industry it serves. It is an open question as to whether Nasdaq is really the "Market for the Next 100 Years," as the NASD's commercials proclaim.

In the past, exchange automation has not been warmly received by Wall Street's trading community in part because it seems to threaten to bypass them altogether. Yet these systems exist because of the massive distrust Wall Street has inspired. Most buy-side traders and even consumers invested in the market think that securities professionals may trade ahead of order flow. Automated systems like Steven Wunsch's auction system possibly preclude that.

Wunsch has produced software that allows buyers and sellers to link up in a daily securities auction. The system mimics electronically the buy and sell calls of the NYSE and other exchanges before continuous trading was established. Such a system, according to Wunsch and others, can produce far more "robust" prices than can the present specialist system of the NYSE, or the Nasdaq market-making system. That's because it generates more bidders per security.

Wunsch's system is open only to institutional investors. But for some industry observers, the vision remains of a true electronic market that might allow consumers to treat brokerage firms a little like banks—as places where accounts were established and from which funds could be borrowed for the consumer's individual investment activities.

Junius Peake has given thought to this process. Automated systems already available allow investors to tap into the market using simplified trading terminals at home, he points out. In the future, he says, there is nothing stopping the industry's so-called discount brokers from guaranteeing the consumer's account up to a certain limit; then the individual would be free to trade to that limit directly into the automated exchange—bypassing both the full-service broker and the trader.

This trend has also been facilitated by the industry's own structural changes. After Mayday, a whole group of brokers sprang up to take advantage of the industry's new, flexible rates. These discount brokers didn't try to advise customers on what to buy or sell, or even market products of their own. For this reason, they could offer to buy and sell stock on the customer's behalf for less commissions than their full-service competitors.

The most well-known discount broker is Charles Schwab & Co. Inc. This firm, started in San Francisco soon after Mayday, has grown to national proportions. While Schwab has continued to keep prices low, it has begun offering customers a variety of computerized systems. Some track the prices of securities in this country and around the world; others link the customer directly to Schwab's order-routing services.

Beyond this, Schwab—which has more than 100,000 customers—has started to disprove the old securities wisdom that held stocks were sold, not bought. Because, the idea went, stocks were a speculative investment and difficult to figure out, most people needed help to overcome initial caution and confusion. But Schwab does not employ brokers in the regular sense: It does not have its employees canvas the country with "cold calls" to find prospective clients. It simply offers a cheap, efficient way for investors to place securities orders. Schwab's success shows that there is a considerable segment of the public that is looking for a cheap way to trade and that does not necessarily miss so-called full-service brokers.

Former Merc executive Glen Windstrup, who is working to automate the futures markets, also has his eye on providing nonstandard automated services to investors. Windstrup left the Merc in 1984 to build automated futures systems for small physical exchanges. His system does away with the physical exchange floor, much as automated equity systems transcend the need for groupings of individual securities executives.

He thinks there's no reason why executives within the agricultural community should not have access to the futures markets the same way that professional traders and brokers do. He's currently trying to sell his system to feedlot executives who purchase grain in abundance and therefore have a need to lay off their risk on the futures market. "I'm hopeful within two years we'll have feedlot placements," says Windstrup. "But it's a challenge. There's a lot of mistrust to overcome."

The mistrust that farmers and others feel toward the futures industry is similar to the mistrust of the securities industry toward automation. "It's always been this way," says Peake's colleague, Mendelson. "The industry fears change and fights it—especially the exchanges."

Yet the change on the way may be even more startling than Peake or Mendelson envisions. When TV first came along, radio actors brought stools to the set and perched on them, reading their scripts in front of the cameras. It was only later that actors began to act. When automation was envisioned for the markets, it was not clear even to the clearest-eyed visionaries that an automated system would function much differently from the physical exchange. Orders would meet electronically. Buys and sells would be matched. The lowest sell would take out the highest buy as soon as possible. The nation, and then the world, could participate in a vast, simple electronic market.

Today, industry professionals and academic observers are starting to see new and more complex possibilities in automated systems. In Cambridge, Mass., Evan Schulman has constructed Lattice, his system that routes orders automatically to the exchange or system with the best price. It is a private version of the ITS system, but one with far more complexity and connections. Jefferies' Quantex system routes orders from Jefferies' Posit Crossing Network to a new "Institutional Indications" facility.

Certain institutions place buy and sell "indications of interest" within the Quantex/II system: These indications are electronically placed in a workstation at an ITG New York data site. As customer orders that have not been filled by ITG's Posit cross electronically "swim" through Quantex/II, some of the orders meet up with complementary indications of interest placed there by the institutions Jefferies has invited in.

When customer orders trigger the indications of interest, an electronic signal is sent back to the institution's own computer via dedicated line. The institution's computer decides if the price and size of the order swimming by is right; if it is, the system signals ITG's computer in New York that it wishes to buy—or sell—and the match is made. Both the institution and the customer receive electronic confirmation that the order is done. Remaining orders, not taken out in ITG's morning cross nor in the Quantex/II real-time matching system, swim farther down the electronic river to the Big Board's SuperDot, which will guarantee a fill at the market price.

This explanation illustrates the growing complexity of the electronic nets that are now being set up. Markets are no longer places, for all practical purposes, where deals are done between single buyers and sellers. Rather, such systems are capable of processing the orders of many customers and trades at any given electronic instant. Such nets don't respect rigid terms like "dealer" or "institution." An order from a Wall Street firm does not have much of an advantage over an order from any other industry entity.

It is amply clear that the realities of what the future of securities automation holds has not yet sunk in among the general public. For the general public, orders are handled, usually one at a time, on the floor of a physical exchange. Yet combine sophisticated indexed investing techniques with layers of electronic options—as market guru Christopher Keith has done—and the implications start to become clear. What TV was to radio back in the 1940s, so electronic systems today are to physical exchanges. The surface has barely been scratched.

International Trading

As the OTA *Bulls and Bears* study points out, the first international financial services were provided by Paul Julius Reuter, who used carrier pigeons to fly stock market quotations between Belgium and Germany. In 1851, an underwater telegraph cable connecting England and France let Reuter deliver market data and financial news back and forth between England and the Continent. Today, Reuters is one of a number of companies offering worldwide market data including Japan-based Quick, Knight-Ridder Inc., Automatic Data Processing Inc., Dow Jones & Co.'s Telerate, Inc., and Citibank's Quotron Inc.

Internationally, the trading efforts of exchanges, brokers, and other private-sector groups continue to grow. In 1987, the Merc said it would develop, along with Reuters, an electronic futures and futures options network called Globex. The system was initially accepted by Merc members as an after-hours trading system. Some five years later, with new partner the CBOT, Reuters is finally readying Globex for international installation.

Matif, the French financial futures exchange, has already agreed to use Globex. In this country a local exchange, the New York Mercantile Exchange, has also installed a system that may rival Globex domestically. Other automated trading systems include the Irish Futures and Options Exchange, the London Futures and Options Exchange, and the Tokyo Grain Exchange.

Another kind of joint venture involves the CBOE and its Cincinnati Stock Exchange. They've agreed to form a joint venture with Reuters and Instinet to create a worldwide system for trading options on the CBOE and equities traded by the Cincinnati.

Even the New York Stock Exchange has plans for automated international trading. It has developed a multistep process to develop an automated 24-hour trading system by the year 2000.

In Toronto, Canada, an automated system has been in use throughout the 1980s. Toronto's Computer Assisted Trading System (Cats) matches the orders of less active stocks: It also displays limit orders along with the name of the broker, and there are market makers to make continuous quotations in some stocks. Large trades are negotiated by telephone, like Nasdaq, and then they can be entered on system.

Cats' ground-breaking electronics were assembled in bits and pieces over a ten-year span by the Toronto Exchange's president, Jay Bunting. Bunting joined the Toronto exchange in 1969 and soon realized—much as the NASD had—that to make an impression on Canada and to continue to be competitive, the exchange needed to find a way to stand out. Bunting decided on automation and launched a slow but stubborn campaign to convert the exchange's members to his point of view.

The original system was put in place in 1977. About 200 terminals were distributed to 70 Toronto member firms. The network gradually gained acceptance because the traders making markets did not resist the electronic quote information the network provided. Later on, however, the Exchange acted to place half of the traded stocks on the system for purposes of electronic trading. This meant that market makers who had dealt stocks on the floor now had to trade by screen. Some adapted and some did not, but even with all the changes, only 30 percent of the volume was eventually being traded electronically.

Early in 1990, the Exchange went a step further and put its electronic systems on the floor in the midst of the crowd. A broker who wishes to buy or sell a stock gives the order to an Exchange official who punches it into the system. The Exchange is now in the process of pushing its automated network even further.

The big fear among firms and exchanges of losing their special place brokering the cash flow unfortunately results in systems being chosen not for their efficiency but for the promise of generating the most business for the dealer.

In Canada, in one of the more interesting developments of the early 1990s, Donald Unruh, formerly vice president of international trading at the Toronto Exchange, has licensed exchange-simulation software he has developed to a consortium of European dealers. The dealers may eventually recommend new electronic markets for the European Community.

Unruh, who helped Bunting build the Cats system, became Toronto's marketing chief and sold and constructed electronic exchanges in France, Argentina, and Brazil, based on the Toronto model. Unruh quit the Toronto market when his bosses decided the Exchange was in business first of all to serve its members—not to replicate Cats in other countries.

Unruh spent the next two years perfecting his software, which is designed to research the efficiency of various aspects of the market. To develop his software, Unruh used a Simscript computer language—the one used by military planners for battle management simulation in the European tactical theater. Unruh says Simscript could also be used by automated exchanges to track market manipulation.

Unruh's market study may help determine what kind of market model is truly preferable. The preferable system should have several characteristics, he says. For one thing, it should minimize the gap in the marketplace between what the highest-price buyers want to pay for securities and the lowest-price sellers are willing to accept for their stocks or bonds. This is called the spread, and it is considered to be a primary indicator of efficient markets.

But the best market would also be the most liquid market and also the fairest. A truly fair market gives the buyer the lowest possible price and gives the seller the highest possible price. Such a market also places a priority on timeliness. That is, a fair market may truly operate on a first-come, first-served basis. Unruh points out, however, that time-priority may not be the only kind of fairness. There may also be fairness in giving an edge to customers who routinely buy and sell large blocks of stock.

Additionally, a fair market should use capital efficiently. Some analysts have claimed market makers and specialists, in trying to stabilize a stock, only retard a stock's downward movements and therefore cause buyers to purchase the equity before it has reached its natural bottom price. Unruh notes one way to determine the efficacy of such market makers is to figure out the spread of the markets in which they operate.

Since the spread at the NYSE is extremely tight, and since the capital used by specialists is relatively small, Unruh says the Big Board's controversial system may have much to recommend it. Unruh already has evidence market-making does help with the buying and selling of stock. In the first test of his proprietary software, he used Toronto exchange data to determine whether the presence of market makers helped the market. In the case he tested, the total market increased by 60 percent and customer business increased by 20 percent with market makers present.

"Right now there is no way to determine what markets work best other than by trial and error," says Unruh. "And just because one market's spread is better than another's doesn't mean there isn't some other system out there that would be better than both. That's what I'd like to find out."

Alan Loss, who owns a consulting and conference firm, Amtech Systems Inc., is more cautious than Unruh about using spread as the way to define the best market. "You have to build in characteristics that will attract not only investors and issuers, but also people willing and able to make markets," he says. "What good is transactional efficiency [low cost and fast access to a market] if your order sits in the system for hours or days waiting for the other side of the trade?"

Canada may have had some of the first real automated systems. But competition for international trading resides mostly in Europe and Japan.

The Tokyo Stock Exchange was the world's largest market in value of investments coming into the end of the decade. Like the NYSE, the Tokyo Stock Exchange handles about 86 percent of the volume and value of all transactions in Japan, some $3 trillion.

The TSE's less active stocks are now computerized via a real-time automated price-matching system called Cores, for Computer Assisted Order Routing and Execution System. Of close to 2,000 issues, perhaps 1,600 are traded electronically. The bluest chip issues, about 150 of them, still trade on the floor and constitute about 80 percent of share trading. The TSE also trades government bond futures by computer now. Additionally, the Japanese also have an OTC Nasdaq-style phone-automated system called Jasdaq.

Japan's Osaka Securities Exchange trades several stock index futures based on stocks trading on the TSE. One of the indexes is the Nikkei 225 futures. In 1988, the Nikkei 225 fell nearly 200 points in 15 minutes of TSE trading, then ran up 300 points in a final 30 minutes. Program trading was blamed: The TSE, like the NYSE, instituted regulations to slow computerized trading between indexes and cash markets.

Europe is also grappling with automated trading. The London International Stock Exchange (ISE) after the 1986 Big Bang deregulated commissions, adopted an unsuccessful version of the Nasdaq style system—the Stock Exchange Automated Quotation system (Seaq). As with Nasdaq, big trades are made by telephone, while little orders can be electronically routed to market makers. Meanwhile, the London International Financial Futures Exchange (LIFFE) has developed an electronic trading system that emulates open outcry trading.

London's ISE, despite its problems, is among the largest electronic markets following the Tokyo Stock Exchange, Osaka, and Nasdaq. But the German exchanges, the Paris Bourse, and the Swiss Exchange are also automating their markets. The European community as a whole is considering a "European trading arena" including, eventually, an integrated market.

Ironically, it is in Eastern Europe that some of the most interesting experiments in automated trading are taking place. In Poland, for instance, at the Warsaw stock exchange, members have adopted an electronic single price auction remarkably similar to Wunsch's system. While Warsaw's exchange may eventually switch over to real-time electronic trading, international sources say that the Exchange also plans to let banks trade from around the country and perhaps from around the world. Thus electronic nets take root in previously barren soil; technology allows countries with no market experience to leapfrog those with much.

The technology for global trading is mostly in place. Communications and computer-communications systems for market dissemination are set up. What now need to be determined are international standards to insure that buyers and sellers will honor their trading commitments.

Clearing, the function whereby a trade is deemed accurate by both parties, and settlement, in which cash trades hands, is one of the less glamorous but one of the most important parts of what must be harmonized before global trading can really take off. A number of international bodies are working on these issues. Studies have been completed by the European Economic Commission and the Federation Internationale des Bourses de Valeurs, the Group of Thirty, the International Society of Securities Administrators.

What is worrisome to some is that international investment is rapidly outstripping the regulatory and industry infrastructure necessary for safe trading. If clearance and settlement don't keep pace with global cash flows, sooner or later some investors will lose a great deal of money.

The situation is complicated by what is emerging as one of the financial industry's hottest markets of the 1990s: derivatives trading. Derivatives are financial swaps or informal option instruments customized for specific purposes. Wall Street sells derivative financing to corporations and institutions and then hedges its own risk using exchange mechanisms such as futures and options.

Already warnings from such regulators as the New York Fed's Corrigan are being sounded about the billions of dollars' worth of off-balance sheet instruments that are being traded around the world. It's not that financial innovation is bad, but in a closed system, where few have power over many, innovations can grow at a dizzying rate. Wall Street "drives a stake" through each new product just the way America's car companies used to continually exaggerate every stylistic innovation into exhaustion; taillights turned into fins and then into ungainly flying wedges. A more truly competitive, international, automated environment might alleviate some of industry's destructive exaggeration.

One of the more optimistic scenarios for the development of global trading has been championed by Peter Schwartz of the Global Business Network. Schwartz told the OTA that it is possible what will emerge, worldwide, over the next decade or two will be some kind of stratified two-tier market: A relatively unregulated group of perhaps 100 to 1,000 transition or global companies evolving on top of a regionalized market structure. In such an environment, it's possible that some of the world's largest players would serve as their own regulatory agents. Consumers investing through such entities would receive the protection not of a regulatory authority but of the agent itself. In such an environment the free market could prove to be the safest harbor of all.

Looking Ahead

In 1960, according to the OTA, it cost perhaps $75 to do a million computer operations; in 1980, it cost one tenth of a cent. Digital information, the process of taking information and turning it into binary-coded electronic signals for use by trading systems, has allowed computers to use market data in bits and pieces. AT&T, MCI, Sprint, and other communications carriers are making their existing networks available for high-capacity digital lines.

Planning and building a properly functioning automated system is not easy. But many of the problems of implementing electronic systems have come from industry resistance, more than technological or systemic hurdles. The NYSE itself has lobbied hard to insure that its structure and dominance remain intact. The Big Board has sent its chairman, William Donaldson, out for interviews and onto TV to explain the merits of a single physical exchange receiving the largest possible order flow. And SEC chairman Breeden has said, "It would be good public policy to create public oversight of margins, eliminate exclusivity and unify regulation of stocks, options and futures. . . . Prudence, not punitiveness, should be our goal."

These comments sum up the nub of the country's current dilemma over its evolving marketplace—at home and eventually abroad. Because of historical trends, the country's top regulators and politicians, mostly lawyers, have decided they have an affirmative obligation to "prudently" manage the securities industry.

In place of an invisible hand—and because of the current gridlock of our political system—enormous power has devolved on individual regulators and members of congress convinced of their mandate. In the 1980s one man, John Dingell, effectively stymied legislation aimed at doing away with Glass-Steagall, despite congressional sentiment for the move.

Perhaps regulators, properly informed about the securities industry, can anticipate trends in the free market and adequately create regulations that will apply in almost any circumstance. Yet the experience of the 1980s seems to show this is not the case. Free markets are a powerful force. The revolution in the financial industry will move more quickly in the future. And if it is stymied in this country it will move ahead elsewhere.

As I write this, the SEC is about to release the first version of its Market 2000 report which will reportedly emphasize equities and deal with issues such as market fragmentation. Market fragmentation has been made an issue by large industry players including the NYSE. By claiming that orders must be concentrated in one physical location in order to generate a "best price" the NYSE wraps its own self-interest in the banner of the public good.

In reality, electronic systems are being started by entrepreneurs around the world. If the free market is allowed to operate without overwhelming regulatory interference, these systems will slowly form linkages that will bring orders together in sufficient size and quantity to allay the fears of even the most ardent fans of price and time priority. It is somewhat disheartening to see, then, the industry's chief regulatory body stepping forth with yet another study. Such studies are often a prelude to regulation. And regulation, in the case of market structure, can offer big industry players a chance to stifle innovation that threatens the current set-up.

The SEC's chief congressional overseer, John Dingell, has indicated his agreement with fears of market fragmentation. The SEC, through no-action letters, has allowed the spread of small electronic systems despite Dingell's apparent displeasure. But the study may again bring to the fore the SEC's Rule 15c2-10, intended to regulate such systems. Already, the SEC moves slowly when it comes to new systems. It took Wunsch over two years to get his system approved. Chicago's Globex, developed in part under the watchful eye of the CFTC, took six.

Gobex and another system, the Electronic Joint Venture (EJV), are a special case. EJV's owners are some of Wall Street's biggest firms including Goldman Sachs, Salomon Brothers, and Shearson Lehman Brothers. EJV's effort to place Wall Street analytics and data on the desk of institutions—and Chicago's attempt to extend the dominance of its exchanges worldwide—are examples of the industry itself fighting back against the creative anarchy of automation with structures of its own.

Globex's main sponsors, the CBOT and the Merc for instance, get to decide what does and doesn't go on Globex. Far from opening up the securities industry, Globex is actually a Trojan horse for extending domestic control of powerful national players into the international arena. Inevitably the industry will encourage regulations to enshrine these efforts, much as the NYSE has attempted to keep certain regulations in place to protect its franchise—at least up to now.

Wide-ranging regulations aimed at industry-structures often help the biggest industry players at the expense of smaller ones. And regulators ultimately encourage big business which is seen to be more conveniently regulated. Of course, vital markets are often the product of small as well as large efforts. And the creation of market systems need not be left to major exchanges; indeed, it shouldn't be.

The SEC should probably resist the temptation to implement broad policy declarations. Managing the market by fiat is something even Eastern Europe has given up. Instead, the SEC should probably concentrate on urging physical exchanges—large and small—to automate. Internationally, the SEC should help the financial industry regularize clearing and settlement. Additionally, the SEC should closely examine the way investment instruments are marketed to the public—including rules that currently constrain many funds, and especially mutual funds—both domestically and internationally. Funds that cannot switch back and forth between markets, funds that must remain invested in specific securities at specific proportions due to regulations, may be more at risk in this day and age than are those that are less constrained.

Today, automated markets are just beginning to reflect the richness of the technologies they utilize and the breadth of the new portfolio management theories they accommodate. As the industry expands and changes, as new investment theories and new ways of investing and speculating become prevalent, this country must muster a consensus of trust in the free market. The alternative, as "futurist" Schwartz has pointed out, is that capital will eventually flow away from American markets. Domestic exchange systems will suffer more rather than less stresses and strains in the decade ahead.

30

■ ■ ■

INSTITUTIONAL INVESTORS

"The buy side in the 1980s became less reliant on Wall Street."

■ TIMOTHY MCCARTHY

Timothy McCarthy has had a long and varied career on Wall Street, first on the sell side with Merrill Lynch, as vice president, manager of corporate financial services, and now on the buy side with Fidelity Investments.

McCarthy is president of Fidelity's National Financial Institutional Services, which manages Fidelity's institutional electronic trading and clearing capabilities.

Here at Fidelity we may in any given day be buying or selling up to 30 million shares. We may trade over 10 percent of all equity in the country. Because of our situation, it seemed important to know where the other sources of liquidity were being generated from.

We commissioned some primary research, and what we found surprised us. One surprise was the volume of off-exchange-listed equity trading, more than 20 percent, and going up. We've talked to the regulators and told them they need to be capturing this data, and I believe they're developing systems to do that. The NYSE is requesting permission to require data from its members. It's important. The country ought to know where shares are traded, what systems are competitive.

Trading directly between buyers and sellers, usually through electronic means, is becoming more, not less, prevalent. There are three springboard trends that have fueled this evolution.

First is the growing power of institutional investors like Fidelity. This trend began during the 1970s and increased in the 1980s as it became clear the investor was turning to intermediaries like mutual fund companies. Take Fidelity. In 1980, we had $5 billion under management, and now, some ten years later, we have over $150 billion under management. There's been a massive increase of money under management, not only at funds but also because people are tending more and more to invest through their pension funds.

The result of this increased money under management was a huge increase in fee income, and more money means more resources. The buy side began buying its own research, setting up its own brokerage arms. The buy side in the 1980s became less reliant on Wall Street. A lot of these powerful buy-side firms just felt they were locked out, that they didn't have the information available to the sell side. They started saying, if I can't play with these people on an equal basis I'll trade directly with others like me who have enough liquidity. The power shift combined with electronic trading made it possible.

Then there's the growth of quantitative trading. If you look at the growth of the largest money managers, institutions like Wells Fargo, they've grown through their use of quantitative strategies. They're doing easier, cheaper trades that way. They have less need of broker-dealers for research, they often don't need client-facilitation. Wall Street's services are less important. Quantitative trading gives the buy side more power—they can trade electronically because that kind of trading lends itself to electronic transactions.

Finally, there's the economics of electronic trading, and the economics of indexing. A lot of firms can trade, using automated systems because they can now afford the technology. The combination of increased buy-side power, quantitative strategies and automated systems have led to irreversible changes in the securities marketplace. A big change is, of course, a blurring of the distinction between the buy and sell side. Fidelity owns a brokerage, Merrill Lynch runs a huge amount of funds. Market rules like Rule 390 of the NYSE and Glass-Steagall, separating banks from brokers, these are almost Swiss-cheese rules at this point.

I don't think that electronic trading is going to put exchanges or specialists out of business. For one thing, electronic systems tend not to be very efficient at closing the spread for thinly traded stocks.

Electronic trading works best for the easy stocks, the liquid issues. Of course, in many instances, the electronic exchanges have got it reversed. The specialists or market makers tend to hang on to the liquid stocks while the issues attracting smaller volume are traded by screen.

When we really go to screen trading on a global level, investors will find out where there's less liquidity, and I think you'll have people in there making a market. You'll develop hybrid systems. Maybe combinations of physical exchanges and automated systems.

31

■■■

ELECTRONIC TRADING

"Money managers will develop a rich tapestry of trades."

■ EVAN SCHULMAN

"The father of program trading." Evan Schulman is labeled that way by some in the industry for his work at the Batterymarch funds in applying computer programs to the stock market. Schulman, good natured and low key, hastens to point out that his programs never included the futures market or even the options market. He was strictly an equities trader.

It was heresy, what we did—but we had to bring down transaction costs. What I decided was this. Since brokers have always boasted of their trading skills, one way to test their belief in these statements was to have them bid for the right to trade baskets of stock.

Our simulations indicated that by following very naive trading strategies, brokers could, on average, earn profits in the order of one percent. Those with skill could earn more. My expectation was that the better brokers would be willing to pay our clients for the privilege of executing their orders.

Anyway, I went to New York to make the pitch to our biggest broker, the one who handled most of our orders. I remember I was met in New York by a huge Cadillac. I got the full treatment. The ride into the city, then lunch at an expensive restaurant. When it got around to coffee, I started to make the point that the broker should pay us. One of the partners asked me to repeat what I had to say three times. He was very polite. He said, "I can hear the words but I can't put them together in a meaningful sentence." They weren't impressed with the idea of a firm paying an institution for order flow. I took a cab back to the airport.

I majored in economics at the University of Toronto. I went to the University of Chicago for a year of graduate work. That's where I met the famous economist Milton Friedman. I taught for a year and then I moved into the real world. First I went to the Royal Trust in Canada, then to Keystone.

When I joined Batterymarch, it had $100 million in funds from institutions and private investors. I joined because I wanted to do more computer program trading. I was running $1 billion at Keystone, but Batterymarch was where I wanted to be. It was funny. I spent more time negotiating the kind of computer equipment I wanted than my salary. What we did was work out a system at Batterymarch where we turned the portfolio management process over to the computer every morning. The computer would make the trades. But we didn't do any arbitrage. Only equity program trading.

Now we're in the process of testing our own system. We're bundling exchanges through our own computerized network. That way institutions will be able to put orders in, and the computer will be able to mind those orders and find the best market and the best price. What we are, I guess, is a kind of electronic broker.

Our company is called Lattice. The idea is that once you develop a rich tapestry—a lattice—of new trading techniques, you'll get a surge of trading and liquidity in the market. Current systems to access trading floors stand in the way of institutions providing liquidity for our markets. Once money managers have this access they will develop a rich tapestry of trading techniques to turn trading from a cost center to a profit center. The result will be a deeper and more liquid equities market.

■ CHRISTOPHER KEITH

A Hypothetical Trading System

Technology will create its own systems. You can build a system where you could put in 50,000 shares of Dimwit and the system itself would allow you options you never could have on a trading floor.

This idea is based on the concept that whatever an exchange wants, you can find on the other side without risk, so long as you're willing to pay for it. There are tiers of risk and tiers of reward. That's why the NYSE has survived all these years.

A system like this combines the virtues of Jefferies' Posit and Instinet's Crossing Network. These are price and time priority systems like they have up in Canada. You can put in an order to buy and sell and no one will match it, not for weeks. But there are ways to combine the advantage of a crossing network with guaranteed execution.

There's a way to build mature systems much more complex than what people have currently designed.

Essentially, it would work like this. Institution A would like to buy or sell stock using our network, which makes its cross at say 11:00 in the morning. It puts an order into the system and then receives back information on who is willing to buy or sell the stock institution A is dealing with. The information in the system on who wants to buy or sell the stock comes from big firms like Salomon or First Boston.

Institution A has many choices within the parameters of the system. For one thing, institution A can buy a kind of trading insurance from these big issuers. That means, for a price, say a penny a share more than what he would ordinarily pay to fill a buy or sell order, he can guarantee that the deal for the securities he needs to buy or sell will be completed by 11:00. If institution A does not want to buy insurance from the big dealers, that's all right too. He can simply leave his order in the system and take his chances on a successful cross at 11:00.

There's a third option. Institution A can decide to go on stand-by. That means he can inform the system that he is willing to fill leftover orders after the cross. That's not as good as insurance, which guarantees a fill, but to encourage it, the firms might make it even less costly than if the institution left his orders sitting in the system.

This kind of system is good because it will attract order. Successful markets tend to concentrate order flow. The NYSE's order flow has been in part attracted by the Big Board's own success, but also by Rule 390, which mandates that firms trade with specialists.

Why would this system attract order flow? First of all, some other systems tend to repel order flow because people know what is being traded and sometimes who is doing the trading. This system makes proper use of anonymity because the institutions querying the system are anonymous. Not only that but the big dealers can constantly update what they are willing to buy and sell for a variety of securities because they are constantly getting queries from the institutions and whatnot.

In other words, since they are offering a surety of a penny a share if they guarantee that institution A will be able to cross at a certain price, some institution will pay that price. The firm will then know more about the order flow in particular securities—good knowledge to have if you want to make money in the markets.

In this kind of system, information about buying and selling would constantly change based on electronic and phone queries from institutions and dealers. Computers would become part of the process, rather than just serving as electronic bulletin boards, as they do with Nasdaq, or linear matching systems like Cats price and time priority systems. Finally, computers would start to be part of the process rather than a conveyor of the process. That's what good system design is all about.

■ RAY KILLIAN

Ray Killian is head of the ITG subsidiary of Jefferies which offers buyers and sellers electronic access to trading opportunities. Jefferies is remaking itself into a leader of electronic trading; in the process it is rebounding from a past that saw the banking and trading operation lose its founder, Loyd Jefferies, to stock manipulation charges in the late 1980s.

Through its ITG utilities, Jefferies is making some of Keith's hypotheses real.

I came with Jefferies in January of 1985 from Goldman Sachs & Co. where I was involved with institutional sales.

We don't do any proprietary trading at ITG; we don't do any at Jefferies either. We may facilitate a client's order at Jefferies by buying a small portion and then reselling it, but we're not trying to make a profit for our own account. At Goldman we had the same mentality—it was more or less to facilitate a trade. Goldman always had the attitude the client came first. You have to know how to balance the interest of the clients and the firm. That's hard to do.

I've seen a lot of different phases of this business. But the way the game is played is changing. I'm not so sure there's going to be that much of a need for any single intermediary between the buyer and seller in the future. What's evolving is that liquidity and sources of liquidity are becoming more complex and not so easily identified. A broker's job is not so much one of executing an order per se, though that's an important part of it, but rather to help the client find the liqidity and as often as not liquidity will not be found in the so-called central marketplace. That's a myth; the central marketplace no longer exists as we once knew it. What does exist is a whole series of electronic links, between foreign entities, regional exchanges, NYSE and others. These sources of liquidity exist for a reason and they will be segmented from each other so long as there is a reason for them to be separate. Institutions, in other words, will use a crossing network for one reason, and will use Reuters Instinet for another. Instead of visualizing a physical exchange, you have to think of an electronic highway. As an agency broker, I want to be the traffic cop on those highways.

Here at ITG, what makes us different is that we have a little clearer view of that world. We see the whole question of execution in the equity environment as one of facilitating access. Institutions and traders have a big problem, sifting information. How do I understand what liquidity is, how do I get there fast, coordinate what happens in the options market with the equity market?

That's what we're trying to do at ITG. We've been trying to do it since 1985 when I came on board as institutional sales manager. That's when the guys at Jefferies on the quantitative side came to me with the idea of a crossing network. That network later became Posit, our own black box system in which at a specific time during the day, anonymous buy, and sell orders meet.

Since Posit, we've gone on to build other systems. What we really want to do is offer the client one system, one box, with all our services sitting on it. We have that situation now with our Quantex service. Quantex is an order routing system that allows institutions to route, buy and sell orders to the floor of the NYSE using SuperDot.

But Quantex also includes a front end, an analytics package called MarketMind that allows the user to program trading strategies that the software can then automatically follow and even execute. MarketMind was developed by Integrated Analytics in California, and we bought Integrated in 1991.

MarketMind sits on a UNIX box, and we've added other services to them like Thomson's First Call, which allows an institution to automatically call up research from leading broker-dealers about specific equities.

We've added about 50 different analytics and market data options to Quantex. We're still adding. We want to be a conduit for liquidity—we want institutions to put our boxes on their desks. That's why we recently added Quantex/II, a service that allows an institution to route an order to the broker of his choice. We make money when an order is routed to us for execution; we charge three or four cents a share. But we'd rather have our box on the desk of the institution—give that buyer a choice as to where he can execute rather than not have a presence on the desk at all.

We've added one service that's kind of a composite between a black box and real-time trading. We've found some institutions to provide liquidity—they place indications of interest in the box in the morning. Orders flow from our Posit crossing network to meet the orders of the institution. An electronic query takes place between the system and the computer of the institution providing the order. If the size and price are agreeable on both sides of the trade, it happens electronically without any human intervention.

This service, and other services like it, are miles away from the kind of trading done on a physical exchange. People assumed that computers would simply mimic the trading done on an exchange floor but that's not so. It's a little like the way TV was back in the 1950s. People used to read radio scripts on the air. But that changed, and electronic trading will change the way buy and sell orders meet as people start to understand what the technology can do.

■ BERNARD MADOFF

One of the most successful, if controversial, forces in the domestic automated market is Bernard Madoff, who operates his New York-based firm dealing in the bluest of the Blue Chips, the NYSE's top 400 stocks. Madoff, who pays brokers to trade with him, got his start in the over-the-counter market. He trades Nasdaq stocks as well as the S&P.

Electronics are key to modern trading. The world moves quickly today, and you have to take into consideration what is happening. The domestic-infrastructure has not yet grown to support that growth world-wide, but that's coming too. It has to come. Electronic trading systems are part of the solution to the problems the markets faced in the 1980s. Having everything on an electronic system would not have averted the crash, but it might have prevented some of the disparities and problems that occurred.

Being involved in the national market system and being one of the earliest sponsors of screen-based trading, my firm started making markets in listed securities in the 1970s. We've grown to where we are the dominant force in the automated marketplace, off-exchange, primarily for listed stocks and convertible securities. I employ about 40 traders, and we work out of what's known as the "Lipstick building," in midtown New York.

One hundred percent of our trading is proprietary. The computer automates the process of trading and monitors the risk of the trade. It also helps us design hedging strategies which are of primary importance to a large proprietary trader. We don't get many large orders—our average order is under 1,000 shares, which means that hedging strategies can be utilized efficiently. The key to our system is that we are trading a broad enough base of securities to utilize index options and futures so that we can hedge or risk through other market vehicles.

All of our trading is human directed. The computer assists the trader in spotting the opportunities, but the trader makes the decision as to the type of strategy to utilize and whether or not to trade either the long or short side of the market.

Since our profits come from our own trading, we don't need to charge our customers for our services. But we need their orders. The order flow is the commodity that all traders need to turn profits, but some exchanges charge for their services anyway. Specialists on the floor of the Big Board charge brokers nearly two cents a share to hold limit orders, whereas we charge nothing to hold limit orders.

Wall Street's biggest firms pay floor brokerage fees to trade on the NYSE. We don't charge customers a penny, in fact we actually pay brokers to trade with us. We can do that because our profits came from trading the order. The more order flow we get the more potential trading profits we have. Business really went up after the 1987 stock crash when brokers needed the extra penny a share we were offering them and appreciated the efficiencies of our system.

My mainframe-based computer system is what makes our business possible, and it cost millions to build—and millions to maintain. My brother Peter oversaw the complete programming of the software and network integration. What it does is seek the absolute best price for a buy or sell order available from quotes across the country. All our clients are hooked directly into our own systems. Ninety percent of our business is done with firms trading on the client's behalf. And 90 percent of our business is handled internally.

Recently we've added another function that has greatly increased our business. We've built a price improvement system. That means when any order comes to us with a spread greater than an eighth, our system automatically stops the order and exposes it through the inter-market trading system—the system that electronically links the different exchanges—to see if there is a better buy or sell order somewhere else. If there is, then we will execute it.

Previously, our system would scan ITS to find the best price, but it wouldn't expose the order. Now we expose the order for a minute to see if someone will make a better offer, electronically. This is just what the NYSE said could not be done by electronic trading systems. They say their auction system allows buyers and sellers to meet inside of the posted spread on the ITS, but now we're able to give our clients the same advantage over the entire gamut of exchanges and market-makers using ITS.

We'll always have competition, but we keep on evolving. Right now, we're doing very well, sometimes capturing up to 20 percent of the market in certain securities.

32

■ ■ ■

AUTOMATED AUCTIONS

"It can make a fairer market for everyone."

■ STEVE WUNSCH

Steve Wunsch, mountain climber and former Kidder Peabody program trading salesman, is in the process of launching a new national exchange from Arizona. Wunsch's company, called AZX Inc., offers investors—first institutional and then retail—a wide variety of instruments to trade at a single point in time. Trading is done over computers. Wunsch's so-called "single price auction" connects investors from all across the country, bypassing the broker-dealer community that usually acts as go-between for buyer and seller.

I worked for eight-and-a-half years at Kidder Peabody where I was responsible for marketing index futures and program trading for customers.

The idea of single price auction came from the problem facing most investors—getting buyers and sellers to the market at the same time. In a single price auction you bring one or more traders to market at the same time and that attracts others, and the more people are concentrated in terms of when they trade the less need there is for intermediation—bid offer spread, volatility, market impact, whatever.

The idea grew out of trying to figure out how to implement a sunshine trade. A sunshine trade is a means of trying to create what you might call a do-it-yourself single price auction in a market structure that doesn't provide for one. We tried the sunshine trading first in

190

the futures markets and then in equity trading. But as it turned out it's not easy to create a full gathering of buyers and sellers simply by announcing ahead of time what you're going to do.

It was in the process of thinking about how to implement sunshine trading for more than one customer at a time, I came across the notion of using a computer to collect all of the orders or all those who would like to trade at that time. You could find a single price to trade that way, the clearing price of the market, and it would be a single price.

At that time I had no knowledge of the history of call markets. It was a couple of years after that, I ran into some academics who informed me of the history of the market structure in which call markets figured prominently. I've learned since then that every market began as a call market.

Markets moved away from being call markets because they were organized by broker-dealer intermediaries. Call markets don't have bid-offer spreads, market impact, and volatility. In continuous trading, prices move all over the place and enable price manipulation, front-running, the whole market volatility package that dealers make their living from.

Once markets become dominated by dealers there's no incentive to design the market in the public interest. The market is designed not for the buyer or the seller but for the intermediary.

I pursued the idea of a single price auction because it was obviously a better way to do things. In effect everyone agrees it's a better way to do things. But so many people told me it was impossible because of the huge institutions who would be opposed to it. That made it more attractive. I left Kidder in February of 1990, and at that same time Kerry Yndestad and Chris Moran, two computer executives, left Cray Research to help me build the system.

It's a system that theoretically could be offered on any platform, but we've offered it so far on a PC platform. Users dial into our system over phone lines. The evening auction takes place at five: they can dial in from four-o-clock on and view the order books and place orders. They have to put in their account number, the size of the order, and the price. We're operating every day now. The orders are executed in terms of first price-priority and then time-priority. The bids above the auction price and the offers below it are filled.

It's certainly true that the validity of prices comes from the number of people trading at any given time. There's no reason why you couldn't have a worldwide call market. Markets began as call markets. The reason markets became intermediated in the first place was they couldn't grow in the absence of technology without resorting to intermediation. Now that you have technology, it's quite possible to create a worldwide market in a single room on a single computer, with all participants trading at the same time, receiving the same price, and having the same access. One of the great things about an electronic call market is that it allows the buy-side, sell-side, retail investors—active and passive investors—all to trade at the same time and price. It can make a fairer market for everyone.

33

■ ■ ■

EXCHANGE AUTOMATION

*"The ability to trade options and stocks on the
same system."*

■ JIM JONES

*The NYSE had trouble finding a chairman to take over for John Phelan
when he retired at the end of the 1980s. "They got a lot of turndowns,"
said one Big Board watcher. But Jim Jones, a U.S. congressman for
twenty years and chairman of the House Budget Committee, has an
even tougher job. Assuming the post of chairman of the American
Stock Exchange early in 1990, Jones—a pleasant, low-key man—is
faced with the challenge of taking the nation's second-biggest exchange
and making it an important international force.*

The industry here and overseas is changing dramatically in the
next four years. It's going to be a high-risk, high-opportunity environment.

The industry has gone through certain periods in which external
events changed the way things are done. One of these events is the
post-Sputnik 1960s which created all sorts of technology. We had a
whole new system on Nasdaq based on automation. I think the event
of the 1980s that is germinating is the creation of a true world marketplace.
The question is how to get ahead of the crowd.

A lot of consolidation is going to happen as a result of Europe
1992. In this country there will be a winnowing to perhaps not more
than two auction-based markets and one electronic market taking on
the respectability of the auction market. The regional exchanges will

have a very difficult time. I think there'll be a lot of new players in the game.

As we look to our strategic challenge, it's clearly in the international area, and we have to look at structural alliances. We now have two linkages with Reuters. The first one includes the CBOE too. That gives the individual the ability to trade options and stocks on the same system. If we are successful in getting other foreign exchanges on the system it becomes a global network. If you're looking for market share and revenues it's good because it can become a dominant system.

The NYSE didn't move as fast as we did in products like options. I'm not sure why. Maybe because they're bigger. It's like the difference between turning around a battleship and a PT boat. I think we are more flexible and have traditionally been more innovative especially with our derivative products like the Nikkei warrants that allow you to get on board the Japanese market and decide which way it's moving.

I'm not that familiar with the internal workings of the NYSE, but I can tell you with this exchange I spent the first eight months "painting the noose to focus the mind." The world is changing radically. You can always go back and see how the steam engine affected the horse and buggy trade. Today, there is no longer an industry. At the Amex, the resistance to some of our new ideas has been virtually nothing from the floor. I've told them, this is the way the world is evolving.

But personally I find it hard to believe that the human element of the marketplace is going to be dropped. We're definitely going to be putting a lot more money into technology. We'll be going to more automated systems, but I think it will be a blend. My feeling is that there will be a combination of automation and the auction system where you will have human beings involved. How it will sort out is hard to tell. We're studying these issues—we're in the process of developing a strategic plan to take the Exchange into the 1990s.

I think at this exchange we have an opportunity to reach out to the individual investor. Automation can be of supplementary help. The day-traders, for instance, are a source of liquidity, very much so. Hopefully we'll come out with a bold approach. If we are able to do some of the things we plan to do, it will not be without controversy.

■ RALPH MCNEAL

Ralph McNeal is a venture capitalist who at one time was president of General Foods Corp.'s North Street Capital investment subsidiary. Along with a dozen or so other entrepreneurs, he says he's been planning to build his exchange for nearly a decade—exploring foreign exchanges and investigating automated technologies to find the best combination for his automated capital exchange.

What we've planned is an exchange that will be a combination physical and automated trading facility. Every month, for one week or so, brokers and members will participate in physical exchange trading. For the rest of the month trading will take place from a variety of sites around the U.S. where the members and brokers are located. We'll have three market-makers: one in the east, one in the west, and one in the middle. We'll have automated safeguards to assure everyone's safety and honesty.

Companies would come to us, smaller, growth-oriented companies. They'll have a capital need of $2 to $25 million, and they'll have already gone the venture capital route by the time they hit us. Historically, they'll stay with us three to five years before moving on to a bigger exchange.

We've examined a variety of options for the automated portion of the exchange, but we haven't made any decisions. We've looked at Germany's new automated exchange and also Vancouver, Canada's new network. We've taken a look at Instinet. We haven't ruled out an auction-style effort similar to Wunsch's. There's lots of options.

We want to construct our own rules, create our own securities tests and build our own group of exchange brokers responsible to the entrepreneurial community that we want to serve. It wouldn't be worth doing, if it weren't tough to do.

What we intend is to offer 100 seats over a period of five years. These seats have been applied for by entrepreneurs around the country in 25 cities in 13 states. These members in turn will hire brokers to buy and sell the stock to be traded on the exchange. Since the brokers will work for entrepreneurs with a stake in the companies they are bringing to market, the amount of customer abuse by the middle-men can be held down.

There are over 40,000 OTC companies that would be eligible for trading on this exchange and another 500,000 private companies who have nowhere to turn for investment capital except banks. I hope this exchange will be able to raise as much capital as a deserving company needs. It'll be led by experienced entrepreneurs—brokers and members won't hesitate to raise as much capital as a company needs.

Since we'll mostly be trading small blocks of stock, I expect there'll be considerable small investor participation. We're looking at small pension funds and other institutions who want to participate in growth opportunities but currently can't find enough of them.

34
∎∎∎

AUTOMATED FUTURES

*"**F**utures trading wouldn't just be restricted to members
of the big exchanges."*

∎ GLEN WINDSTRUP

*Glen Windstrup worked for 18 years at the Chicago Merc before
leaving in the early 1980s to build and market his own PC-based
automated futures trading system worldwide. He has had startling success
selling the system, most recently in New York, where it is the centerpiece
of the New York Mercantile Exchange's electronic after-hours trading
system.*

I helped build and run the trading systems at the Merc—I learned
automation is a great thing, but you have to beware, too. The psychology
of the pit may be hurt by automation. We've attempted to build into
the automated trading system, things which could not be done in the
pit. Take automated spreads, which analyze and hook and execute a
buy or sell order based on the price differential between them, automatically at the discretion of the trader.

It took the Merc and Reuters a lot of time to come up with
Globex, the worldwide trading system that they've been trying to install.
In 1984 or 1985 they started talking. Globex is ambitious. It has the
assumption of a much larger user base than the systems I've currently
installed. It has appeal to a large number of people who want to trade
the same thing. The CBOT is also involved with it. The negotiations
have gotten quite complex.

But it's simple business economics: Reuters is a for-profit organization, and it wants to make a lot of monthly income off the hardware. The Merc wants costs kept down so more traders will use the system. That's a big conflict. That's why it's taken them so many years.

Our company is different. We move quickly and we're lighter on our feet. Globex will have a very real value-added component for a certain kind of user, but my futures trading systems are smaller and cheaper. Traders can customize my systems—I would think they'd be able to hook our computers into the Reuters systems if they want, when it happens.

The way we're set up is that our software can be used by standard IBM-compatible microprocessors and phone lines. That means we can be installed conveniently in various regions worldwide. I've placed automated systems in Australia at the Sydney Futures Exchange, at the London FOX (futures and options exchange) and trading floor systems at the Winnipeg Commodity Exchange. Domestically, we've placed our automated system at the New York Mercantile Exchange.

We hope, in the future, to facilitate the interaction between the futures exchanges and the spot market, which deals in physical deliveries. I'm hopeful, for instance, that within two years I'll have feedlot placements. Farms and cooperatives can use these systems. Peoria and Sioux City could look at the same data. Futures trading wouldn't just be restricted to members of the big exchanges.

By putting this information on a terminal, it allows many to relate to many instead of many to few. We increase liquidity and price discovery. This makes the markets more efficient, and it may bring down prices because you're bringing down, in some cases, exchange overhead.

Electronic trading will ultimately enable many more interrelationships than is currently possible on a physical trading floor. Regulators will be able to monitor multiple markets because systems like ours install complete and comprehensive audit trails. And with systems like ours, you have access to the full order book—at any time a regulator can see the entire book of orders, which is quite useful when you're trying to make a determination about a market event.

35

■ ■ ■

INTERNATIONAL TRADING

"These days there's a whole new universe of technology."

■ DONALD UNRUH

Former vice president of international trading at the Toronto Stock Exchange, Donald Unruh has licensed exchange simulation software he has developed to a consortium of European dealers. The dealers may eventually recommend new electronic markets for the European community.

I've helped automate most of Europe. I served as the vice president of the Toronto exchange for 12 years. I put in the Cats system and I automated the equity and bond market for France. I developed the proprietary systems for Toronto, France, Spain, and Brazil. In fact Spain's system is a national market system linked to Madrid, Barcelona, Valencia, and Bilbao.

These days there's a whole new universe of technology. I can now, for instance, design an automated system that would allow for trading rules changes on the fly depending on conditions in the market. Cats will support up to 30 different types of limit orders, all or none orders, stop-loss orders. But I can do much more now.

There are supercomputers and supercomputers on a chip which are able to do pattern analysis using the methods of the brain itself. They're able to spot anomalous behavior in the market; but there is no one using supercomputers for such applications from the Japanese—NEC. Dow Jones is moving in that direction. Telerate runs an

artificial intelligence system that reads news data and correlates that
data with price action. It develops a kind of early warning about
possible upcoming deals. Dow Jones reporters have spotted several
mergers that way, I believe. And a system like Cats will actually
halt stocks and follow the paper trail in certain situations. So guys
tend to modify their behavior. The industry doesn't want too much
of this.

Change comes slowly. Before the Big Bang I stood up in front
of these firms in the City of London and I told them my model
suggested they were going to get killed if they went ahead with a
Nasdaq-type system and tried to compete at the spreads then found
on the NYSE. What happened? Equities market-makers lost more than
$1 billion in equity capital in their first two years of operation. Inter-
professional spreads shrank to within 0.1 percent of the NYSE.

They don't have a lot of small participation in the advertised
London market, although share-ownership has gone public, with
privatizations, and 20 percent of the population owns shares today.
It's not like in the U.S.—buy a share of America. And since the big
orders were clearly visible, every time you bought or sold you got
picked off. Everyone was just waiting for a large order to come across
the screen. They're trying to change it now.

Anyway, my system was very rough then. Now it's more refined.
I finally left the Toronto exchange in June of 1989. In the past, there
have been academic studies, but no one has ever developed a computer
model that will allow researchers or market professionals to make
their own assumptions about the best market structure or order flow,
and then test them on a computer.

Right now there are no ways to determine what markets work
best other than by trial and error, and just because one market's spread
is better than another's doesn't mean there isn't some other system
out there that would be better than both. That's what I'd like to find
out. A preferable system should have several characteristics. For one
thing, it should minimize the gap in the marketplace between the highest
price buyers want to pay for securities and the lowest price sellers
are willing to accept for their stocks or bonds.

This is called the spread, and it is considered to be a primary
indicator of efficient markets. That's the academic perspective: The
lowest average spread between all the buy orders and all the sell
orders is the most efficient market. And it should behave predictably
when markets are under stress—but no one else has evaluated alternative

market structures under peak trading conditions. Some surprises can be found here.

By that criterion, the NYSE is still the most efficient market in the world. But they've been irresponsible at the NYSE. They're not evolving, and they're going to lose their edge. It has internal gridlock because of politics.

The best market would also be the most liquid market, and also the fairest. A truly fair market gives the buyer the lowest possible prices and the seller the highest price. The best market would also place a priority on timeliness—operating on a first-come first-served basis. That's the traditional approach. But there may also be fairness in giving an edge to customers who routinely buy and sell large blocks of stock since they provide liquidity. The liquidity in turn reduces market impact, that is, the price concessions needed to place large orders quickly.

To build my program I used Simscript II.5—a specialized simulation language which is the same language being used by NATO military planners for their battle-management simulations of the European tactical theater. I used the simulation system to write the software. It is a live, PC-based trading system which can automate exchanges doing in excess of ten trades per second, or 50,000 trades a day.

■ ROGER BARTON

Roger Barton is managing director of business development for the London International Financial Futures Exchange (LIFFE). He came to the exchange in 1982 and later assumed the title of managing director of technical services. In this capacity, he worked on systems, including the exchange's after-hours automated pit trading. LIFFE completed a merger with the London Traded Options Market in 1992. LIFFE's volume, both on the floor and on the screen-based system, is growing at a very healthy rate.

During our fifth year we did a strategic study and determined we should develop an automated trading system. We determined this first because it was clear that automated trading would become increasingly important. The second reason was that we felt we should have a trading capability after the close of business hours.

The requirement was to set up an automated trading system that could potentially be implemented in a flexible manner—initially for products after hours and at a later date for contracts better suited to automated trading than pit trading. That turned into the Automated Pit Trading systems we now have.

We looked at various systems already in production. We felt that automated order matching systems were OK for quiet products, but for products with potentially high volume—including major products outside normal trading hours—we wanted to produce something which had greater speed and flexibility. We had the idea of producing a system which retains the principles and dynamics of open outcry on a screen. Traders are represented by icons on the screen, and each trader is able to buy and sell on the screen by manipulating the icons.

The Chicago Board of Trade attempted a similar route with its Aurora product. One major difference between the two systems was that in APT traders cannot choose their counterparties, whereas in Aurora this was possible. What we came up with was a system in which traders are represented by icons on the screen and they have to manually pick off buys and sells on the screen. The difference between our system and say, the Chicago Board of Trade's system, Aurora, is that our system is anonymous. That makes it harder to prearrange trades.

We developed a model and showed it to members in the Spring of 1988. We implemented it in November 1989. What we did was we said we would implement the system for one product, the Bund, the German government bond. The Bund trading worked out, so two weeks later we implemented the Euro mark. In 1990 we introduced seven or eight contracts after hours and then in April of 1991, we introduced Japanese government bonds during the day.

We did make some changes for daytime trading. We developed Atom, an automated facility that allows the system to automatically store and match orders, a function we had previously left out. Now, if your buy or sell order finds the right price in the system, it can be automatically executed. We like to think now the system combines the open outcry of the physical exchange with the kind of order matching that only an electronic trading system offers.

There were a lot of members who weren't sure APT was going to be profitable, but members taking it have found it at least washes its face. Quite a few members have ordered increased numbers of terminals.

The London Traded Options Market, LTOM, is currently part of the London Stock Exchange and is merging with LIFFE. Both are financial derivatives markets, so there should be economies of scale. Many of our customers also trade options.

We've started development of an options automated system. The existing APT system needs to be further enhanced to include order-routing and analytics like the equity options pricing model. Eventually our members will probably be able to trade options and futures on one platform, one system.

We're developing at quite a pace, and I believe the APT, in its after hours use, has attracted additional volume to our market.

36

■ ■ ■

INDEXING

"Picking winning managers is difficult. Indexing becomes the counsel of despair."

■ PETER BERNSTEIN

Peter Bernstein's father founded the well-known investment firm of Bernstein Macaulay, and Peter took over in 1951. In 1967, the firm was acquired by a five-year-old Carter, Berlind & Weill—a firm that included young Sandy Weill, who would later build a powerhouse brokerage called Shearson and go on to run the financial conglomerate Primerica Corp. Bernstein gave up active money management in 1973 for consulting and writing.

A huge amount of the investing community looks down on indexing. But indexed money is $300 or $400 billion now, about 15 percent of the market. That means, however, that 85 percent of all money managers still think that active managers can outperform the market.

I'm attracted to indexing on two scores: the market is substantially efficient because there are too many bright people in there all trying to outguess one another—so the competition is very hot. Beating the numbers with any consistency strikes me as impossible unless you are a plunger—and then you could lose big. And second, people who know how to get rich can do so by doing it themselves. Most of the investment advisers I know have gotten rich from selling their services, not investing.

Of course, every year, some managers are going to outperform the market. And there is something to the hot hand theory—they did well last year, so there's a better than even probability they'll do well this year. But that still doesn't tell you about next year. Anyway, picking winning managers is really extremely difficult, even if it is possible to beat the market from time to time. In this sense indexing becomes the counsel of despair. There's nothing I know that can predict a Peter Lynch. And there will be more Peter Lynches, but I think it's impossible to identify them ahead of time.

Indexing really began to spread after the rocky markets of 1974. People were really shaken up by it, particularly after the big rise in the market in the late 1960s and 1970s. Then the bubble burst and people had egg on their face. They said, "There's got to be a better way."

During the 1980s, the percentage of managers beating the S&P 500 began to decline—and the move toward indexing ballooned. Nowadays people are no longer simply indexing plain vanilla indexes—they've become enhanced indexers. This is an entirely new area of investing that, in my opinion, has only just begun to grow. There's been an evolution into novel and sophisticated products for controlling risk relative to return.

I want people to understand what's going on—and to be made aware of what they might do to these new kinds of products down in Washington. You can't simply shut down the markets the way some of these politicians have suggested.

Indexed investing is succeeding because it makes sense in terms of cost and is getting results. Indexed investing is very inexpensive. If my expected margin of beating the market is 100 basis points, and then I spend a lot of money trading in and out of the market and paying for it in transaction costs, I may lose my profits in the mechanics of investing.

But index funds on the whole are less volatile than undiversified portfolios and have far less turnover. You can predict trading patterns relative to the market. Informationless trades that rely on tracking a given group of securities—rather than specific information about how specific securities might do—are bound to generate lower transaction costs because the brokers' spreads will be tighter. Informationless trading can be much less expensive. If you know something, you want to get that stock into your portfolio today. Then you're paying an additional price for your need to hurry. It's hard to beat an index for economy or efficiency.

Anything that interferes with liquidity raises the cost of capital. Collars, sidecars, the kinds of trading halts that the regulators and exchanges have put in place, all make it more difficult for stockholders to buy or sell equity instruments. When you can't transact, securities become less valuable, and I see no reason why they should end up less volatile. I'd rather have the option of trading 24 hours a day than see exchanges shut down for any length of time. Would automated markets help—I would think so.

Of course, there's no trend in life that you can extrapolate out forever. It's a fact that as customized, indexed, derivative instruments become a larger portion of domestic and international trading, there will eventually be a backlash.

There's a limit to how commoditized the market can become before the profits to be made from those forms of investing will diminish. Corporations may actively seek to invest in less easily traded instruments. The returns for old-fashioned stock-picking may get higher. And, in the end, those fancy instruments have to be priced against the traditional cash market. But new regulations, ways of trying to organize or protect the marketplace won't help. People will just circumvent them. You have to let the free market take its course.

It's possible that the 1980s insider traders wouldn't have made so much money if there were more people with more money to invest and more systems to help them figure out what was going on. The profession of investment management is clean, but it operates in a sea of fraud. More automation, more liquidity in these new derivative products will alleviate difficulties. If market manipulation is held to be harmful, then you can alleviate it by opening up the system, not shutting it down. That's the way to deal with fraud.

■ WILLIAM JAHNKE

William Jahnke is chairman of Vestek Systems, a San Francisco-based portfolio systems and risk analytics firm with several hundred clients domestically and abroad. Vestek was founded by a group of former Wells Fargo employees: Jahnke worked in the original Wells Fargo group that experimented with program trading back in the 1970s.

There's magic out there, the magic of capital ideas. According to the efficient market theory, you can't beat the market. You can figure out, perhaps, how to invest in something that others only catch on to after you have. But once you figure out a way to beat the market, others will catch on too. You can't keep winning; sooner or later the opportunities will disappear.

Now there's an alternative. The alternative is to try to invest so broadly in the market that you can track its overall performance. That way you can predict that you'll never do worse than the market as a whole. Since markets, especially stock markets, tend to go up in time, you're virtually assured that what you're investing will turn a profit over time. This kind of investing is called passive investing because it involves quantifying risk and reward—trading baskets of stocks to match the performance of market indexes. Combine passive investing with automation and computer power, and it all falls into place. And it did in the 1980s.

But now I think there is a grounded fear that people will react against this kind of investing. There's some prospect that reactionary forces will prevail, despite the fact that the horse is out of the barn—market forces and technological forces will ultimately win out. The academic community already understands these arguments. Sooner or later the regulators and politicians will too.

People have always reacted against new technologies. There was once some call for eliminating the telephone as a way to get rid of trading volatility back in the early 1900s. The introduction of the telephone was viewed as a way of overwhelming the specialists on the floor of the Big Board. Its access was supposed to be tightly controlled.

These days you can use a computer through the gamut of investment decisions. You can use it for research and portfolio decisions—deciding what it is you want to invest in. Then you can use it to figure out what indexes, combinations of indexes, you want to track. Once you've figured out the indexes, you can create a portfolio of representative securities to track the chosen index. You can calculate the risk—the beta we call it—of how far off, on average, from the index, your performance will fall.

What we help institutional investors do is pick indexes and provide systems to manage passive strategies. Once the portfolios are invested, we can help keep track of how those portfolios are doing. We store our clients' portfolio information in our computers, and they gain access to that information and to the software with which they can manipulate that data, through high speed modems and phone lines connected to PCs at the client site.

That's our business. We charge clients for their computer time. Now we're starting to offer packages of our portfolio management software and analytics for use at the client site. The client can use the system without being hooked up to us. In the future, more and more clients will be able to perform quantitative activities on their own. Vendors will be packagers, providing mixes of services and software.

Some people see technology as a threat to their vested interests; some see the involvement of technology as causing a collapse within the securities industry. In fact we're going to see a restructuring of the industry.

There's always a distribution of players. There are leaders and followers, less of the former, more of the latter. Then there are those lobbying against change. The goal of lobbying is to slow things down by pointing to flaws and problems.

People say quantitative investing involves speculation, as if that were a dirty word. The role of speculators is to take risks others are not willing to take. They are the ones seeking out opportunity. Anyway, the least speculative kind of investing may be to buy some of everything—which is what passive investors are trying to do.

Derivatives have come under attack. But derivatives open up a new dimension of opportunity for the management of risk and for the leveraging of positions and so it is not surprising that there is a wealth of opportunity for those who make use of these strategies. There's just so much latent opportunity in derivatives.

We needed some things to take place before all this could happen. We needed the theoretical underpinnings. We needed the tools computers have provided. We needed people who knew how to use those tools. Finally we needed a convergence of interests within the financial community. In the case of indexers, it happened to be how to provide cash management and investments at the least possible cost. In the case of Wall Street, it had to do with risk control, with laying off the risk of their market exposure.

It's true, passive investing makes for a huge change in the way business is being done. And it's happened relatively quickly. Batterymarch developed a trading program where brokers and other interested parties could dial in to Batterymarch and take a position against their list.

The kinds of trading that Wells did in the mid-1970s and later had to do with laying off the execution risks by having brokerage houses compete for the trade, a package trade—the package being more than one security, a basket of securities, a program trade, in other words.

Any system takes a while to adjust. Any new technology can be abused. But automated systems, automated trading, and the ability to capture the trade electronically reduces significantly the opportunity for manipulation.

Markets are inherently risky. There's nothing, ultimately, you can do to make any market safe. Automated trading is happening as we speak. There are systems being built and the volume of trading is growing. I hold a fundamental belief that the technological answers will prevail. In the final analysis, they will best serve the interests of the beneficial owners of the assets being managed.

37

■ ▨ ■

SWAPS AND DERIVATIVES

"Every day someone says the market will blow up."

■ PAUL SPRAOS

Paul Spraos, a former investment banker, is founder and publisher of Swaps Monitor, *"the newsletter for the financial risk management professional," founded in 1987.*

Both swaps and other derivative off-exchange instruments are vehicles for transferring risk. The use of this market has grown tremendously—with more than $3 or $4 trillion in various kinds of swaps now outstanding. Wall Street is the middle man in such transactions—either providing a tailored instrument directly for a customer or arranging with a third party to supply it.

The terms swaps, OTC derivatives, and off-exchange instruments mean essentially the same thing. They refer to a family of instruments whose members include interest rate and currency swaps, commodity swaps, and equity options. These instruments are private transactions which take place over the counter, and are individually tailored to meet the precise needs of two parties.

The date I use for the start of the modern swap market is August 1981. Two things happened in that month. The first was the introduction of the first IBM PC, which allowed people to make complex calculations fast enough to keep up with the market. The other event was a very famous currency swap between IBM and the World Bank, which gave the product legitimacy.

The options and futures exchanges have benefited massively from swaps and derivatives growth. The Eurodollar futures contracts on the Merc are so successful in part because they are widely used to hedge interest rate swaps and options.

Despite the obvious benefits, the Chicago futures exchanges have been very hostile to the growth of off-exchange products. They don't seem to recognize that off-exchange and exchange-traded instruments are complementary to each other.

You can think of it this way. Futures are liquid but blunt. Off-exchange instruments are less liquid and more sophisticated. Each needs the other. It's unfortunate that some of the exchanges don't see this.

In the summer of 1989, the CFTC came out with a set of safe harbor rules which basically said that as long as you meet certain conditions a swap, and certain other derivatives, will not be subject to CFTC jurisdiction.

A major safeguard included in those tests is that the swaps cannot be marketed to the general public. Swaps are complex instruments and I think it's good public policy that widows and orphans be appropriately protected.

The CFTC came out with these safe harbor rules despite pressure from the Chicago exchanges for greater regulation of the swap market. The credit for that goes to the CFTC—they are not in the pocket of the industry they regulate. Of course the swap market lobbied actively too, led by The International Swaps Dealers Association in New York. I suppose, for the Chicago exchanges, the fear is that swaps and derivatives pose a competitive threat.

But the Chicago exchanges are only one side of the equation. The New York commodity exchanges have seen the advent of swaps and embraced them. They've adopted contracts specifically to meet the needs of the swap community.

Although there are protections against swaps being used by individuals, the benefits of these instruments nevertheless trickle down to the personal level. Here's an illustration: Banks will allow you to lock in your rate at the time you apply for a fixed-rate mortgage. But in doing so, they run a risk that interest rates may move in the wrong direction. But, using swaps and other derivatives, that's a risk that can be hedged by the lender, providing an option for the borrower which might not be available as cheaply otherwise.

When people get burned it's normally for one or two reasons. Either they try to take more risk than they're able to handle, or they don't understand the risks. But I don't think you can force swaps and derivatives to trade on exchanges. If you try, or if you impose some artificial regulation, the market will simply flee overseas to a more favorable environment. The immediate effects will be a loss of jobs and the possible disappearance of the huge competitive advantage for the U.S. of having an efficient hedge against risk.

As Wall Street firms gain more understanding of risk, they're able to offer more products. In the early '80s you could swap interest rates or currencies. By the late '80s you could also swap commodities and equities. In the future you'll be able to swap many other things as well.

Of course it's easy to slam Wall Street. I call it the California Earthquake phenomenon. On any given day, for the next few years, someone, somewhere, can probably predict an earthquake in California and sooner or later someone may be right. That doesn't make the person a genius, that just makes him lucky. From the predictor's point of view, it's a no-lose situation.

The same thing is happening in the derivative markets. Every day someone says the market will blow up. But anyone can predict an earthquake, and the naysayers must explain why. And I haven't heard any sensible reasons as to why.

For all the attention that is given to the risks that are supposedly associated with swaps, two things are forgotten. One is that there is no such thing as reward without risk. The other is that swaps are very important risk-reducing instruments. For example, suppose that one financial institution is exposed to the risk of interest rates rising, another to the risk of them falling. By entering into a swap, both can reduce risk.

What I'm saying is that OTC derivatives don't necessarily increase risk. The reality is much more complex. I'm no expert on exchanges and exchange structure, but I think it's clear that many of them are not as efficient as they could be. They've been hampered by the effects of time and changing technology on an inflexible regulatory regime. Imposing greater regulation on swaps isn't appropriate because there's no evidence that it's needed or that it's good public policy.

38

■ ■ ■

CLEARING AND SETTLEMENT

*"**M**arket volatility is the tip of the risk iceberg."*

■ ALAN LOSS

An engineering graduate, Alan Loss began his career in the Management Services Department at Arthur D. Little and was then hired by the New York Stock Exchange as the youngest vice president in its history. He now owns his own firm, Asset Management Technology Corporation (Amtech), which consults on securities issues and runs an annual global financial industry conference.

In the place of what is today a series of many exchanges, clearing houses, and settlement agencies, we'll eventually see a global market. It could even be one that would give you the ability to transact underlying instruments and derivatives on a single screen.

It's not going to happen overnight. Despite the efforts of regulators and industry organizations such as the Group of Thirty, we don't even have agreement between institutional and retail firms as to how soon settlement—when money changes hands—needs to happen after a trade, three days or five days. We can't even agree in this country, let alone agree with the rest of the world.

But it's bound to happen. Here's an example. Back in the 1960s when I was with ADL, I helped design an electronic pink sheet quotation network, a system now called Nasdaq. The NASD members had a vested interest in keeping pink sheet prices off such an electronic system. But we kept at it. We had meetings with dealers around the country and finally convinced enough of them to come on board.

We told the critics that we agreed with their forecast, namely if you create a central system it would force competition that would narrow the spread, meaning less profit for the dealer. But the narrower spread between buy and sell orders—and an automated system would generate more interest in the market—and the profits of dealers would also go up. They would lose a little on each trade, but they'd make it up in volume.

Businesses are supposed to optimize long-term profits. If you can convince a significant group that it's in their long term interest, such as coordinating and integrating international trading, clearing and settlement issues, it will eventually happen.

In the meantime, there are great risks. One of the studies we're doing is called "The Hidden Risks of International Investing. "Pension fund foundations and endowments are using apparently sophisticated asset allocation models to allocate their assets based on the relative risk and return of various markets. The only risk factored into these models is market volatility. Market volatility is the tip of the risk iceberg. Think about the potential write-offs of investments in emerging markets. In Hong Kong, after the 1987 crash, the market was closed for three days—until the authorities pressured the members of the clearing house to contribute $250 million so that it could reopen. Think what would happen if a market was closed at the time that funds had to price and report their positions. How many would dump their holdings—would say, take me out at any cost, for fifty cents on the dollar. People don't get it.

Here's another example. Say you're involved in international arbitrage. You buy an instrument in one market and sell it for a derivative, in another. But if your trade doesn't settle in both markets, you only complete one side of your trade. You've bought a lot of something but you haven't sold anything else to offset the position. That means you're not hedged. You think you're in a position to make a riskless profit when you go to bed. Instead, you wake up and you own a lot of risk.

In Italy, for instance, they recently had a significant percentage of trades that failed to settle on time. Their problem of late settlement was publicized. Now they've spent a lot of money and improved. But it's not the case elsewhere.

It's very worrisome that in this country clearing and settlement risks and potential costs aren't taken into account in asset allocation models. Only some of the largest international investors understand and habitually factor in international settlement risk. They take a haircut—up to thirty percent. That means they'll reduce any perceived profit on trades in some countries up to that amount and then see if it's still worthwhile doing the trade. It keeps them out of a lot of trades; it also keeps them out of trouble.

In this country we have a built-in advantage, one we should be using. You've got this shoe company in Country XYZ and another listed on the NYSE. If the expected return of the foreign company is greater than the U.S. company, U.S. institutional investors will purchase it. It offers higher return and diversification. That's fine, but it also offers credit risks, systematic risks, legal and regulatory risks not confronted when one purchases a security in the United States. Clearing a trade at National Security Clearing Corporation and settling it at Depository Trust Company is not "risk-free," but it's far less risky than clearance and settlement system facilities in most markets abroad.

The NYSE and NASD should emphasize the reliability of our clearance and settlement system. In this country we have an elaborate regulatory system to back up the clearance and settlement process. If clearance and settlement is good, people can sleep nights.

In order to get more overseas companies listed on the NYSE, the Big Board is seeking to have the SEC relax reporting requirements for these companies. Instead of having to report to the public four times a year, the NYSE is asking to list overseas companies who are now required to report less information, and less frequently. So far, in their attempt to protect the public interest, regulators don't even bring up the reliability of our clearance and settlement systems. If a U.S. investor wants to buy a foreign company, it's safer for them to buy it in the United States. Why should Fidelity Investments trade with Dreyfus and the California pension plan, Calpers, in Jakarta when the trade can be done in the United States?

We should work within the current structure in this country to bring order to a common market. I'm all for new networks but a lot can be done with what we've built. We don't have to tear down the NYSE, just make it more responsive to investors and less captive to member greed and fear, especially the fear of change. Emphasize to the public and to the international investment community that U.S. markets have much to offer.

Let's not pressure regulators to lower standards. That's not the answer. Regulators aren't at fault. Actually the customer is to blame. They're the ones who have to bring pressure on overseas markets to improve their clearance and settlement processes. If the customer doesn't differentiate between the non-market risks, that is, credit, systems, and regulatory and legal environments in Mexico and Jakarta, Italy, France, and New York, why should anyone try to improve?

■ THOMAS A. RUSSO

Thomas Russo is one of a few in the financial markets industry with experience on both sides of that industry's regulatory divide. In the 1970s, he was a staff attorney at the SEC's Division of Market Regulation and subsequently became the first director of the CFTC's Division of Trading and Markets. He has published numerous books and articles concerning securities and commodities regulation with a focus upon how our regulatory system applies to derivative and hybrid products.

Russo assisted in the 1987 Brady Commission investigating the stock market crash and has been a partner at New York's Cadwalader, Wickersham & Taft law firm since 1977.

The clearance and settlement of financial instruments normally takes a back-burner role in the minds of most people. This is so because clearance and settlement issues are probably the most complicated and the least glamorous issues around. Also, because money ordinarily is made in sales and not in the "back office" aspect of business it is not surprising that these issues often fade into the background. Nevertheless, in light of the reality that the clearing and settlement process goes to the heart of a transaction's financial integrity, its importance cannot be overstated.

In the United States, much needs to be done in this critical area. There are economically equivalent instruments traded on various domestic exchanges that are subject to substantially different clearing mechanisms. In fact, there is a lack of certainty as to the extent of clearinghouses' financial obligations with respect to instruments traded on exchanges affiliated with those clearinghouses. Many of these concerns were mentioned in the reports after the 1987 stock market crash, including the Brady Report. We need to have a much more concerted effort in this country regarding clearing issues so that participants in our marketplace will understand what a particular mechanism does guarantee and how that guarantee will work in a financial disaster scenario.

On the international level, the United States has a clear competitive advantage over other nations in this area. Even though our clearing and settlement systems are disjointed and, to some extent, lack the clarity that some would like, they are far superior to equivalent systems abroad. Effective customer fund segregation, net capital and margin rules, give the United States' markets a well-deserved reputation as the safest in the world in which to do business.

In contrast to the United States, most countries have not developed a statutory body of law with respect to market integrity and customer protection issues. Regulators, exchanges, and self-regulatory organizations have rule books in the United States that are much thicker than those abroad and we have a body of case law that helps clarify some of those rules. Thus, there is much more certitude in the United States regarding the financial integrity of transactions and participants in the marketplace than in other countries.

As with most competitive advantages, one can only rely upon them for a short period of time, because competition itself undoubtedly will close the gap. The result is that this nation's leaders must devote the time and energy necessary to continue to improve in this area to maintain our competitive advantage.

Perhaps just as important as improvements in our clearing process is the need to solve the fundamental problems of our regulatory structure. Financial products are governed by a number of laws, some of which are, on their face, contradictory. Many financial products are subject to regulation by the SEC, while others are regulated by the CFTC. Because there is significant overlap in the regulatory reach of these two agencies, many products could be governed by both the SEC and CFTC. This has caused not only uncertainty with respect to new product development but has, on several occasions, resulted in litigation involving both agencies.

This regulatory monopoly given to exchanges in conjunction with the uncertainty surrounding the definition of "futures contracts" has proven burdensome for those who seek to develop products that could only be traded efficiently and practically on securities exchanges or, alternatively, in the over-the-counter market. The reality is that if a product is considered to be a futures contract, it will be forbidden to be traded in the United States even if it were proposed to be traded on a securities exchange with all the protections afforded under the federal securities laws. This has caused a chilling effect on financial innovation in the United States and an exodus of new products to overseas markets.

Over the past several years, the SEC and CFTC have found themselves in court over the issue of which agency should have jurisdiction over particular products. But the fundamental issue with respect to innovative products should not be which agency has jurisdiction, but rather, whether the offer and sale of the product meets fundamental customer protection, safety, and soundness criteria. It perhaps makes more sense to have a coordinated regulatory structure or, indeed, one regulator for financial products, with the primary goal of permitting new products to trade where the public is protected and the safety and soundness of the market is preserved. Such a system stands in stark contrast to our present structure in which resources are wasted fighting over which agency has jurisdiction.

Our present regulatory structure was developed, essentially, in the 1930s. During that time, a "futures contract" meant instruments that managed risk primarily with respect to agricultural products, and the term "securities" primarily meant stocks and bonds. In the last decade, however, the futures industry evolved into a financial services industry, while the securities industry became involved with derivative financial products. In short, the products offered both industries became much more of a "scrambled egg," making distinctions between the definition of a security and a futures contract increasingly difficult. The regulatory system, however, continued to draw the same clear lines based upon these definitions. Having a regulatory system that has not kept pace with the products it regulates hampers creativity and, sadly, has made us our own worst enemy.

One good example of how we hurt ourselves competitively without corresponding benefits arises in the area of mutual funds and commodity pools. Presently, it is possible to create a mutual fund that trades stocks and bonds and to create a commodity pool that trades futures. If one should want to set up a public vehicle to trade both, however, our laws forbid doing so. This, obviously, makes little sense because today identical vehicles can be established, one to trade securities and the other to trade futures, when the regulatory structure governing each provides substantially equivalent protections. Because either structure provides adequate protections, it appears nonsensical that U.S. entities cannot do it all under one roof.

39

■ ■ ■

EXCHANGE COMPETITIVENESS

"Our industry ought not to be so reluctant to change that we give up the dominant position we have today."

■ DONALD WEEDEN

Perhaps no single individual in the financial industry had more of an impact in the late 1960s and the 1970s than Donald Weeden, the son of "third market" pioneer Frank Weeden. With his brothers, Don Weeden took over the family firm and entered into a historic debate with the SEC, Wall Street, and the NYSE over the securities industry's regulated commission structure and other practices that restricted participation in the nation's financial marketplace.

Weeden won a Pyrrhic victory. In 1975, Congress deregulated the commission structure of the securities industry, but by the late 1970s Weeden's own firm had begun to fail. Today, Weeden & Co. is back in business, but as a full-fledged member of the Big Board.

One of the things the NYSE understood before anyone else was that giving out real-time information on trades was an enormous marketing tool. It drew listing, brokers, it drew the volume of business away from other markets. The old ticker tape came with NYSE prices. Everybody watched that and then naturally went to New York to execute that trade.

The other thing NYSE understood was the continuity of the market. The NYSE set up their specialist system so you could always find the market, no matter how small. In other exchanges there was no one who wanted to take responsibility for trading a small stock or taking the other side of an order. New York understood that if they could give customers execution on a higher percentage of stocks, it would drive investors to trade at their market. So they built this specialist system that gave them continuity, and drove orders in their direction, and they've done very well.

Now it's funny, the New York has no interest in a composite tape that would reflect European prices. Of course, if you had a composite tape reflecting prices that occurred before the opening in New York, maybe it would satisfy people in Europe and farther East sufficiently so they would do their trading prior to New York's opening.

But the question before the court is how to create the fairest market. I think in order to create the fairest playing field, you have to have equal and real-time disclosure of market information for everyone, and you have to have a system that allows for access to the market place as equally as possible—and as equally in cost as possible.

A market like that may not eliminate volatility. But you'll have a level of liquidity that you don't have today. Liquidity has traditionally been confined to a narrow group of people.

The key ingredients for a fair market are a composite tape, a composite limit order book so everyone can see what the backlog of orders are, and the price at which those orders may be executed and, finally, electronic access to the market.

If I were the buy side, and I felt I could put orders in, or withdraw those orders, I would put more limit orders in. I wouldn't even mind if people saw them if I had immediate access and control over my orders. I think you would find there would be an entirely different situation than what occurred in 1987 and 1989 during the crash and mini-crash.

Now the NYSE has put limits on the market. That means we'll stop the market because we haven't thought out a system that disseminates information and can handle order flow coming in, or provides a sense of fairness to the people who are the logical providers of liquidity.

All we have to do is create a system in this country that can operate 24 hours a day and we set some standards that overseas participants would have to meet to be part of that system. That's the big competition now, to see who will provide the technology and regulation that will be the most attractive to equity investors, institutional and retail.

The NYSE should support a system that would allow multiple market makers. It should take the 100 biggest stocks on the exchange and give everyone equal access to trade them. They should institute an electronic limit order book accessible to all. If they did this, and they extend the time that the system was open, it would attract business to their market. In my opinion, it would so improve our market system in terms of quality that it would force overseas corporations to meet our requirements for listing.

The liquidity would draw them, as it has in the past. Having higher standards will also draw them as it has in the past. But now the NYSE is asking the SEC to allow it to lower standards to attract overseas listings. It's moving exactly in the wrong direction, away from the higher standards that insured its growth in the first place. It runs against past experience of what has drawn business to their marketplace.

It's funny that congress got ahead of the SEC in its understanding of what was needed back in 1975. The SEC has always had a bias toward the industry as most regulatory agencies do. They've handled that conflict of interest as well as any regulatory body I know. But they move slowly, and congress got ahead of them.

What the SEC should do is say, we were given the responsibility to move toward a national market system. In two years we'll eliminate Rule 390. Two years will allow the industry to sit down and think about what will happen when that occurs and prepare to remove the trauma that will take place then.

If 390 is not done away with, someone else will eventually come along and create a better market. There are four logical producers of the better market: the NYSE, Nasdaq, Tokyo, and some kind of consortium in Europe.

The problem with Europe is that they've been fighting with themselves. The weakness of Tokyo is that people have difficulty trusting it. Tokyo, with all of its problems today, is going through a traumatic readjustment and might emerge a stronger competitor. Europe is organizing itself. The NASD has taken great strides toward improving its market, and I believe it may soon be able to take the offensive as the emerging market of the future.

I'm indifferent as to who emerges except that I believe it would be a mistake for the U.S. to allow some other market entity to emerge as the international marketplace. I would rather have it be New York or the NASD. I think the NASD is demonstrating a more forward-looking attitude than New York.

Look, people don't go overseas to hide something—they go there to avoid regulations that the industry has built into the system to serve their own interests. They go over there to facilitate legitimate needs.

If our automobile industry had read the tea leaves better and not been so caught up in selling big cars through dealerships and all the other ways that created lower quality and higher prices—if they'd taken advantage of the technology and been willing to give up some profitability to retain market share—we would never have had this Japanese problem. We lost our opportunity. It will take us decades to get back our superiority.

Our industry ought not to be so reluctant to change that we give up the dominant position we have today.

40

AGENCY BUSINESS

"We have all these high-tech trading products being developed by Wall Street and offered to the investment community. Some of the permutations in the market, the swings, the disasters, are a result of this marketing."

■ HOWARD SCHWARTZ

As a soft dollar broker, LJR provides investment research and related services receiving as compensation orders to buy and sell stock from money managers. But it also does business directly with pension plans, rebating 50 percent of commission dollars to those plans as incentive for continued order flow.

LJR is an agency broker that does no trading for its own account. LJR's president, Howard Schwartz, sees a growing adversarial relationship between Wall Street firms that serve as agents of institutions, protecting their interests and educating them about the securities industry, and firms which combine proprietary trading with agency business—raising questions about front running and other abuses.

The knowledge level in the markets is absolutely the core of understanding markets. First, there's the sell side—Wall Street. Then there's the buy side, the traditional investment managers, the banks, and insurance companies. Then there's a third component, the ultimate consumer, the retail customer or, in our case, the pension plan itself. The knowledge of the ultimate consumer is getting better, but it is still on the wrong side of the learning curve, and with so much money on the table, this is a dangerous situation.

We have all these high-tech trading products being developed by Wall Street and offered to the investment community. Some of the permutations in the market, the swings, the disasters, are a result of this marketing. Portfolio insurance, for instance, was an idea that never came and cost investors billions of dollars.

With the exception of the big corporations, the Amocos and IBMs, the top 100 maybe, most corporate staff is thin, they don't have a lot of time to spend on investment concepts. As a practical matter I have found that the average consumer, who is called the plan sponsor, the amount of knowledge they have is minimal due to all their other responsibilities. It's a little scary sometimes when you consider the amounts of money.

The problem is much more acute in the public sector versus the corporate. I happened to be making a presentation to a large municipal pension plan in a major city. There had to be twenty people sitting in the room. I remember in my introductory remarks I was going to be discussing the idea of commission recapture programs, where we, Lynch Jones & Ryan, approach a pension plan and suggest that we rebate a portion of their fund's commissions directly to them. This helps the plan gain control over a whole range of expenses.

I didn't get past the first two minutes of my introductory remarks and a hand shot up in the back of the room. I acknowledged it and the man stood up and said, I have a question, something I don't understand. You want to talk about equities and fixed income. I thought we only invested in stocks and bonds.

It wasn't a joke. This person was a trustee for a four or five billion dollar fund, just not educated, and he had assumed this responsibility out of a sense of civic pride, civic responsibility to his fellow workers. But here was a total lack of understanding of the process. And it's not gotten a lot better.

Due to lack of funding, this need for education is generally unmet. Consider the magnitude of the situation. You could probably with some sense of assurance take the hundred largest public and private plans and figure they're running well over $1 trillion.

Now that's a formidable amount of money and influence. It is essential to the process that we have to raise the level of understanding among these large plans, so they can better deal with what they're up against. The ultimate consumer, pension plan or individual, still does not understand the business, but should because it's their money. They're terrified of it and that's why there's so many consultants to help for a fee. You're dealing with billions of dollars on a daily basis. It's beyond the ken of any human being. Do you have any doubts as to why there's something like 10,000 money managers, all actively marketing their services, going after this pot of gold?

Ideally, Wall Street itself can facilitate the educational process by acting as an agent for the consumer. One of the big complaints of the 1980s is that there were so many lousy investments foisted on the public by Wall Street. Everybody was hurt, offended, surprised, whatever you want to call it.

But the institutional consumer himself or herself was responsible. After Mayday, the consumer, the plans, and the money mangers, beat up Wall Street relative to agency commissions. You're overpaid, you're overpaid. As a result, commissions went down as far as they could go. Then Wall Street went into other businesses to get a return on capital.

Wall Street started to invent new products. Some of them are good, some are lousy. But you can't fault Wall Street for being in business, for wanting to make a living. The feeling is that if you've driven me out of this business, acting as a commission broker, I'll find another one. So what happens, Wall Street comes up with derivatives, with other products.

Now all this is more complicated by technology. Personal computers have given Wall Street more opportunities to develop rocket science investments. But the professional investor can't complain about it, not now. They changed the business by making agency trading less profitable for most firms by driving down commissions.

How did we respond as a firm? By becoming the lowest cost provider we could and sticking to what we do best—agency trading. We were never doing proprietary trading, and I don't think we will in the future. We began to see we could emphasize our role as an agency broker, as a truly honest broker for the buy side.

There are two kinds of proprietary trading, no matter what else you may call it. The first is acting as a dealer where you facilitate a trade by buying or selling a security from a customer who needs to make the trade right away. Then there's straight proprietary trading, today usually computer driven, where you're buying or selling for the firm's own account to try to make a profit.

Straight proprietary trading is probably the most egregious assault on the investing public that was ever invented. Because you're taking the brokerage firm and putting it in an adversarial position with the investor.

More people should go to jail for front-running. I believe that computer-generated strategies lead to more abuses in that area and they're more difficult to track than you can possibly imagine. I also believe that the concept of the Chinese Wall does not exist in any firm. It's nonsense. If you go into some of the big trading rooms and you go on the tour and they'll show you, there's the institutional desk, there's the proprietary trading desk, there's the administrative desk, there's the correspondent clearing desk, they're all in the same room.

Have you ever been in a trading room and heard them shouting out the orders from one end to the other? I mean please, it's a joke, an absolute joke. That they can continue to push that kind of nonsense and have anyone believe it is a joke.

In 1986, we began to approach the pension plan directly. Our primary product back then was the Institutional Brokerage Estimate Service, IBES, which gave money managers an estimate of what top Wall Street analysts were saying about specific company prospects. We also had a core soft dollar business providing other research services to money managers.

We decided to approach pension plans directly because of an informational bulletin from the Department of Labor in 1986. What that bulletin said was that pension plans had the responsibility to get control over their own transaction activity. We came up with the concept that one way to do this was to help them get their arms around the commissions that were being spent.

We show pension plans how to gain control over their commission costs. We explain that they should have their money managers direct transactions to us subject to our ability to provide best execution. We emphasize this is their money and from the perspective of a plan sponsor, there is no such thing as soft dollars. So if the money manager does not need the money for research the plan should recapture these dollars to use and benefit the plan's participants. Thus, what we will do then is rebate half of those commissions back to the pension plan. It becomes their responsibility to use the dollars to reduce fund expenses. They're in control.

If a pension plan manages money internally we can also do this directly with them. Since we don't manage money, we don't try to woo pension plans away from money managers. The investment management community adds value to the process. That's what I believe.

Some pension plan professionals think relationships between plans and money managers should be structured differently. Marvin Damsma at Amoco has a lot of interesting ideas. He believes pension plans should take money in-house and use money managers as advisors. There are some people that already do that and pay them a flat fee or a percentage of profits.

But things change slowly. A good example is that the world is the same as it was ten years ago when you get out in the real world beyond the canyons and cliffs of Wall Street and Los Angeles. The way most of these organizations deal with this incredible rate of change on the outside is by making decisions more and more slowly. They take more time. They're trying to understand and avoid major mistakes.

The key to facilitating change is education. We see ourselves as an agent for education. We see business opportunities in the changing environment. Where it makes sense from a brokerage perspective for a pension plan to take control of its investment destiny, we'll try to help. That's what we've been doing for five years, and our business directly with pension plans now accounts for 40 percent of this firm's revenues up from zero five years ago. I'd anticipate that trend will continue, and we'll use technology to facilitate that trend.

On Wall Street, things are changing too. From our viewpoint, we'll continue to spread the message to customers that it's absolutely essential you separate proprietary trading from agency trading. The technology today, combined with proprietary trading, leaves the consumer ill-served. The most serious problem is that Wall Street is product oriented not customer oriented at this point. They've forgotten about representing the customer.

■ A PLAN SPONSOR OFFICIAL

A small group of pension fund activists have been quietly talking throughout the 1980s about how pension plans can be run more effectively. Currently many pension plans leave the management of the plan's money to money managers who often have close relationships to Wall Street. But activist pension plan executives are increasingly dissatisfied with this arrangement.

The current alignment of Wall Street, money managers, and pension plans gives rise to too many trades with too little value. Why not let the pension plan arrange its own investment strategy—so long as proper safeguards and oversight remain in place. (To encourage appropriate risk-taking, the government's pension guarantee might be reduced in such cases.)

Under this concept, money managers would provide ideas; Wall Street would provide execution along with various automated trading networks. And extra profits raised through this system would cut the corporation's contribution to the plan, making stockholders happier. The big question: Would Wall Street and Washington let it happen?

Under prevailing structures of pension management, the sponsor is not in completely in control of his strategy. As a result, plan sponsors may be missing opportunities to enhance efficiency and returns. The sponsor's limited control of his fund's total performance results from both structural constraints and operational weaknesses which lead sponsors to set up a form of horse race among money managers.

The multiple-manager system can—and often does—lead to over-lapping strategies, inefficient trading, and other problems which form a barrier that keeps the plan sponsor from investment success.

Perhaps it's time for a change, a new way of looking at things in which money managers and sponsors establish a revised relationship. This could entail the purchase of a manager's services as usual plus the purchase of broader portfolio advice which a sponsor could use to modify the investment strategy. If constructed in the proper framework, the sponsor could adjust portfolios on a real-time basis, a real benefit on the way to achieving successful results. It would make sense to receive buy and sell information from money managers along with broader portfolio advice. You could determine for yourself whether you wanted to try out those ideas or track them hypothetically.

Additionally, managers have ideas that could be useful to sponsors, but have limited methods to communicate them. For example, bad or inferior stocks could make good short-selling candidates. The key is to be able to identify and process ideas in a new way. This would clearly require extensive use of technology and various other cost-centers. But the potential to improve returns is expanded significantly.

It's a new data-processing world we're in. Using technology, we can now accumulate a great many ideas and process them, and focus them so they can be implemented in a quick and efficient fashion.

Here's the future the way I see it. If I don't do it, someone else will. And once you've built the first one, you can build the second one.

No one has ever seen this before. But people say, Gosh, when you build it, let me know. Of course, it's not cheap. You have to bet a lot of money on the potential it will work.

41

■ ■ ■

THE FUTURE OF FINANCE

"A place where consenting adults can have safe sex cheaply."

■ PETER SCHWARTZ

Peter Schwartz, president of Global Business Network, is a "futurist" and business strategist. His current research encompasses energy resources and the environment, information technology, telecommunications, finance, and entertainment. From 1982 to 1986, Schwartz headed scenario planning for the world's largest company, the Royal Dutch/Shell Group of Companies in London.

In the 1980s, the scale and scope of the securities industry changed dramatically. But there was a fundamental misconception about the permanence of those changes. It reminded me of what happened in the oil business in the 1970s. Oil companies thought oil prices would keep going up; instead they went down. The securities industry planned for a strong growth scenario that went along as predicted for a while and then went off the tracks.

I don't think the executives in the securities industry or its market regulators are willfully blind to the evolution of the marketplace. It's not the guild blindly protecting its past—it's just that they believe the system they have created is actually superior to what's coming. That's why you get plausible arguments about the virtues of the system in place, the virtues of the physical exchange or the specialist system. That kind of belief makes things even more dangerous and far more difficult.

230

The danger is that this blindness, this belief in the perfectibility of our current domestic system, will retard the evolution of our financial markets in the international arena. Regulatory obstruction can retard capital flows—money and jobs will go elsewhere. In the meantime our markets will behave worse and worse. We'll lose efficiency in our own capital-raising mechanism at the same time as we'll lose some access to the new systems that are being created internationally.

It seems to me that a couple of things are quite fundamental in shaping the future of the markets. The first one is the increasing rapidity and size of capital flows, the second is the ability to integrate and operate our evolving automated markets, and the third is the eventual stratification of the marketplace.

When I was advising the London Stock Exchange, after the Big Bang, I spoke at length with an American securities executive running an overseas subsidiary. He told me, "What we want is a place of our own where consenting adults can have safe sex cheaply."

What he was trying to say was the rules for adults—the world's largest corporations, banks, and money managers—should be different from the rules for the small investor with $50 to invest in IBM. That's currently starting to be the case anyway. The bulk of international global trading is inefficient, unobserved, and ripples into our domestic market in ways we often choose to deny.

What we're going to get, probably in a piecemeal fashion, is a market for consenting adults with more than $100 million to invest, who have the sophistication and systems to trade in the global arena. These adult players will trade in an environment with a minimum of rules where the biggest risks are counterparty risks—can I trust the guy on the other side to honor his commitment.

What this market will seek out—and demand from international regulators—is capital adequacy requirements. Trading rules, the rules of fair practice, the Glass-Steagall legislation, the host of regulations enacted in this country over the last 50 years will probably be irrelevant in the global trading arena.

In addition to capital adequacy, the other big thing global traders will be interested in is insuring they are trading at the lowest possible cost. Efficient, automated systems for executing and settling the trade will be of high value to them. They won't wish to be constrained by boundaries, they'll want efficiency—a minimum of rules and a maximum of efficiency.

All this has tremendous implications. For one thing, we'll have to stop thinking of companies as domestic or foreign. When a company's stock is mostly owned by investors outside of this country, then how can you define that company as American? Additionally, we're not going to have the control over the international arena that we're used to having over our domestic economy. Inevitably, we'll have an internationally managed marketplace, probably managed by some subset of American, German, English, and Japanese regulators. The French want in too, but they're probably not going to be a factor.

The closest analogy I could probably make is to the unregulated foreign currency market, where large institutions trade among themselves without regulations or publicity. The critical issue is how this new structure will be regulated. I think what will happen is that the industry's International Organization of Securities Commissions (IOSCO), will empower a standing committee to put together the rules and regulations necessary to make a true international trading arena practical. This committee would discuss capital adequacy and what can be counted as capital. It would be a voluntary system, of course. The worst that could happen would be that countries could boycott other countries who refused to accept or follow the guidelines.

But this new trading environment will probably look radically different from the one we now accept as standard. For one thing, with true automated systems functioning in a professional environment and manned by professional traders, you won't have a lot of the market crimes we now pay attention to. Things like insider trading, parking stock, and other kinds of market manipulations will be detectable to sophisticated traders. And if not detectable, the market may tend to regulate itself, just the way exchanges used to do before government got involved to protect the small investor.

These international players will all know each other. If one of them acts up for too long, the others just won't do business with that firm. It's going to be like a physical exchange was, except it will be done on a global scale.

There will be another market, probably not as interesting as this international market that's emerging. That will be a domestic, possibly regionalized, market that will be evident in most countries including this one.

The international markets will be vastly different from those we are accustomed to domestically. They will trade a variety of customized, index instruments, highly hedged, in many derivatives, equities and bond markets. The old definitions of what constitutes a stock, a bond, a future—those definitions will fade, probably along with definitions of what makes up a bank, or a money manager versus a Wall Street firm, or a futures or commodities firm. A lot of these definitions we're used to thinking of in this country were imposed by regulations that won't exist in the international arena.

But the domestic market will be more familiar. There will probably be physical exchanges, at least at first, alongside electronic communications—eventually even domestic markets will begin to take on some of the flavor of the international marketplace. But the change will be slower and, depending on the liquidity of the domestic market, investors may find it less risky to invest there.

The international market will certainly be a riskier market. One of the troubles we have with markets is that we don't want anybody to lose. Well, it's the nature of markets that there's loss. That's how markets work. Investors with a higher tolerance for risk will probably be able to access the international market through mutual funds. Of course that will entail changes in the way we regulate mutual funds, and what we allow our small investors to invest in. But there's no reason why we shouldn't allow our citizens to invest in a global economy.

The process is very similar to what this country went through in the late 1800s when we finally began to establish a true national economy. The way we did business changed. Our systems changed, and so did our regulations. These changes will probably be good for the world. Efficient third world companies will attract surges of capital from huge private entities, instead of depending on handouts from world organizations. The market itself will decide which countries are more efficient, where capital should flow.

The risk is that we won't move fast enough in this country. If we don't, if we restrain our banks and corporations, they won't take part so fully. Our own access to capital will diminish.

In this country, we'll continue to see great pressure on our domestic exchanges and firms—as we strain to make them international players without giving them the regulatory power to compete. We have to recognize the future and let it come. That takes courage and foresight and the will to compete.

42

■■■

COMMERCIAL
BANKS/INSURERS

*"The politics of regulation go back to Andrew Jackson,
and it's extraordinarily bad politics. The U.S. was founded
by debtors who distrusted centers of financial power."*

■ WILLIAM SIHLER

*Professor William Sihler, professor at the Darden Graduate School of
Business, University of Virginia, recently co-authored an insightful look
at the financial industry, The Troubled Money Business.*

*While Sihler and co-author Richard Crawford deal at length with the
nation's shaky banking and (somewhat less shaky) insurance system,
the book's conclusions have a direct bearing on Wall Street.*

*The authors' main conclusion: The nation's neat package of commercial
banks, savings and loans, insurance companies, and investment banks
is being replaced by a new system of pension funds, mutual funds,
the financial subsidiaries of nonfinancial companies, and investment
management companies. The upheavals of the 1980s, including the
nation's massive S&L problems, can be traced to this evolutionary
process.*

   Once we had a financial system in which everything fit together
and everything had an assigned role. S&Ls provided loans for housing;
commercial banks were in the consumer lending business and also
loaned money to private business; investment banks raised cash from

the public for investment in private and public enterprises; insurers took in public money and guaranteed a return in case of trouble.

Now efforts to regulate our current system the way we regulated the previous system are causing problems. We're trying to mandate certain requirements for our banks that make them less competitive in the marketplace. As a result, they can't attract the capital they need to survive.

S&Ls are dead, the fundamental flaw of borrowing short and lending long killed them. Commercial banks and insurance companies are struggling. In fact, these two kinds of financial enterprises are becoming more alike. Insurance companies are actually a form of a bank, except that commercial banks have traditionally taken shorter risks, insurers the longer. Insurance customers tend to "deposit" money for the long term—insurers take in deposits in the form of premiums and then sometimes, years later, pay them back out.

Now insurance companies are taking in deposits for shorter periods of time. Insurers are offering more and more group policies as opposed to traditional whole life policies. A group policy is a more unstable funding source because the company purchasing the group policy might take its business elsewhere next year. Whole life customers tend to be with an insurer for a much longer period. Insurance companies now have the same kind of uncertainties as commercial banks except they have no Federal Reserve window, no government lender of last resort, the way the commercial banks do.

Additionally, insurance companies are struggling because of new societal ills that they are expected to insure, but for which their policies and current structure are unsuited. This is leading to new, and sometimes smaller, companies with more flexible policies aimed at fewer individuals in some cases.

Insurers, commercial banks, and S&Ls have a less stable base of investors. Once commercial banks took almost no risk at all. They funded seasonal inventory and receivables: the customer sold the goods and paid the bank back. Later on banks took the daring step of making term loans, longer loans not paid down by the liquidation of assets but through a portion of earnings. Insurers handled the longest risk of all, since life insurance policies might only be paid out decades after the initial deposits were made.

Now the most stable funding sources belong to mutual funds and pension plans, especially pension plans. These plans have the most stable funding of all since they don't have to pay investors back at all short of death or retirement, and investors are barred from removing their assets. That's a financial intermediary with a long time horizon.

But mutual funds are attracting a good deal of relatively stable investment as well. Demand money is moving into money market funds offered by mutual funds. These funds have no requirement for capital because all their funds are counted as equity. A mutual fund company like Fidelity can reinvest its depositors' money just the way a bank can, but it has no community obligations to consider, no risky loans to make out of a sense of social conscience. Additionally, a firm like Fidelity doesn't have to pay for banking insurance or carry a certain mandated percentage of assets in cash to insure solvency.

Because of these requirements, a bank's cost of capital is higher than a mutual fund's. Government has even prohibited banks from paying market rates of interest on their deposits. In the case of money market accounts at banks, you can't make more than three withdrawals per month. Consumer demand moves to the more flexible funds, the mutual funds.

Global commercial banks aren't doing a good job of lending to companies anymore. That function is being taken over by the regional banks, even the small regionals. The big banks are getting into investment banking and underwriting. They're trying to do some of what Wall Street does. J. P. Morgan, Bankers Trust, Continental Bank in Chicago, they're all trying to move away from their traditional business base. The only trouble is that they're still hampered by the rules of our previous financial system.

The government tends to defend the status quo. The 1991 Bush banking bill got nibbled to death. It called for more interstate banking, for letting the banks do more. But in the end the banks got almost nothing. The securities firms gained access to the Fed Window, which they wanted, thanks to their powerful protector John Dingell.

The securities industry is remarkably healthy. Initial public offerings are 50 percent higher than in 1987, the previous high. The other thing is $300 billion in securitization. It's astounding. Business has doubled, and Wall Street gains a fee for each securitized deal it brings to market. It started with collateralized mortgage obligations but now almost anything can be securitized, credit cards, anything. Asset-backed securitization is extraordinarily profitable.

There's an old saying, "capital like liberty does not last long where it is not valued." Capital tends to flow where it is respected. In the Great Depression, government and the Federal Reserve did all the wrong things. They didn't respect capital, and they aggravated what was already wrong—they raised taxes, embargoed trade.

What people don't understand is that we already had a highly regulated financial system before the 1930s. The politics of regulation go back to Andrew Jackson, and it's extraordinarily bad politics. The U.S. was founded by debtors who distrusted centers of financial power.

Andrew Jackson disbanded the Second National Bank of the United States in 1833. That left banks in individual states. Instead of a federal banking system you had a state and even a city banking system—the Bank of New York, the Bank of the Manhattan Company. Every region wanted its own bank, a money center that could attract the deposits of wealthy people and lend money to build up business. It was a state's rights issue to some degree, part of the argument between federal and state government.

The result was that when the Great Depression came, all these little state and city banks were vulnerable to collapse. Europe didn't have as much of a problem because its banks were bigger. They didn't distrust size so much. Of course, if banks are too big, you don't have competition, but if they're too small, you also have problems. In this country, our banks were too small, because of our regulatory bias. When the Depression came along, the little state banks all started going under. So we regulated more, and that got us to where we are today.

Now we have a skewed playing field where banks can't compete. We can keep regulating, but ultimately the consumer will pay the bill. The market is going to evolve, anyway. Basically the consumer goes where he's respected. Money moves. You can't keep it in one place.

Regulators should get out of the way where they can, and they should try to strengthen all market participants. It does no one a service to let insurers and commercial banks go the way of the S&Ls. Further consolidation and more efficient use of capital is what our system needs right now. Our commercial banks, especially, should be allowed to compete on an equal playing field with our securities firms.

43

■■■

AUTOMATED BONDS

"Wall Street was against it."

■ DAVID JEFFREY

A graduate of Dartmouth, David Jeffrey worked for five years in industry, finally at Joseph Seagram & Sons Inc., as a financial analyst in the corporate treasury department. He later founded CapitaLink, an electronic single price call auction to allow corporations to sell debt directly to buyers, cutting out Wall Street and its banking fees. He now works for Wunsch.

At Seagram I watched how Wall Street's bankers competed to create innovative deals that would tempt a company to raise funds using those structures. It took me a while to decide there was a simpler way: let issuers raise money by appealing directly to buyers, forgetting about the middleman.

Wall Street was quite effective though—they wouldn't compete on price. Instead, a firm like Salomon would get a huge piece of new issue business in the fixed income market by differentiating their ideas from the ideas of their competitors, by adding one more wrinkle.

What was ultimately happening was these deals became so convoluted that they were harder and harder to evaluate. The investor might purchase an instrument with a good yield, but the product might not turn out to be so attractive.

238

I think these products were most attractive to the investment banker. The more complex, the more difficult to mimic, the more he could create a franchise in the business. They gave them nicknames, and that legitimized them further. Now they could shop the product around and get other companies interested in issuing debt using that particular technique. Of course, sooner or later, other firms would copy even the most intricate product and give it their own nicknames. The franchise would erode, the game would start over.

I've always been interested in finance. My thought process finally became: I've seen a lot of simple financings and a lot of complex ones, and the straightforward ones seem just as good to me, and not so expensive.

It seemed to me you ought to be able to save still more money if you could simply put the buyer and seller of primary issues together in some electronic fashion. The issuer in the market I was involved with tended to be a Treasurer who was pretty sophisticated about the markets. The purchasers of corporate bonds were mutual funds and sophisticated institutions. These two groups didn't really need someone in the middle.

It seemed to me the only thing that was lacking was an automated system to take the place of Wall Street. That's when I founded CapitaLink in 1985. By 1988, we had received some funding from an affiliate of J. P. Morgan, the big commercial bank—they owned 25 percent of us—and we were up and running in our final form.

The final service consisted of a host computer system which was hooked to clients through a modem. Clients would receive our DOS-based software to run the system. We knew the system would work best for large companies issuing commodity-type bonds. Say firm XYZ issues a small round lot of $100 million. They would generate a prospectus that we could mail out. Then at a designated time, the issuer would pick a half hour period and tell the clients to log on and bid for the issue.

Unfortunately, we never did a completed auction—we had about 140 customers signed up to be bidders including 25 regional brokers. And as far as issuers go, we had about 12 filed with the SEC to use us. Some of our customers got very close. But the concern about a failed auction was very real. Before a customer would use the system, he'd ask us to canvas our buyers to insure there was interest. Of course that defeated the purpose of an auction. You're not going to say what you're going to bid in advance. We couldn't count on it, anyway.

The trouble was, if a company offered debt to the public, and the issue didn't sell out over the system, the issue would have to be withdrawn. That wouldn't look very good for the company, and the Treasurer would be unhappy since he'd have to tell the CEO he'd used this new system and it hadn't worked.

The fact that Wall Street was against it made a big impact on the minds of the treasurers—they were told it wasn't a good idea. They were told, if they had a failed auction, that Wall Street firms would have trouble underwriting other issues. Using our system could jeopardize their ability to finance. So treasurers were rightfully reluctant. It wasn't clear the risks of using the system, at least for early users, outweighed the benefits of cheaper financing.

You know, we came very close with one company. But it was reported in the press that Merrill stopped it by providing a very cheap bid to the issuer. So the issuer went with Merrill instead.

Eventually, in late 1990, we had to shut down. I went to work for Steve Wunsch. I'm a vice president of fixed income, developing an electronic market in the fixed income area—but in the secondary market. It works a lot like Steve's equity system. It makes a lot of sense since there aren't the same kind of concerns among the clients. In the secondary market you don't have to worry about a failed auction because everyone remains anonymous. If it fails, if no orders cross, nobody gets hurt.

The bond market is a pure OTC market, in any case. There's no formal reporting of prices, no formal physical exchange. What we're going to generate for users are actual market prices. For the first time, users of our system, specifically institutions, will have the same exposure to bond prices, real-time, that Wall Street has. They won't have to call around to try to get a price. They'll see the market demand right on the computer screen. That kind of information is valuable. I suppose we'd be able to sell it, too, elsewhere. For us, this kind of market is ready-made; the possibilities are limitless.

CODA

■ ■ ■

WHAT I LEARNED

We are headed into an exciting, uncertain time. If we are to make the most of it, our powerful financial industry—and those who regulate it and are beholden to it—will have to change to keep up. Problems must be recognized and dealt with; current systemic rigidities should be recognized and alleviated.

The market crash of 1987 was at least in part the product of too much information available to too few people. So was the S&L crisis, so were the financial scams like limited partnerships and penny stocks. More information, more players, less privilege for a regulated few—these are some of the building blocks of tomorrow's richer, healthier markets.

Regulators and politicians need not operate by fiat. Market participants should quietly and steadily work toward dismantling distorting market regulations: Glass-Steagall and Rule 390, among others. Pension plans should be encouraged to make better use of emerging market technologies. Internationally, efforts to assist the financial industry in regularizing clearing and settlement practiccs should be encouraged. Ways to better track underlying exchange-derivative instruments that are used to hedge off-exchange deals should also be implemented. Possibly the release of information about off-exchange transactions should be made mandatory.

This last point deserves greater explanation. Right now, nobody really knows much about the derivatives markets, how Wall Street is hedging the instruments it develops for clients, how much risk has already built up in the system. The idea that Wall Street's finest financial minds can be trusted to toil away in secrecy for the greater good of the marketplace is not a sensible one, given what has occurred just in the recent past. Despite the protestations of knowledgeable observers like swaps reporter Spraos, it's probable that the unrestricted growth of derivatives trading, off-exchange, especially in a worldwide trading environment will eventually lead to uncomfortable market disruptions. This is not because the use of derivatives is in any way wrong or unethical, but because, given the current market structure, only a few players really know what's going on—and then only for their own trading book. And that's because the derivatives explosion is fueled in part by the same pension plan/money manager/Wall Street layer-cake structure that fueled the market innovations of the 1980s. Portfolio insurance, the rage of the last decade, proved chimerical because of the simplicity of the concept, the rigidity of the market structure to which it was applied, and the ferocious marketing by Wall Street. Wall Street may well drive the same stake through the heart of the derivatives market that it drove through M&A, junk bonds, and naked options.

The idea that Wall Street can sell everyone insurance against risk is foolish unless one accepts that Wall Street in the 1990s is a kinder, gentler place, dedicated to shouldering the burden of the very risk it is removing from others. As a matter of fact, Wall Street always sheds the risk it takes on—usually for a fee—just as soon as possible. Wall Street's risk is thus transferred elsewhere, usually to other Wall Street clients, and usually at a profit.

Risk exists; it migrates from market to market and instrument to instrument, depending on what transactions are involved and how various markets relate. Eventually, there comes a time when risk can be staved off no longer. In a rigid, overregulated market and industry environment where strategies tend to mimic one another despite the many minds at work, that day of reckoning may come sooner rather than later.

Competition, rather than regulation—in an undistorted market environment—can be a great creator of fiscal discipline. Both the FX and fixed income markets function adequately, thus far, without the kind of regulatory attention our options, futures, and stock markets have been subjected to. The greatest possible financial creativity with the greatest possible disclosure is probably a sensible alternative to continual waves of regulation following regularly on each market disruption. Using automated systems and the fullest possible disclosure, our securities exchanges can gradually begin to operate more as pure markets and less as adjuncts to the financial industry.

In *Stealing the Markets,* Mayer points out that reporting requirements on all trades should be imposed on tax-favored institutional investors, including insurance companies and mutual funds. Such reporting requirements should be extended to trades in foreign securities and in commodities, currencies, and options as well as trades of securities subject to SEC registration. The identity of brokers in all trades, as well as commission, should be part of a restricted public record, Mayer says.

Such requirements would do much to insure that the kind of worldwide trading environment that futurist Schwartz envisions is realized. In the nineteenth century and for most of the twentieth century, the technology did not exist to make prices and other market information rapidly available. As a result, it was relatively easy for the financial industry domestically and abroad to manipulate markets and make a profit at the expense of the unsuspecting "ultimate" consumer. In this country, a cartel-like group of interrelated financial firms apparently manipulated the nation's largest stock exchange for decades, milking profits and contributing to the system's fragility until the system collapsed in 1929—bringing on all the regulation that helped cause the collapse of 1987.

But in the twenty-first century it may be that there is less to fear from large financial institutions trading with one another in an international environment. If prices are truly made available, if competition is rigorous and not paid lip service to, if new players are not barred from dealing with each other on an equal basis through electronic trading nets, it is possible that the revolution of democratic markets that swept through the world in the late twentieth century will continue to evolve.

We should not be afraid of bigness. Big players will always attempt to manipulate the market. But the more big players there are, the more capital invested in all kinds of products through all sorts of instruments and automated nets, the harder it will be for any single entity, or group of entities, to control the markets. This is especially important in the coming decades as neural networks and other computerized strategies begin to reshape the market in ways almost unimaginable to us now.

Booms, busts, and fraud will always take place. But the public should be educated by the media, it should be informed by politicians, and it should insist that regulators substantively address—through forceful, creative deregulation—the evolution of our marketplace.

The thesis of some market analysts is that markets have a purpose—to provide pricing information to investors: Markets therefore need to be reclaimed for the benefit of the larger capitalist enterprise. Yet there is another way of looking at markets, a less sympathetic way, but possibly a more practical one. This vision does not hold any one instrument or product dear. The stock market itself, with its painstakingly apportioned doses of equity information, is gradually giving way to a commoditized investment environment that lumps equity together in various indexes. Regulations that freeze markets in place, that try to determine what can and can't be sold in a domestic or global marketplace are ultimately doomed to failure—though probably not before causing considerable mischief.

As Wayne Wagner points out in his afterword to this book, we do understand certain rules about markets. But rules, like markets, can evolve—in a free-market environment. I'm not sure Don Weeden's, or even Wayne Wagner's, prescriptions for our markets, even our equities markets, are the last word.

Competition is not a bad thing, not even for capitalists. The alternative is to continue to pile regulation on top of regulation in a vain attempt to "prudently" anticipate the problems of global financing and electronic trading.

Product-rich, efficient, competitive, automated markets, agency representation, and a true code of professional ethics could bring us closer to where we want to be.

WHAT'S TO BE DONE? WHO'S TO DO IT?

■ WAYNE H. WAGNER, PLEXUS GROUP

Today's markets are restructuring in directions set not by the insiders, but by the serious, analytic, and cost-sensitive market users. These efforts to rebuild Wall Street raise awareness about one of our nation's critical issues: the evolution of our financial marketplace and industry. Mr. Fadiman does a service in pointing out that technology and modern economic theory are radically changing the way our most powerful institutions do business. We must embrace these changes as the opportunities they truly are.

The regulatory environment hasn't been especially helpful. Six different Acts cover various aspects of financial markets. Each creates its own domain and its own coterie of intensely interested parties. The path of innovation is thereby artificially narrowed. Only those changes perceived to be to the benefit of the existing interests slide easily through the channel. As a result, huge amounts of money sometimes get poured into relatively few investment schemes. This leads to market instability, bad results, and unhappy investors, both individual and institutional.

We need to widen the channels by blasting out the obstructions. Modern computing and communications can shatter the artificialities of the set-up by simply putting buyers and sellers in touch with each other under the conditions that make them most comfortable. As a result, responsibility for the control of the order is migrating to money managers and pension sponsors. Different types of questions are being asked, such as "Is it cost effective?" Investors are increasingly aware that having a good idea and having a good idea in the portfolio are different. A new science is dawning: the design of markets and the systematic study of investment implementation.

It sometimes feels that the market evolves at tectonic speeds. Yet, it does move—mostly in lurches—into a better solution to changing market needs. When change can't work within the rules, it works by exception. Thus most changes occur on the periphery of the traditional domains, and is often greeted by stiff opposition and limp foot dragging. However, once change is made, the exchange community finds new ways to make money. This usually comes as a complete surprise to the curmudgeons and doom-sayers. What they fail to appreciate is that people will pay willingly for valuable services.

Quantitative analysts and other innovators have nurtured a profusion of new investment ideas over the past quarter century. We can now choose from a multitude of new investment vehicles and inventive new ways to finance business. Techniques that didn't even exist 25 years ago manage most of today's assets. Bit by bit, we learn to apply the speed and flexibility of new communication and computational power. Each innovation strains the boundaries of the way things are done. Too often, the result is a compromise of the new understanding and advantage at the point of implementation.

Markets exist to serve the needs of investors and issuers. To those who have invested money and time in the old procedures, however, change is always a threat. Their immediate goal becomes to preserve their investment. The result is to reject change, breed inefficiency, and enforce a one-size-fits-all approach that chafes increasingly diverse investors and issuers.

Institutional Investor quoted John Phelan in September 1989: "Technology and communication bring efficiency. Money is made in the inefficiency." This is the toll collector mentality: What originally was a means of financing and maintaining the bridge becomes an entitlement. Who's to pay for this, John? What happens when they choose not to pay?

When the tolls are onerous, someone builds a new bridge. Similarly, large innovative investors who feel the deck is stacked against them—fixed commissions are a sterling example—will be drawn to upstairs, off-exchange markets and other alternatives. Meanwhile, the portion of trading best served by the traditional exchange dwindles steadily.

I doubt there is such an entity as the optional, for-all-time best market structure. Fortunately, we don't need infinite wisdom. All we need is a flexible, open environment in which to test new ideas. If useful, they will earn their place in the spectrum of trading alternates.

The essence of exchange is a transaction. Anything that facilitates a transaction creates liquidity. In the previous chapters, the interviewees put forward a list of promising liquidity-producing ideas:

- Free flow of information about securities and their prospects.
- An agreed place/time where buyer and seller can find each other.
- Low transaction costs, which make more ideas actionable.
- Availability of dealer services to facilitate transactions when desired.
- A guarantee of fidelity so that promises to trade are kept.
- Broadly diseminated information about trade completions and statements of interest.
- Relentless sweating down the costs of approaching the market or settling the trade. (Why not next day?)

Recently—and after compiling the above list—I came across the 1975 list of market improvements suggested by William Schreyer, then President and now Chairman of Merrill Lynch[1]:

In our view a national market system must have the following elements:

1. *All orders come together so they have the opportunity to interact;*

2. *Automatic execution, particularly for active, liquid issues with narrow spreads;*

3. *Locked-in trades with automatic comparison and clearing so that stock certificates can be immobilized or eliminated to a substantial degree;*

4. *Fair and equal opportunity to compete for all who have capital and willingness to make markets;*

5. *Full limit order protection so that the public customer has an incentive to come into the market; and*

6. *Market information, such as firm bids and offers, size and transaction reports, promptly and accurately available to all.*

---

1 Quoted by Junius W. Peake in "Market Center Competition: Order Flow or Listings?" Unpublished paper, March 1992.

The words are different, but the commonality of my list to this 17-year-old list is remarkable. Conclusion: We know what to do, we only need focus to move forward with it.

We need many of the current facilities. Tim Metz applauds the specialists who stood up and defended the market in October 1987. So do I. But I'm reminded of the brave Polish horse calvary riding out to meet the Panzer divisions in 1939. The firepower wasn't adequate for the need.

Most markets seem to function better with dealers, particularly on the extremes of very thin markets or very large institutional markets. Dealers seem to arise spontaneously. The advantage of constant presence and short horizon create a trading edge on which dealers make money. In the process they build bridges and create liquidity. We need no artificiality to create a dealer's edge.

For better or worse we're heading toward markets of greater concentration. The chances for simultaneity of action—through narrowed channels—becomes frightening. We are not prepared to deal with it. Capital, and large amounts of it, will be needed to facilitate trading. One potential source of capital is the institutional investors themselves. Locking them out of a capital-providing role—as we do now—is a prescription for disaster. During the October 1987 crash, corporations stepped in with buy orders for their own stocks to relieve the pressure on the market-makers. It helped save the market then, but the process needs to be less ad hoc.

The franchise used to be the building in which the exchange conducted business. There was a time when the better capitalized, knowledgeable, fiduciary persons were on the exchange floor. Increasingly the better capitalized, most knowledgeable institutions are off-floor and outside the reach of the exchange. Institutional investors and corporations need to take their "seats" alongside the current stakeholders. Their needs create new problems, and they need to be active participants in the solutions.

Pension investment, for instance, was once a way-station in a career in the Treasurer's office. Increasingly, it has become a profession of its own. The better pension sponsors are true professionals, and advance within the pension industry rather than Treasury. The power over the pension assets is now heading with deliberate speed into the hands of the pension sponsor. With it will come the power over the commission and, ultimately, the exchanges.

Do we need a physical floor? It's already crowded by the current population. Most thinkers believe it's doomed, but they've believed that for 30 years and counting. The bond market seems to work quite well with phones. Donald Unruh installs electronic exchanges all over the world. Yet on the electronic-exchange Paris Bourse, 30 percent of the volume and most block trades are arranged through dealers in London. We seem to need some human touch to connect wary buyer to wary seller. Imagine the changes that will accompany the spread of videophone technology!

One of the most sacred beliefs of the exchange is in the value of intermingling large and small trades. We try to bathe the elephant and the ant in the same bathwater. One of them is inevitably going to be disadvantaged. *Small* needs quick execution and does not fear exposure. *Size,* in contrast, needs to carefully orchestrate a quid-pro-quo exposure, even if it takes longer. If size cannot protect itself, liquidity is extinguished. Both size and small then suffer. We separate the retail and institutional traders in bonds, to no one's apparent disadvantage. Why not the same in stocks?

As Mr. Fadiman's interviews show, the leverage of the securities industry inevitably gives the elephant the advantage. The nonprofessional seems destined to the role of Michael Lewis's Fool in the Market: less skilled and informed than the sell-side trader. As money managers and pension plans become better investors they depend less on Wall Street for advice. For individual consumers, the answer may be the "two tier" structure that Peter Schwartz mentions in his interview.

The securities market is fragmenting, not only for stocks but for other instruments as well. Since the end of the negotiated commission, a spectrum of trading ideas and venues has emerged to serve specific needs. So far, these solutions have been fractionalizing, pulling part of the market away. More niche markets are coming, and the successful ones will draw away liquidity. Fragmentation in an electronic age need not choke liquidity. Markets serving disparate functions can now be linked, and are being linked in some cases. Orders are beginning to swim electronically from one net to another. What we now think of as market fractions are evolving into useful modes in larger networks.

To the exchanges' credit, they have moved forward when the path became obvious. Like tectonic plates, they appear immovable, then shift suddenly. The pressure is building. Our exchanges need to watch the signals so the future path doesn't lead to London, Tokyo, or Toronto.

We can't expect the exchanges alone to play the leadership role in this scenario. The inside is a frightfully difficult place from which to perceive even the need for change, much less the direction, magnitude, or means. Change will probably come from more "damn fractionalizers." Their appeal will be to those whose interests need to be readdressed: large scale investors and issuers.

Who's to provide the focus, the stretching of the minds, the *creneau*? Mr. Fadiman wants reporters to call attention to the financial industry's larger problems and potential solutions. In this thorough effort, I believe he makes a case for his profession. Yet we should not leave the final word to any single group, inside or outside the industry. The challenge is too complex and the stakes are too big. We have an idea where we're headed, but we will need the most expansive and inclusive discussion possible to build—and rebuild—our financial system.

In our impatience to restructure, we shouldn't forget that the most potent tool for change is a free and vital market. Evolving global investment will release powerful forces. Instead of trying to deflect this raw energy, we should tear down impediments standing in the way. By removing obstacles instead of maneuvering around them, we can take our share of the coming global boom and reap its benefits. By granting more participants economic equality, we will not diminish the market or ourselves. As my friend Evan Schulman says in his interview, a "rich tapestry" of traders and trading techniques can provide a deeper and more liquid market. We needn't be fearful or suspicious. History is showing us the way.

SELECTED BIBLIOGRAPHY

Adams, James Ring. *The Big Fix.* New York: John Wiley & Sons, 1990.

Arbel, Avner, and Albert Kaff. *Crash.* Carol Stream, IL: Longman Financial Services Publishing, 1989.

Barro, Robert, et al. *Black Monday & The Future of Financial Markets.* Chicago: Mid-America Institute for Public Policy Research, Dow Jones Irwin, 1989.

Bernstein, Jake. *How the Futures Markets Work.* New York: New York Institute of Finance, Simon & Schuster, 1989.

Bernstein, Peter. *Capital Ideas: The Improbable Origins of Modern Wall Street.* New York: The Free Press, Macmillan Publishing, Inc., 1992.

Burroughs, Bryan, and John Helyar. *Barbarians at the Gate: The Fall of RJR Nabisco.* New York: Harper & Row, 1990.

Chase, C. David. *Mugged on Wall Street: An Insider Shows You How to Protect Yourself & Your Money from the Financial Pros.* New York: Fireside, Simon & Schuster, 1987.

Crawford, Richard, and William Sihler. *The Troubled Money Business.* New York: Harper Business, 1991.

Downes, John, and Jordan Elliot Goodman. *Dictionary of Finance and Investment Terms.* New York: Barron's Financial Guides, 1991.

Ehrlich, Judith Ramsey, and Barry Rehfeld, *The New Crowd.* Boston: Little Brown & Co., 1989.

Fitzgibbon, John Jr., *Deceitful Practices*. New York: Birch Lane Press, Carol Publishing Group, 1991.

Galbraith, John Kenneth. *The Great Crash, 1929.* Boston: Houghton Mifflin Co., 1988.

Gastineau, Gary. *The Options Manual,* 3rd edition. New York: McGraw Hill Book Co., 1988.

Greider, William. *Secrets of the Temple: How the Federal Reserve Runs the Country.* New York: Simon & Schuster, 1987.

Haas, Lawrence. *Running on Empty: Bush, Congress and the Politics of a Bankrupt Government.* Homewood, IL: Business One Irwin, 1990.

Herzfeld, Thomas. *The Investor's Guide to Closed End Funds.* New York: McGraw Hill, 1980.n

Johnson, Philip McBride, and Thomson Lee Hazen. *Commodities Regulation,* second edition, vols. I & II. Boston: Little Brown, 1989.

Lewis, Michael. *Liar's Poker.* New York: W. W. Norton, 1989.

Metz, Tim. *Black Monday: The Catastrophe of October 19, 1987 . . . and Beyond.* New York: William Morrow & Co., Inc., 1988.

Mayer, Martin. *Stealing the Market.* New York: Basic Books, 1992.

Morris, Charles. *The Coming Global Boom: How to Benefit Now from Tomorrow's Dynamic World Economy.* New York: Bantam Book, Bantam Doubleday Dell Publishing Group, Inc., 1990.

Pilzer, Paul Zane, with Robert Deitz. *Other People's Money.* New York: Simon & Schuster, 1989.

Powers, Mark J., and David Vogel. *Inside the Financial Futures Market,* second edition. New York: John Wiley & Sons, 1984.

Sales, Thomas. *Lies Your Broker Tells You.* New York: Walker & Co., 1989.

Seligman, Joel. *The Transformation of Wall Street: A History of the SEC & Modern Corporate Finance.* Boston: Houghton Mifflin Co., 1982.

Sloane, Leonard. *The Anatomy of the Floor: The History of the Efficient Pandemonium of the Men and Women at the Nerve Center of the New York Stock Exchange.* Garden City, New York: Doubleday & Co., Inc., 1980.

Spicer & Oppenheim. *Guide to Securities Markets Around the World.* New York: John Wiley & Sons, 1988.

Stewart, James. *Den of Thieves.* New York: Simon & Schuster, 1991.

Strassman, Paul A. *Information Payoff: The Transformation of Work in the Electronic Age.* New York: The Free Press, 1985.

Train, John. *The New Money Masters.* New York: Harper & Row, 1989.

Vise, David, and Steve Coll. *Eagle on the Street.* New York: Charles Scribner's Sons, 1991.

Wagner, Wayne, ed. *The Complete Guide to Securities Transactions: Enhancing Investment Performance and Controlling Costs.* New York: John Wiley & Sons, 1989.

Walter, Ingo. *The Secret Money Market: Inside the Dark World of Tax Evasion, Financial Fraud, Inside Trading, Money Laundering & Capital Flight.* New York: Harper & Row, Ballinger Division, 1990.

Warfield, Gerald. *How to Buy Foreign Stocks & Bonds: A Guide for the Individual Investor.* New York: Harper & Row, 1985.

SELECTED SPEECHES AND STUDIES

Study: *Findings of the Committee of Inquiry.* Chicago Mercantile Exchange. Preliminary Report: December 22, 1987; Final Report: Spring 1988.

Study: *Program Trading.* Subcommittee on Telecommunications & Finance, Committee on Energy & Commerce, 100th Congress, First Session, July 23, 1987. Washington, D.C.: U.S. Government Printing Office, 1988.

Various papers, Junius Peake, Morris Mendelson. The Office of Technology Assessment, U.S. Congress, Washington, D.C./1990. Electronic Bulls & Bears.

Financial Innovation & Uncertain Regulation. Selected Issues Regarding New Product Development. Thomas Russo and Marlisa Vinciguerra. From *The Texas Law Review*, copyright 1991, volume 6, May 1991.

STORIES FROM:

The Economist, Investment Dealer's Digest, Chicago *Times, Investor's (Business) Daily, Forbes, Barron's, The Wall Street Journal,* The *New York Times, Washington Post, BusinessWeek, Fortune, Institutional Investor. Wall Street Week* newsletter, et.al., *Securities Week, Water's* newsletters.

GLOSSARY OF TERMS

active money manager: (vs. passive) manager who chooses securities by pulling together a variety of fundamental and economic data.

after-hours trading: buying and selling securities after the close of a specific physical exchange.

agent: intermediary between a buyer and a seller.

agency trade/broker: a service performed by Wall Street firms for its customers; the facilitation of a trade by a broker with no proprietary dealing interest.

anonymous order: a buy or sell order that does not reveal the identity of the customer.

arbitrageur: in the 1980s, a financier usually seeking to profit on the upwards movement of the stock of a company "in play," often while laying off risk by selling security short.

arbitration: the process of taking a securities grievance to an industry forum, usually an exchange, rather than to a court of law.

ask: (vs. bid) offer to sell, "asked price."

asset: something that can be bought or sold.

auction market: a market in which securities are bought by the highest bidder. The NYSE is a double auction system since the specialist presides over many buying and selling agents.

audit trail: a paper trail tracing who bought and sold what security in a specific transaction. Can now be done electronically from start to finish in almost all instruments.

best execution: best possible price for purchase or sale of securities.

bid: (vs. ask) offer to buy.

bid stabilization: practice of selling short to cover against share redemption.

bifurcated regulatory structure: the delineation of regulation between the SEC and the CFTC whereby the SEC regulates the securities industry (Wall Street) and the CFTC regulates the futures industry (the Canyon).

Big Bang: London's Mayday, October 27, 1986. More anticipated than celebrated.

blind pool: a limited partnership with no specific investment goal (vs. specified pool).

block trade: the purchase or sale of a large number of shares by a trader. Usually at least 10,000 shares, $200,000 worth of bonds.

blue sky (rules): state securities laws on sales and issuance of securities.

bond: corporate, government, municipal security that offers regular interest to investors as well as final payment. Bondholders have no corporate ownership privileges; stockholders do.

broker: a securities salesman employed by a firm to sell financial products, usually for a percentage of the commission.

broker-dealer: a broker acts as intermediary between buyer and seller. Dealer buys and sells for own account and also underwrites securities.

"bulletin board": a screen-based system accommodating indications of interest.

buy side: any part of the financial services industry not primarily identified with securities firms. Those institutions are not able to buy or sell directly on the floor of a physical exchange in this country.

calls: in options, the ability to purchase, on a certain date or dates, certain security or securities at a specified price.

cash market: terminology applying to the underlying market from which a derivative instrument receives its value; i.e., to equity instruments when speaking of financial stock index futures.

cash settlement: receiving cash for the market value of an instrument at a certain point in time. Often refers to the futures or options markets where instruments settle monthly or quarterly at face value.

caveat emptor: Let the buyer beware. Fundamental rule of securities industry.

Chinese Wall: Wall Street's unspoken mores demanding that those who deal for the company do not take advantage of the customer in the process. Sometimes defined by regulation.

clearance: the process of ascertaining that the buyer and a seller of a security agree on the trade. Usually performed by a clearing firm.

client facilitation: originally the idea of purchasing a large block of securities from a favored institutional customer with the intention of quickly reselling same; meaning changed in 1980s to involve the process of facilitating a client's program trade.

closed-end fund: a fund, typically listed on an exchange, often composed of securities whose total value is more than the actual price at which the fund's shares are trading. Since closed-end fund managers have no obligation to redeem shares at net asset value, fund participants are often forced to sell for less than their shares are actually worth.

collar: a trading halt imposed on a market after it has moved up or down too much (mostly down). Red China's exchange windows in some cases are reportedly open for trading when the market rises. When the market falls, only one window stays open.

commercial bank: bank that takes deposits and makes loans in addition to private placement business. As opposed to a *merchant bank*, which places its own capital at risk in private deals, and an *investment bank,* which places its capital at risk in underwriting public issues.

commission: broker's percentage of fee paid to firm for purchase of a financial product or for executing a trade.

Commodities Futures Trading Commission (CFTC): established in 1974, after SEC turned down responsibility; regulates commodities and financial futures. Oversight includes fair practice, disclosure, and maintenance of orderly markets.

commoditization: a trend where something jealously guarded, like information or technology, becomes more easily available to the general public and therefore worth less to its industrial guardians.

commodity: goods of a nonfinancial nature such as grain or metals, often traded on a futures exchange.

consolidated quotation system: primary and regional exchange best bid or ask for specific securities.

consolidated tape: primary and regional combined prices of listed securities as they have just been traded.

continuous trading: process of buying and selling securities throughout the trading day.

correction: used to imply that stock market movement (invariably downward) is overdue and sensible price adjustment has occurred. Upward movements are never described as corrections:; compressed correction: term of art used almost entirely by Wall Street bankers and brokers to refer to the 1987 stock market crash.

credit: the ability to get a loan.

cross: trading a security.

crossing network: an automated utility facilitating a securities trade.

custodian: bank physically storing financial instruments.

day trader: local in a futures pit; a futures trader in business for himself. Also retiree hooked on trading.

dealers: (see broker-dealer).

debt: longer-term fixed income securities (see bonds).

deregulation: the political philosophy of reducing burdensome corporate rules imposed by government to let the free market operate more effectively. In practice mostly the lifting of a regulation here and there, often accompanied by a great media din.

derivative(s): securities whose worth is based on an underlying instrument. Prices of options and financial futures, for instance, have some connection to the movements of underlying equity. But many derivatives are traded off-exchange; their popularity is growing along with questions about how well Wall Street actually understands the risks inherent in these OTC customized instruments.

discount broker: an order-taker for a discount broker. Not to be confused with a "full service" broker.

disintermediation: removing the agent between the buyer and the seller.

dividend: shareholder profits on company earnings, often distributed quarterly.

Dow Jones Industrial Average: thirty big NYSE-traded stocks whose average is presumably representative of the market as a whole; price-weighted.

due diligence: the duty of the broker-dealer to determine whether the issue offered for sale is properly represented by financial statements and other information.

efficient market: a market that, in comparison to other, similar markets, is able to rapidly accommodate the buy and sell orders of customers without large price gaps.

eighth: the smallest standard up and down movement of equity prices. No reason, except tradition, why this should not take place in tenths.

equity: in industry terminology, a fancy word for stocks.

exchange: used to be a building, owned or rented by members, where securities were traded. Now can refer to an electronic net.

execution: buying or selling of a security.

fair market: one offering the buyer the lowest possible price and the seller the highest possible one in comparison to similar markets.

financial consultant: mostly euphemism for "broker."

financial future: futures contract including those based on underlying instruments such as long bonds, mortgages or stock indexes.

financial industry: banks, insurers, managers, plans, and firms that constitute the country's money business.

financial planner: a certified professional who draws up investment plans for corporations and individuals often for a fee. On Wall Street, a salesman who offers to help.

financial services industry: enterprise wrapped around a market.

fixed income: (see bond)

flipping: buying of or selling short, securities of a primary or secondary offering and then unloading securities a short time later. Anathema to Wall Street underwriters who claim such short-termism smacks of speculation and opportunism. Wall Street penalizes its own brokers who indulge in this practice on behalf of their clients. By penalizing its brokers, Wall Street may be interfering with its brokers' ability to act in the best interest of clients. This issue, five years on, has not yet been resolved by the SEC.

floating shell: corporate entity with publicly available shares but no purpose.

floor broker: member's designated agent on the floor of a physical exchange.

fourth market: trading venue, usually automated, for managers and other "buy side" entities to trade amongst themselves without a broker.

front run(ning): trading ahead of a customer's trade with foreknowledge of customer's eventual position.

full-service broker: a broker whose firm charges more than a so-called discount company but adds value by delivering financial "advice" through the broker.

future(s) contract: a security whose worth is based on an expectation of future worth of the underlying instrument.

futures pit: where commodities and financial futures are traded; biggest domestic futures exchanges are Chicago Mercantile Exchange and Chicago Board of Trade.

games: package trading, front-running, and the like.

general partner (partnerships): the principal manager or managers of a limited partnership, usually responsible for the idea in which the partnership has invested and liable, in theory at least, for the partnership's failure.

Glass-Steagall: this 1934 Act separated private banking functions from public dealing and brokering functions. Henceforth, banks could not underwrite securities, nor recommend their sale. Today banks can underwrite corporate debt and even, in some cases, launch stock offerings. Glass-Steagall totters, but still stands.

government bond: government paper issued in medium- and long-term tranches; short-term government issuance is referred to as commercial paper.

hedge fund: small, secretive firms using sophisticated financial investing techniques, often in several markets, and primarily concerned with proprietary trading profit rather than agency business.

hedging: the process of purchasing off-setting instruments in several markets so as to protect against losses.

high yield: optimistic industry terminology for "junk." (see junk bonds)

index: a large group of securities, supposedly with similar characteristics, tracked as a group:; *index trading:* buying or selling shares in an index through a futures exchange.

index arbitrage: the process of buying in one market while simultaneously selling in another. For a long time in the 1980s, the SEC claimed, with the media's cooperation, that this practice induced market "volatility." There may be some evidence that the practice exacerbates what has already begun, but not that it can begin it.

indications of interest: a buy or sell advertisement, usually placed on an electronic trading utility.

initial public offering (IPO): the first offering of stock to the public.

inside the bid: trading below the stated sales price or above a stated buy.

insider trading: trading on information that few others have access to, to turn an illegal profit.

institution: any large financial management entity not identified with Wall Street's "sell side."

interest rate: the expense of using borrowed cash or securities.

Intermarket Trading System (ITS): automated trading system exposing orders, through screens, to buy or sell specific securities to specialists and certain member firms across the country.

investment banker: employee, often highly paid, selling Wall Street's underwriting services to corporations or municipalities.

junk bonds: corporate credits rated BB or less.

leverage: credit available to someone who has managed to impress those who lend money, usually for the purpose of making large or risky investments.

limit order: an order to buy or sell a security at a certain price. A *conditional order* adds more specifications.

limit order book: the entire spectrum of orders, at various prices, placed for a security at a specific time and held in secret by the specialist or market maker.

limited partner: investor in public or private partnership; one who acquires a general partner's idea while gradually surrendering his cash.

limited partnership: these come in two flavors, public and private. Private partnerships are restricted to 100 partners or less, along with a general partner or partners; public partnerships may have thousands of investors, usually at $5,000 per, along with a general partner or partners.

liquidity: the ability of a market to quickly accommodate the buyer and seller at an acceptable price.

listing: corporate instrument traded on an exchange.

M&A: stands for mergers and acquisitions, a 1980s financial buzzword implying the activity, on Wall Street's part, of scouting for companies to be bought or sold at a profit. Process garnered fees for all.

market impact: the purchase or sale of a security in such a way that it moves the market as it changes hands.

market-makers: (vs. specialists) market-makers, in NASD terminology, are those traders who stand ready to buy or sell securities for their own account. Unlike specialist systems, more than one market maker may have responsibility to insure an orderly market in a given stock.

marketplace: once upon a time where buyer and seller met.

mark-to-market: pricing inventoried securities according to current market value.

Mayday: May 1, 1975, the day brokerage commissions were formally deregulated and Wall Street ceased to act quite so much like a cartel.

merit regulation: rules allowing state regulators to disallow certain issues from being available to the public in that state if the issue exhibits certain suspicious traits.

money manager: term commonly used to refer to someone who runs portfolios professionally for an institutional fund or pension plan.

mutual fund: these are funds, open or closed-end, that operate under the rules of the 1940 Investment Company Act, which mandates disclosure of performance and investment objectives. Mutual funds are usually run fairly conservatively and offer shares to the public at relatively low cost.

Nasaa: North American Securities Administrators Association. The state securities group that administers and enforces a variety of local securities rules. An older regulatory body than the SEC and one that, along with the CFTC, often comes under attack by the SEC.

NASD: National Association of Securities Dealers, a self-regulatory organization set up by the SEC and the Investment Bankers' Conference to regulate the myriad OTC firms of the 1930s across the country. One goal: "to establish high moral and ethical standards in securities trading." Association later developed an electronic trading net, Nasdaq.

Nasdaq: National Association of Securities Dealers Automated Quotations System. Electronic system, on three levels, that gives brokers and dealers quotes for Nasdaq-listed stocks. Despite use of screens, still mostly telephone market accessible, at the inside price, to no one but NASD members.

national market system: the 1975 congressional mandate to build an automated securities trading system that would offer a fair, un-manipulated market for all. It never happened.

noise traders: term coined by Fischer Black to describe those individuals who trade on meaningless information.

offer: (see ask)

offering: referring to the public or private distribution of securities, usually in the context of an underwriting.

option: the ability or right to purchase a financial instrument at a certain time for a certain price. If the ability is not exercised, it lapses.

order facilitation: in which an agent may help to place a client's buy or sell order by either buying from or selling to itself.

over-the-counter: issues not listed on a physical exchange but traded on the Nasdaq.

package trade: a trade designed in advance, usually intricate, involving the use of computers to peg positions of both the customer and the firm in several markets.

passive money manager: manager who relies on program trading strategies, mostly index strategies that routinely track a broad index. As managers switch to customized index strategies, the idea of a truly "passive" investment strategy is becoming less relevant.

penny stock: In the past, referring to equity selling for less than $1 a share. Issues called "penny" stocks often carry an illegitimate odor and are more easily manipulated by less monied crooks than more expensive issues.

pension plan: industry term for pension funds.

physical stock exchange: a place where buyers and sellers meet physically to trade securities. Oldest and grandest is the New York Stock Exchange, also known as the "Big Board." Once necessary, now perhaps not.

pink sheets: stock information, printed on pink paper, from the national quotation bureau on companies not formally listed on any exchange. Not all pink sheet companies are "fly by night." Pink sheets include huge foreign companies that trade in this country through American Depository Receipts. Also gray, yellow sheets, in regions around the country.

portfolio: more than a single security under management or owned by an individual or group.

portfolio insurance: the once-popular idea that a money manager could hedge stock purchases with stock index futures and then sell futures if stock values diminished—and buy them back at a lower cost. It didn't work.

primary offering: an initial public offering of stock.

private placement: the sale of an interest in a venture to institutional investors, often banks, without a public offering; private placements don't have to conform to the same rules of disclosure as do public offerings.

program trading: the act of trading via computer, usually in several markets, often, but not always, at once. Commonly confused, especially in the 1980s by the news media, with index arbitrage.

promoter: term used by regulators to refer to those in the penny stock business; penny stock "promoter" or "operator," as opposed to legitimate securities salesmen or brokers.

proprietary trading: in which a dealer trades for its own profit, sometimes at the expense of the client for whom it is acting as broker. The nub of the problem.

prospectus: a written explanation of securities being offered.

put (options): the ability to sell, at a certain price, at a certain time, a specific number of securities. (see call)

"quants": professional traders using quantitative analysis, i.e.: computerized investment strategies.

quotes: offers to buy or sell securities.

Real Estate Investment Trusts (REITs): a company overseeing a real estate portfolio for shareholders and passing along profits, if any.

regulatory capture: the process whereby an industry, subject to governmental rules, gradually co-opts the process and begins to influence rule making to its own advantage. The evolution of this occurrence often is not easily discernible to those not directly involved in the industry.

retail market: a market in which the "small" investor participates.

robust price/market: referring to a purchase or market with a good deal of liquidity and interest in specific securities.

round lot: $1,000 par value for bonds or 100 shares of stock.

Rule 390: basically mandates that member firms not trade for their own account away from the Big Board.

S&L: savings and loan; regulated financial institution whose main purpose is to loan money to people who want to buy houses.

Securities Exchange Commission (SEC): created by the Securities and Exchange Act of 1934 to administer that act and supervise the implementation of the rules of the Securities Act of 1933. The SEC is responsible for supervising statutes promoting full public disclosure and for protecting the public against securities fraud. The SEC supervises exchanges, investment companies, advisers, and the NASD. It is responsible for administering the Public Utility Holding Company Act of 1935, the Trust Indenture

Act of 1939, the Investment Company Act of 1940, and the Securities Acts Amendments of 1975.

SEC Rules: rules that involve short selling, solicitation of purchase, short tendering, stabilizing an offering, distribution through rights, confirmation of transactions, credit terms in margin transactions, solicitation of proxies, tender offers, net capital requirements for broker-dealers, customer-protection reserves, prohibition of fixed rates of commission, off-board trading by exchange members, public sale of unregistered securities, shelf registration.

secondary offering: a securities offering, usually stock, made some time after an initial offering.

secondary market: the physical or automated market venue in which financial instruments are bought and sold.

security(ies): bonds, stocks, other kinds of financial instruments, offered publicly or privately.

securities monopoly: (see "financial services industry")

Self-Regulatory Organizations (SROs): exchanges and other securities membership organizations such as the NASD, which are supposed to cooperate with the SEC to regulate their own conduct.

selling/buying sloppy: a feat accomplished by those who wish the market to be aware of what is being bought or sold; often a trader "selling sloppy"—advertising the sale or purchase of a security with all his or her might—has something up his or her sleeve.

sell side: commonly known as Wall Street; those who are the broker-dealer members of physical exchanges and conduct agency or proprietary trading and commission business.

settlement: the process of settling a trade; i.e., taking in the cash on one side and delivering the security on the other.

Shad-Johnson accord: the settlement, reached at the Monocle, over who would regulate stock index futures and other securities-related futures. Shad, of the SEC, agreed that Johnson's CFTC should be in charge. Later referred to as "Second Pearl Harbor."

shelf registration: conforming with SEC requirements in advance of an offering so as to be ready for issuance when market is ripe.

shell company: a public company without a purpose. (see blind pool)

short sale: the sale of a security not owned by the seller, or if owned, not delivered, which is accompanied by delivery of borrowed shares to the buyer. The seller makes the sale with the hope that the security will decline in price.

soft dollar (sales): the provision of research and services from the broker to the institution in return for trading volume and, ultimately, commissions.

specialist: the market maker on the floor of the NYSE; a securities auctioneer with an "affirmative obligation to buy" in order to keep an "orderly" market traveling up and down by eighths, if possible. The specialist stands ready to invest his or her own capital to insure an orderly market, or so the theory goes. Also presides over auction of assigned securities.

Special Study: famous 1963 study that predicted the emergence of an automated fourth market and blasted financial industry business as usual.

speculation: betting on a short-term securities movement versus establishing a position for the long haul. According to some, the investment in any other instrument than stock. Wall Street firms are supposed to frown on speculation, as is Wall Street's regulatory body, the SEC. (see trader)

spot markets: commodities telephone market.

spread: the difference between the quoted offer to buy and the quoted offer to sell.

stock: ownership in a corporation.

stock parking: purchasing and eventually disposing of stock on behalf of a buyer who cannot legally own the equity in question.

sunshine: the idea that prices on all instruments are always publicly available. A very valuable and controversial quality.

SuperDot: the electronic utility that carries small share orders to the floor of the NYSE for the specialist's disposition.

swap: trading one financial instrument for another.

syndicate: a group of firms joining together to sell an underwriting.

Telecommunications and Finance subcommittee: congressional committee responsible for oversight of the nation's financial services industry.

third market: trading of listed securities off formal exchange.

trader: a securities professional a speculator employed by a Wall Street firm.

transactional efficiency: low cost and fast access to a market.

Treasury (Treasurys): government bonds.

Triple Witching: four Fridays a year when index futures, index options, and equity options settle together.

underwriting: the process of purchasing securities from an issuer with the intent of selling them soon; a function commonly performed by Wall Street's banking firms.

"up front" money (brokerage): money paid to successful brokers to lure them to another firm. Usually based on a percentage of commissions the broker has earned the previous year and paid in advance of the broker's new start.

upstairs traders: traders for big Wall Street firms.

uptick rule: rule instituted after 1929 crash mandating a share of stock can be sold only once the market has moved up an eighth in that particular security. Rule instituted to discourage big traders from artificially depressing the market.

volatility: term referring to rapid up and down market movements in the (stock) market. Intra-day movements, as economist Merton Miller has pointed out, should more properly be termed "velocity."

Wall Street: a place where the securities industry congregates on the tip of Manhattan. As physical proximity diminishes in importance, Wall Street becomes more a state of mind and less a place.

warrant: the right to buy additional shares of a security, usually stock, at a specified price, should there be an initial rise in value. Usually issued to a purchaser of an offering as an inducement.

wrap fee: a specific commission, 3 percent or less, paid to a broker in return for money management services.

INDEX